Published in Great Britain and the United States of America in 2021 by
CASEMATE PUBLISHERS
The Old Music Hall, 106–108 Cowley Road, Oxford OX4 1JE, UK
and
1950 Lawrence Road, Havertown, PA 19083, USA

Copyright 2021 © Andrew Richards

Hardback Edition: ISBN 978-1-61200-830-1
Digital Edition: ISBN 978-1-61200-831-8

A CIP record for this book is available from the British Library

All rights reserved. No part of this book may be reproduced or transmitted in any form or by any means, electronic or mechanical including photocopying, recording or by any information storage and retrieval system, without permission from the publisher in writing.

Printed and bound in the United Kingdom by TJ Books

Typeset by Versatile PreMedia Services (P) Ltd.

For a complete list of Casemate titles, please contact:

CASEMATE PUBLISHERS (UK)
Telephone (01865) 241249
Email: casemate-uk@casematepublishers.co.uk
www.casematepublishers.co.uk

CASEMATE PUBLISHERS (US)
Telephone (610) 853-9131
Fax (610) 853-9146
Email: casemate@casematepublishers.com
www.casematepublishers.com

Front cover: A close-up of the Garrison Sargent Major inspecting the 1st Battalion Coldstream Guards Flag Bearers. (OGL v1.0, photo by Owen Cooban)

AFTER THE WALL CAME DOWN

Soldiering through the Transformation of the British Army, 1990–2020

ANDREW RICHARDS

CASEMATE

Oxford & Philadelphia

C000006309

This book is dedicated to my brothers in arms who have left us during or after serving their country and to those that survived and live with the consequences and aftermath today.

Contents

Foreword

General The Lord Dannatt GCB CBE MC DL

'I swear by Almighty God (or do solemnly, and truly declare and affirm) that I will be faithful and bear true allegiance to Her Majesty Queen Elizabeth II, Her Heirs and Successors, and that I will, as in duty bound, honestly and faithfully defend Her Majesty, Her Heirs and Successors, in Person, Crown and Dignity against all enemies, and will observe all orders of Her Majesty, Her Heirs and Successors, and of the Generals and officers set above me.'

With those words, generations of British, Irish and Commonwealth citizens have pledged themselves to the service of the Crown within the ranks of the British Army. I swore those words at the Army Recruiting Office on Springfield Road, Chelmsford, on 28 August 1969 in the lunch interval of a County Championship match between Essex and Leicestershire. By the time the players came out for the afternoon session, I was back in my seat. In the lunch interval, I had joined the British Army. Swearing In counted as a day's work, so I was paid the Queen's Shilling and one pound, two shillings and sixpence were in my pocket, as was the New Testament on which I had sworn the Oath of Allegiance. And so, another soldier's life in the British Army began. A few days later 24184515 Officer Cadet F. R. Dannatt reported to the Royal Military Academy Sandhurst. Thirty years before, my father had sworn a similar oath to King George VI and had reported to Hyderabad Barracks, Colchester. As soldiers, we all start somewhere.

And this book is about soldiers. It is about the generation of soldiers who served in the British Army from 1990 to 2020 – the post-Cold War generation. And what a generation that has turned out to be. The story starts in the dust of the fall of the Berlin Wall but is soon into the dust of the Saudi and Kuwaiti deserts and on through the Balkans, to Iraq, to Afghanistan and many other theatres of operations along the way. But the battles and the campaigns merely provide the backdrop for the stories of the lives of those soldiers who served, fought and some who died in that extraordinary 30-year period. In whatever way military historians might describe them, wars and conflicts have always been intense. For the soldier on the ground the crack and thump of an enemy bullet passing over head or the ear-splitting noise of high explosive makes fighting a very personal matter. An experience that does not end when the fighting stops. But, back to the Oath of Allegiance – we fight for our Queen and our friends and our families; we do not fight for the Government. We are citizens first, but citizens in uniform, and citizens who have become soldiers – that is our life, that is our calling, that is where our spirit of comradeship is born. It is unique. Those who have never served will never be able to fully understand that.

Towards the end of this book, the brilliant author, Andrew Richards, asks an important question. Knowing what he now knows about the life of a soldier and the present circumstances of the British Army, would he join up today? You must read on to find out. I joined for three years and stayed for forty. My middle son served in Iraq and Afghanistan while I was the Commander in Chief Land Command and then Chief of the General Staff. I love all my four children dearly, but do I have a special bond with Bertie – Captain E. R. S. Dannatt Grenadier Guards? Yes, of course, I do. To understand why, you have to read this book.

Preface

Throughout history Britons have been willing to sacrifice their lives in defence of their country. In times of war, generation after generation have answered their country's call, from Elizabethan sailors who defeated the Spanish Armada, to Wellington's Army at Waterloo, General Haig's 'Pals' battalions, and Churchill's 'Few' who cleared the skies above southern England in 1940. Of the many, several generations stand out from the rest. It is hard to argue that the conditions faced and sacrifices made by the millions who fought during World War I were not Britain's greatest. American journalist Tom Brokaw has written of those who fought in World War II in his book *The Greatest Generation*. And who would deny that Britain's greatest generation were those who fought off Hitler – British servicemen and citizens of the 'Finest Hour'? Really, it is not practical or fair to compare either of the World War generations to any other; the scale, scope, and totality of effort required from armed forces and civilians makes them unique.

Young men and women who left school and joined up during the mid- to late 1980s and then embarked on a full career in the British Army did so during a unique period of history. The Army they joined had not changed for decades. Mechanised infantry and cavalry regiments stationed in West Germany carried out the same routines with little change except live-firing exercises at the British Army Training Unit in Suffield (Canada) and maybe a six-month tour of duty in Northern Ireland. For troops based in England, as well as tours in Northern Ireland, there was the chance of a six-month tour in Belize or in Cyprus with the United Nations. This was the type of career that a soldier joining the Army in the late 1980s could have expected had the Cold War status quo continued.

However, with the fall of the Berlin Wall, all those certainties fell away. Unlike the two World War generations, what the Army faced was not total war; there was never any declaration of war, no common foe, or a single enemy to defeat. In fact, it was supposed to have been the end of a war, a time of peace and stability. Politicians started to use the term 'Peace Dividend' in reference to the money not being spent on defence, with government officials even planning on how and where it should be spent.[1] But over the next two decades and beyond, for those in the British Army there was no peace. Military spending was slashed, yet commitments increased exponentially. Those serving not only faced continuous deployment in overseas operations, but they would also be involved in immense upheavals that took place within the Army. The ending of the Cold War, combined with a technological revolution, a changing society at home, and new global threats, meant that the Army of the second decade of the 21st century was unrecognisable from the one many soldiers had joined.

It was not until retiring from the Army in 2002 and moving to the United States that I became aware of this post-Cold War generation. As the events of 11 September 2001 rolled over into military conflicts in Afghanistan and Iraq, I began to understand what many soldiers in my regiment (and the rest of the British Army) were going through. With the help of social media, I have been able to reconnect with many ex-colleagues who have also now retired.

Initially, I had planned to write about the careers of five men who were soldiers throughout the post-Cold War period. These five were a decade younger than me and were either troopers or junior non-commissioned officers in the same Life Guards squadron as mine in 1990. Unfortunately, the Ministry of Defence would not allow me to interview serving soldiers[2] so, sadly, I have not been able to include four of the five men who were the genesis and inspiration for the book.

With this disappointing news a change of approach was required. I widened the scope of the book to include soldiers from all British Army regiments and corps and sent out a questionnaire via my website and social media. I had almost two hundred responses and started to correspond with 50 ex-soldiers whose combined experience spanned most of the British Army's post-Cold War operations.

My interviews consisted of an initial set of questions on the subject I was writing about at the time. Where I had follow-up questions and wanted to know more information, we connected via email, phone, or video chat. I also had the opportunity of taking two trips back to the UK when I was able to meet face-to-face with individuals.

Soldiers who helped me with this book have all been able to pick and choose when, and if, they answered my questions. Some polite persuasion aside, the decision to answer questions has been theirs alone, with no single soldier contributing to every section. Most agreed to talk openly to me, while others were more reticent; some were struggling in the aftermath of their service, and several would only do so if I promised to withhold their identity. Those who wanted total anonymity are quoted in the book with no mention of any name.

As I progressed with the book, it became apparent to me that I would not be able to safely protect the identity of those soldiers if I recorded the interviews in the endnotes – a close scrutiny of dates might inadvertently reveal an identity. And even with consent to publish a name, I have decided to use only a first name and initial of a surname (Andrew B., Charlie D., Eddie F., etc.). In an ever-changing world, personal security for those who have helped me with this book, both now and in the future, is extremely important.

When I first advertised for ex-soldiers to help with the book, I got a big response from fellow Household Cavalrymen that knew me. Although there are several soldiers from my regiment, there is also a wide range of soldiers from across the British Army. These include: The Queen's Dragoon Guards, The King's Royal Hussars, Grenadier Guards, Scots Guards, Irish Guards, Welsh Guards, the Parachute Regiment, Royal Regiment of Artillery, Corps of Royal Engineers, Royal Corps of Signals, Royal Army Medical Corps, Adjutant General's Corps, Royal Military Police, Queen Alexandra's Royal Army Nursing Corps, as well as the Household Cavalry.

Most of the military operations undertaken by these men and women have already been covered in great detail by military experts, journalists, and soldiers who took part in them. Although I cover all the deployments carried out (during this time), it was never my intention to go into the kind of details covered by other books and publications, nor to be a complete guide or historical record of all conflicts and underlying political events. I chronicle history and politics, some events being covered in greater detail than others where I feel there is a need for context and where that history and politics have had a direct effect upon the lives of the soldiers. These are stories of a remarkable generation of soldiers, friends, colleagues, and brothers.

Acknowledgements

My grateful thanks to the many soldiers, friends, and comrades who have helped me with this book. I cannot thank you all enough for the many hours you spent answering my questions, talking to me online, or taking time to meet me face to face when I was in the UK. Without your patience and time, there would be no book; without the service and sacrifice willingly given by generations like yours, we would have no country.

I would also like to thank my friends, family, and 'framily' for being so supportive over the past three years. It has been hard work at times, but with your help, I got there in the end. Also, special thanks to Ruth Sheppard and everyone at Casemate.

Finally, once again, a special thank you to my wonderful wife, Melissa, for the hours spent editing, supporting, and listening as I struggled through to completion. I couldn't have done it without you.

Prologue

Thursday 9 November 1989

I have heard it said that witnesses to historical events watched them unfold before their eyes not fully understanding their enormity. With no comprehension of the consequences, it is only with the passing of time that they fully grasp the event's historical significance. This is how it was for me the night the Berlin Wall came down.

I distinctly remember watching the BBC's *Nine O'Clock News* having just finished training at the rugby club in Barnstaple; I was posted in North Devon as an instructor at the time. Chatting to teammates over a beer with the television on behind the bar, it was obvious that something was happening although no one paid much attention. It was all taking place miles away and had no immediate effect upon us. Those with me at the bar that night were more concerned with our next opponents, telling jokes, or discussing the recent spate of bad accidents on the new link road that had been completed that summer. About an hour later, I drove home, ate a late supper, and then stayed up to the early hours of the morning watching live coverage of what was happening in Berlin.

It took a while, but as I watched I started to understand that I was truly watching history being made. Reporters like the BBC's Brian Hanrahan and NBC's Tom Brokaw spoke to bewildered-looking East German citizens as they passed through newly opened gates. Those from East and West embraced with thousands clambering upon the wall itself. It was surreal to watch champagne corks flying where just 24 hours before such a gathering would have been greeted with bullets flying. Nine years earlier, I had stood on a viewing platform overlooking Checkpoint Charlie and the wall. On another trip I actually passed through the checkpoint in uniform and was able to walk around East Berlin. Born a year after its construction in 1961, I had only ever known a world in which there was a Berlin Wall. Watching coverage of Berliners celebrating at the Brandenburg Gate, I was struck at how quickly this had all happened, and I started to ponder the future as I was about to return to my regiment in Germany. The questions started to come: What now? Had our Challenger tanks become obsolete, surplus to requirements? What about the Russians? What about the Germans? I felt certain that British soldiers would become increasingly unwanted in a country that was surely going to be reunified, but beyond that my questioning was short-sighted.

Like most serving soldiers in their twenties and thirties, I had become accustomed to the Cold War status quo. I didn't know what to expect as the Soviet Bloc collapsed. Although I realised there would be some changes, looking back now, over three decades later, I think there was no way I could have foreseen the full extent of what was going to happen next.

CHAPTER I

The Cold War and Thatcher's Britain

All new recruits enlisted in the British Army are required to stand in a recruiting office and swear an oath of allegiance to Her Majesty the Queen. For centuries this act of fealty remained largely unchanged; fresh-faced young men and women (most not old enough to legally drink in a public house) promised to 'defend her Majesty, her heirs and successors in person, crown and dignity against all enemies.'[1] After receiving a day's pay, known as the 'Queen's Shilling' (roughly £12 in 1988), the newly attested soldiers then went home and waited to receive instructions by mail detailing where and when their basic training would start.

For many school leavers in the 1980s there was never a question of them joining up. One soldier recalled, 'In recruiting terms, I was what's called an intender; someone who was always going to join from a very young age. I had no family who had previously served but I was infatuated with a life in the Army, particularly serving on tanks.'

Doug K. said, 'It was the only career I ever wanted. I would have gone mad in a nine to five job.' Rich G. came from a service background: 'All my family served in the military, mainly Navy and Air Force. But my father joined the Army at 15 … the Army was all I ever wanted to do, and nothing else ever entered my mind as an alternative.' David K. had known he was going to be a soldier since he was an 11-year-old cadet. He wanted to join the Royal Military Police but was told there were no places available at the Junior Leaders Regiment. 'The recruiting sergeant, Queen's Dragoon Guards, put on a video and as soon as I saw a light tank going airborne over a mound, I was sold. QDG it was to be.' Angus T. knew what he wanted to do after he sat in a Chieftain tank gunner's seat aged 11. He applied to join the Army before he left school, but got a letter saying there were no vacancies.

> To say I was devastated is an understatement. A week later I had left school (with nothing) and started at Kwik Save as a stockroom lad. I reapplied the following year and was accepted into the Army Air Corps. A Corporal of Horse in the Life Guards was the recruiting sergeant. He said I could go to the air corps but I would have to wait six months, or I could go on tanks in the Life Guards where there was no wait. I signed up that day.

Simon J. had no real intention of joining the Army at 16.

> I was playing a lot of football and got a YTS scholarship at Swansea City … I quickly realised football was not that exciting so when about ten of my friends decided to visit the Army Careers Office one day, I joined them … by the time the sergeant got to me there were no slots left in the Royal Regiment of Wales so they offered me QDG. I accepted and the rest is history.

Jules H. had a long family history of military service to live up to, so there was never any question. His great-grandfather was a Royal Artillery regimental sergeant major in India, and his great-uncle had died at Arras in World War I: 'I signed up at 16 years old to keep his memory alive.' His older brother, Andy, joined the Coldstream Guards before he decided to follow in his dad's footsteps and join the Household Cavalry. 'For as long as I can remember all I ever wanted to do was ride on the Trooping of the Colour just like my dad.'

Robert C. was another soldier who had been influenced by a family member. His grandfather had served during World War II. 'He introduced me to Army life … he'd been captured in the desert near Alamein and he told me all the stories from a very young age … joining the Army was all I ever wanted to do.'

Any teenager who joined the British Army in the late 1980s grew up in a country dominated by one person. In May 1979, Margaret Thatcher became prime minister. Opinion has always been divided on the changes to British society that took place during her premiership. Once described as the 'Marmite Prime Minister',[2] whether you loved or hated her, after 11 years in power there can be no argument that her influence and the policies of her government transformed the country. Soon after becoming leader of the Conservative Party in 1975, Margaret Thatcher quickly gained a fearsome reputation. Unlike most politicians of the time, the 'Iron Lady'[3] exuded strength at home and abroad.

For the next three years it looked as though the Conservatives would win any election if and when it was called. By the time the country went to the polls on 3 May 1979, it had been subjected to what became known as the 'Winter of Discontent'. The harshest winter for 16 years was coupled with crippling strikes and rampant inflation; by the time spring flowers were blooming, the country was ready for a change. Soon after entering No. 10 Downing Street with a 44-seat majority, Britain's first woman prime minister and her cabinet went about the task of fulfilling promises. Because of the dire economic situation her government faced over the first few years in office, she could not implement the radical changes she would have liked; only later in the decade would the full effects of 'Thatcherism' be felt.

In the spring of 1982, despite an improving economy, Margaret Thatcher was still extremely unpopular. Her attempts to clamp down on trade union power had provoked more industrial unrest. Selling off nationalised industries and a heavy-handed approach to control inflation were hurting the poor and middle classes. Unemployment was rising, and racial and class tensions turned into violent riots in London, Birmingham, Liverpool, Manchester, and Leeds. Despite the political headwinds, Margaret Thatcher and the Conservative Party would win a landslide victory in the General Election of June 1983. It was thanks in no small part to an event that took place 8,000 miles away from Westminster.

For thousands of soldiers who joined the Army in the late 1980s, the Falklands War had a massive influence on their decision. After the task force set sail for the South Atlantic in early April 1982, the British public was engrossed in the ensuing events for the next 74 days. Soldier B. 'followed every minute of the Falklands War', wishing he was old enough to join up. Angus T. said, 'When the Falklands started, I was in the Army Cadet Force, hoping we would be called up – how naive.'

Shaun G. remembers the task force leaving Southampton. 'We went down to the River Solent to watch the ships sailing away to this far-flung island that no one had ever heard of, then went down there again to watch them return.' Jules H. had a morning paper round. 'During the Falklands war I was late for school every day – on my round I would stop and read all the stories and articles about the war.'

With non-stop coverage on radio and television, impressionable young men and women watched and listened, not fully comprehending the grim realities of war. Soldier G. recalls some youthful jingoism. 'The Falklands was fascinating to me because all I wanted to be was a soldier. The dreadful events never really dawned on me at the age of 12 ... only after my first tour of Iraq in 2004 at the age of 35 did I fully understand the true nature of war.' For Stuart B., the cost of the conflict hit close to home.

> The Falklands was a big part of my life and I watched the reports on TV on the edge of my seat. Private Steven Illingsworth, 2nd Battalion, the Parachute Regiment, was a former pupil at Edlington Comprehensive School and was killed at Goose Green. This first sparked my interest in the Parachute Regiment... I knew what I wanted to be when I left school.

Martin M. was just 14 years old.

> The Falklands War was probably the biggest and most influential event of my life. I was utterly obsessed with it; I watched every news bulletin and read every newspaper. Suddenly I knew what I was going to do when I left school ... I was going to serve my country like the brave men I'd watched on the BBC and I was going to go to war. How naive was I?

After the Union Flag flew again over Port Stanley and the last Argentine invaders had left, the task force returned home to scenes of jubilation not seen since the end of World War II.

Even though Britain was gripped with a new nationalistic fervour, not everyone who joined the Army in the late 1980s did so because of the Falklands. Despite an improving economy, the future for industries including coal, steel, ship-building, and large manufacturing companies was not bright. Thousands of school leavers struggling to join a shrinking workforce started to look at a military career as a viable alternative. Shaun G. weighed up his options in Southampton. 'The docks had almost closed completely so the only options available were college, an apprenticeship or the Army – I chose the latter.'

Before Neil S. joined the Royal Engineers he had grown up in Wallsend on the River Tyne. 'There was nothing to do … I was bored at the thought of never leaving my home town … Everyone who left school went to work at Swan Hunters Shipyard; the talk of this closing down and having nowhere to work helped me make the decision to join up.'

It was not only urban areas where jobs were scarce that enticed some into a military career. 'I lived in the north of Scotland … jobs were not that readily available, so the Army seemed like a good idea at the time.' Conrad P. grew up in the mining valleys of South Wales. 'I was leaving school and wanted a job and money; the mines had closed and poverty was rife. So, the Army it was.'

For some, poor employment options were coupled with a real possibility of their lives going in a very different direction. 'I left school with nothing but a bad report and no other option but joining the military. I'd had several run-ins with local authorities and had gotten off with just a warning … the future wasn't looking bright. Luckily I was accepted by the Army before I ended up doing some time.' Paul H. tried to join up as soon as he could for the same reason. 'Jobs at the steel works were drying up and even though most of my family worked there I was not guaranteed a job … I got in with the wrong bunch, was always linked to minor trouble and would have ended up serving at Her Majesty's pleasure – my friends did.'

From the early days of her premiership, Margaret Thatcher was determined to reduce the power of the trade unions. The previous Conservative Party government of Edward Heath had been brought down by industrial action. Although she strengthened anti-union laws, she knew the country was not strong enough to withstand a national strike. In 1981, when the National Union of Miners (NUM) threatened to walk-out over proposed pit closures, she backed down. Many in her own party saw this as a humiliation, but avoiding industrial action bought her time to put in place a longer-term strategy.

The 1983 election gave the Conservative party an increased majority of 144 seats and handed the Labour Party its worst ever defeat. Margaret Thatcher now felt emboldened. Soldier A. said, 'She'd dealt with the Argies, now she was going to deal with the miners.' Over the previous two years coal stocks were quietly brought up to the highest possible levels, fleets of private non-union hauliers were placed on standby, and chief constables were told to prepare contingency plans to move officers all over the country to prevent pickets from forming. She also made a major effort to split the NUM, enticing miners in the Midlands to stay at work. The government further isolated the NUM by dealing with other trade unions individually. The collective bargaining system that gave the Trades Union Congress (TUC) such power in the 1970s was being systematically dismantled.

In March 1984, the National Coal Board announced it was closing 20 inefficient pits. Six days later, local strikes received support from NUM leader Arthur Scargill who called on all NUM members to action. The strike not only split opinion across the country, but it saw violent clashes between police and striking miners as well as fighting among factions within the TUC. It brought the word 'scab' (strike breakers) into the public consciousness and caused infighting within mining communities and families. The enmity caused by the strike is still felt today. Although not affecting the military directly, it did divide servicemen whose families lived in mining communities on both sides. And for those who were still at school, not only was the strike a major event during their formative years, but the resulting pit closures were another reason to leave their home towns and join the Army.

Simon J. lived in Merthyr Tydfil, South Wales, with his mother, who had survived the Aberfan disaster as a child. 'The fallout from all the mine closures hit really hard where we lived on the Gurnos Estate because most families had someone working in the pit. They were rough times with many families suffering. But somehow, we got through it.' Stuart B. lived in the mining community of Edlington, Yorkshire. The local pit that employed a big percentage of the community was called Yorkshire Main. 'It was the deepest pit in Britain and very hard core when it came to the strike … Out of the whole work force only a small handful broke the strike and went into work.'

On the other side of the picket lines, miners who didn't support the NUM saw the dispute differently. Soldier G. clearly recollects his family's involvement.

> Living in Nottinghamshire we were in the heart of the troubles during the miners' strike. My father, grandfather and uncles had all stayed at work. The streets and gardens had tents on them with pickets from all over the country … My relatives used to wind the strikers up, taunting them by throwing their money around the pub and putting wage packets in the straps of their helmets as they walked home through the picket line.

Soldier B. came from a staunch mining family. After basic training, he remembers 'going home at the height of the strike when lots of schoolmates were manning picket lines. They were all skint and on strike, and I was on leave with a wallet full of money.' David K. grew up in a poor part of Wales where steel and not coal was the major industry. 'Following many years of unemployment, my father landed a job as a driver with a haulage company and the money started to come in. During the miners' strike the company my father worked for was sub-contracted to assist moving the coal. Having crossed the picket lines once too often he decided to leave and unemployment beckoned once more.'

The confrontational atmosphere soon turned into open violence that ultimately claimed three lives. Men were beaten in their houses, a taxi driver who was carrying strike breakers was killed when he was struck by a concrete block thrown from a bridge, and television footage of police officers beating strikers with their truncheons was broadcast all over the world.

Soldier G. had a paper round during the strike. One of his deliveries was to the NUM headquarters. 'There was plenty of arguing and fighting. When Mr Scargill came to try and persuade the Notts lads to strike, they built a gallows and threatened to hang him if he stepped foot on to Notts NUM soil.' At the height of the strike a soldier returning to his regiment after a weekend with his family in Nottingham boarded a train to London only to find he was sitting a few seats away from Arthur Scargill. Unable to control his anger, he threw a half-eaten pork pie at the NUM leader. 'He was arrested by British Transport police, handed over to military police, and instantly obtained legend status back in the regiment.'

When the strike came to an end in March 1985, it was obvious who had lost. The country had shed billions in lost revenue with Gross Domestic Product reduced by as much 2.5 per cent,[4] the trade union movement was split and fractured, with its power and influence in British politics greatly reduced. But Margaret Thatcher had achieved her aim of breaking the unions. By the time she left office she had reduced working days lost by industrial action from 29 million in 1979 to 2 million in 1990.[5] Although Soldier G.'s family was on the winning side, the tragic irony that all miners suffered in the end is not lost on him. The last Nottinghamshire pit closed in 2015.[6] 'The industry is no more even though the Notts guys kept the country in coal and power in those dark days. Loyalty was never going to stop the economic downturn in coal. Even today I know families that don't talk because of the strike.' The last deep coal mine in Britain closed in December 2015 as the country relied more and more on clean, renewable energy sources. In April 2018, the final nail was driven into the coffin of the coal industry when the United Kingdom was powered for over three days in a row without coal being used.[7]

Towards the end of the decade the harsh aftertaste of the medicine Margaret Thatcher had administered to the country became unpalatable. Even with the economy booming and millions now owning their own homes, the country was deeply divided. Between 1979 and 1990, poverty increased; those living below 60 per cent of median incomes rose from 13.4 to 22.2 per cent.[8] The north–south divide had become a gaping chasm; in the south, 'the haves', and in the north, 'the have-nots'. The Labour Party had become virtually unelectable in the south, and after the bad blood caused by the miners' strike, the Tories were hated in the north. There was a common perception that if you were invited to 'Maggie's get rich party', worked hard, were money-minded, and highly motivated, then there was a whole new world of opportunities. But there was also a growing majority who thought, 'Don't grow old, get ill, or become unemployed under a Tory government.'

In Britain, the decade would end with a political miscalculation and divisions within Thatcher's own party over Europe. In 1989 it was announced that local council rates would be replaced by a 'Community Charge', which came to be known as 'the Poll Tax'. It was extremely unpopular and seen as placing a greater burden on poor people than the wealthy. It was introduced in Scotland in November 1989 and in

England and Wales a year later. Huge demonstrations and protests took place; the Poll Tax riots culminated in London on 31 March 1990. The public, her cabinet, and her party all questioned Margaret Thatcher's leadership, and it would ultimately signal the end of her premiership.

***

This generation of soldiers not only grew up during the Thatcher years; they grew up when the Cold War was at its height. The Soviet Union invaded Afghanistan in December 1979, and Ronald Reagan was elected President of the United States a year later. Any thaw in Cold War relations that had occurred during the *Détente* of the late 1970s ended abruptly. Reagan openly escalated the Cold War with a massive increase in American military forces, including proposed deployment of nuclear missiles in Europe and the Strategic Defense Initiative (SDI) known the world over as 'Star Wars'.

A major facet of Reagan's foreign policy was a continuation and strengthening of the 'special relationship' between the United States and the United Kingdom. His staunch ally, Margaret Thatcher, buoyed by her success in the Falklands, obviously enjoyed being treated as an equal partner. She was more than willing to align the United Kingdom with the United States as it ramped up the Cold War.

The escalating tensions between east and west were felt by everyone. Forty per cent of adults said they thought that a nuclear war was likely to happen before the end of the decade.[9] Even schoolchildren like Shaun G. feared what might happen, as 'The threat of nuclear war seemed so real.' In their barracks on German soil, British soldiers knew they could be 'crashed out' at any moment, deploying to previously sited defensive positions where they would attempt to fight off any Soviet invasion. 'It was a surreal experience as a young soldier when that call-out siren went off. It still sends shivers down the spine even now when I think about it.'

A series of events took place in 1983 that brought the world to the brink of nuclear war. Not since the Cuban Missile Crisis in 1962 had the world come this close to a global catastrophe. Despite both sides almost killing millions of people, it was these events that would ultimately lead to the end of the Cold War.

On 1 September 1983, the Soviet Union shot down Korean Airlines Flight 007 as it strayed over Soviet airspace, resulting in the loss of 269 lives including a sitting US congressman. On 26 September, the Soviets' unreliable satellite-based early warning system malfunctioned and incorrectly alerted the Soviet command centre that the United States had launched five intercontinental ballistic missiles.

Able Archer was a NATO Command Post exercise that took place in West Germany in November 1983 and practised the release of nuclear weapons. It had been planned well in advance but it could not have come at a worse time. In Moscow members of the Politburo genuinely thought NATO was preparing a full-scale nuclear attack using the war games as cover.

Two events before the start of *Able Archer* would increase Soviet suspicions further. Security surrounding all American installations across the world was stepped up after the bombing of the US Marine barracks in Beirut on 23 October. Just two days later the Soviets started to see an increase in communications between London and Washington, D.C. They saw this as another sign, when in fact it was Prime Minster Thatcher, calling President Reagan to complain in the 'strongest possible terms' regarding America's invasion of the Caribbean island of Grenada. As Exercise *Able Archer*'s scripted scenario played out, the Soviet Union took defensive measures moving troops towards the west. Its ships and submarines sailed from Baltic ports, and bombers were placed on the highest readiness. As the exercise moved towards its conclusion – which included a simulated nuclear response from NATO forces – the Kremlin prepared a real response, targeting individual cities and military targets all across the western hemisphere; the Soviet leadership was convinced it was about to be attacked. As the final act of *Able Archer* was taking place – a simulated NATO launch of 350 nuclear missiles – the Soviet Union was poised and ready to retaliate for real. Once the imaginary missiles struck their targets and 'Endex' was declared, all radio traffic ceased. An accidental nuclear war was prevented only by a few Russian spies who managed to convince their leadership that American-led NATO forces had no intentions of starting a real war.[10]

When word got out just how close the world had come to a nuclear war, on both sides of the Atlantic came a realisation that they needed to dial back the rhetoric. When Margaret Thatcher was briefed, she was so concerned she immediately began a campaign to lobby Washington to ensure it could never happen again.[11] President Reagan had intentionally started an arms race as an attempt to bankrupt the Soviet Union. It was working but almost came at a terrible price – one he was not willing to pay. As the full implications of his aggressive anti-Soviet stance and the Kremlin's deep paranoia were revealed, he was genuinely shocked.[12]

Just days later President Reagan watched a private screening of the ABC television film *The Day After*. The film depicts a fictional conflict between NATO and Warsaw Pact forces that soon escalates into full-scale nuclear war. Not only did the film have a profound effect upon the American people, but it also deeply moved the American president. He thought it was extremely effective and left him deeply shaken.[13] The combined effect of seeing the film and knowing how close the world had come to disaster changed his views on nuclear war. From early 1984 Ronald Reagan adopted a new approach towards the Soviet Union. He was now anxious to talk to a Soviet leader – he wanted to convince him the United States had no intention of attacking the Soviet Union.[14]

The single most important milestone on the road towards the end of the Cold War took place on 11 March 1985. Just hours after the death of President Konstantin Chernenko, 54-year-old Mikhail Gorbachev was elected by the Politburo to become the eighth (and final) leader of the Soviet Union. After Brezhnev, Andropov, and

Chernenko, the Politburo understood that the party needed someone younger. But very few could have foreseen the changes this son of a Ukrainian peasant farmer would bring to the Soviet Union and the world order.

Almost immediately Gorbachev set about trying to introduce reforms. *Perestroika* and *Glasnost* are words that became commonplace in political language around the world and ushered in a genuine thaw in east–west relations. He understood that any domestic reforms had to be linked to a new foreign policy, matched by reduced military spending, and the ruinous occupation of Afghanistan had to be brought to an end. Just a month later, the new Soviet leader unilaterally suspended deployment of its intermediate-range SS-20 missiles to Europe, and later that year he proposed that both the United States and Soviet Union reduce their nuclear arsenals by half.

In November 1985, Ronald Reagan and Mikhail Gorbachev met for the first time in Geneva. Although nothing concrete came out of their talks, with the major sticking point being American insistence on developing SDI, the two leaders had struck up a personal relationship and agreed to more talks. They met again in Iceland at the Reykjavik summit in October 1986, and although nothing was signed the groundwork had been put in place for the historic signing of the Intermediate-Range Nuclear Forces Treaty during the Washington summit of December 1987, which was ratified a year later in Moscow.

In July 1989, Mikhail Gorbachev announced his biggest foreign policy reform – an end to the Brezhnev Doctrine. The Soviet Union would no longer interfere in the internal affairs of Warsaw Pact members. In countries like Poland, the Solidarity labour movement had been dangerously pushing back against the Soviet regime since 1980. At last it seemed like their time had come. Inside the Soviet Union there had been protests in the Baltic states and the Caucasus region that were now turning into campaigns for independence. Subjugated for decades, separatist movements sprang up throughout the Soviet Union threatening to tear the country apart.

On 20 January 1989, President George Herbert Walker Bush became the 41st President of the United States. He had been Ronald Reagan's vice president for eight years and had beaten Democrat Michael Dukakis two months earlier. Often seen as a lesser politician than Reagan after two terms in his shadow, Bush was unfairly perceived by some to lack an ideological core. But as history now reflects, President Bush was right for the job. What he lacked as an ideologue he more than made up for as a pragmatist. He steered his country into the 1990s as the world's only remaining superpower.

Less than a month after Bush took office, Russia withdrew its last troops from Afghanistan. After invading the country to support the communist regime a decade earlier, Russian forces now crossed the Amu Darya River in the dead of winter. The defeat of a global superpower had not happened since the American withdrawal from Vietnam. And like its disastrous folly in Southeast Asia, where China and the Soviet Union had supported the North Vietnamese, the United States played a similarly major role in Afghanistan. Throughout the Soviet occupation, the United States had been secretly funding and arming both Afghan fighters and thousands of international 'jihadists' who flocked to the country in defence of their Muslim brothers. With the help of CIA-provided Stinger missiles and $1 trillion[15] spent directly supporting the Mujahideen (Muslim guerrilla fighters), the Soviet position in Afghanistan became untenable. There were some within the intelligence community now sounding alarm bells in Washington, D.C. because arms and funding had fallen into the hands of groups like Osama bin Laden's Al Qaeda.[16] However, President Bush and his government celebrated the victory – it was a step closer to the end of the Soviet Union.

Throughout 1989, the winds of change seemed to be constantly blowing across Europe. The effects of reforms put in place by Gorbachev, now embraced by the west, were felt throughout the Soviet Union and countries of the Warsaw Pact, with far-reaching political consequences. The danger now facing Bush, Thatcher, and every western democratic leader was both unprecedented and terrifying. As the Soviet Union crumbled and fell apart, so did control of twenty thousand nuclear warheads – enough weapons to eradicate all life on the planet.[17]

Throughout 1989, the German Democratic Republic (GDR) was the focal point of attention. Split into East and West Germany after World War II, its border became the front line of the Cold War. In June 1989, Hungary's dismantling of its portion of fencing along the Austrian border was to have huge implications for the GDR. In September, thousands of East Germans travelled to Hungary on the pretence of going on holiday. Up to 13,000 crossed into Austria[18] before the Hungarians realised what was happening. They then stopped many thousands more by closing border crossing points. Long-time East German leader Erich Honecker blocked any further travel to Hungary. Despite these restrictions, the exodus to the west continued unabated; East Germans re-routed through Czechoslovakia to reach Hungary. On 18 October, Honecker was replaced by Egon Krenz, but the situation did not improve. By early November there were daily demonstrations in Berlin. The largest, on 4 November, was attended by almost a million people in Alexanderplatz.

The pressure upon the East German government was growing by the day. To stop the haemorrhage of citizens pouring through the Hungarian gap in the Iron Curtain, new rules allowing limited travel to the west were hastily drawn up by Krenz and some members of the Politburo. On the evening of 9 November, the new regulations were announced live on television. Just before the press conference, the Politburo chairman Günter Schabowski, who was not involved in the drafting of the changes, was given the new regulations to read out. Schabowski was unaware that they were supposed to come into effect the next day, time enough for the border guards to be ready. But when asked by a reporter, he replied, 'As far as I know, it takes effect immediately, without delay.'[19] The effect of his words was indeed immediate. Not only was it announced on all West German television stations, but word quickly spread throughout east and west Berlin. By midnight hundreds of East Berliners had passed unchallenged through the various checkpoints to the west.

By the weekend, the Berlin Wall was all but gone. The East German government had given up any attempts at restricting its citizens' movement and opened all border crossings. Amazingly to some in the west, the East German authorities' plan was working, as most of their citizens now chose to stay in the east. There were those who moved immediately, but most were happy simply to be allowed to travel freely through the wall and return unhindered. Perhaps they stayed because they knew East Germany was finished or maybe they knew that the reality of a unified Germany was just a matter of time.

On 3 December 1989, at the Malta Summit, Mikhail Gorbachev and George Bush declared the Cold War to be over. On the Russian ship the *Maxim Gorky*, Bush announced, 'We can transform East–West relationships to one of enduring co-operation.' Gorbachev was equally optimistic about the future, stating 'The threat of force, mistrust, psychological and ideological struggle should all be things of the past.'[20] Both leaders showed a desire for further arms reduction talks and agreed to meet in June the following year.

***

Soldiers who joined the British Army in the late 1980s came from all parts of the United Kingdom and from all walks of life, with many coming from working-class families that had struggled during the Thatcher years. But even though some came from the most militant labour-controlled communities in the country, most soldiers still held a high respect for Margaret Thatcher. It had nothing to do with her policies; instead, in her attitude and respect for service, she seemed to place an emphasis and importance on the values that are at the heart of military culture. Soldiers like Conrad P. sometimes found themselves having to make a tough decision.

> She was clearly hated in South Wales ... however when I joined the Army I realised the Conservative Party supported the Army much more than Labour did, so I was in a very awkward position. Did I vote for my own personal welfare while based in Central London, or for my ageing parents back home in the valleys of Wales? I often decided not to vote, such was the dilemma.

As the decade came to an end, the world seemed like it had changed forever. At the Malta Summit, Mikhail Gorbachev made a very prophetic statement. At the time it went unnoticed; it was reported but didn't register any more than other statements he'd made during the summit. 'The world is leaving one epoch and entering another. We are at the beginning of a long road to a lasting, peaceful era.'[21]

The first sentence still holds true today; the fall of the Berlin Wall and the end of the Cold War did end an epoch, the origins of which can be traced back to the start of World War I. But the second sentence could not have been further from the truth. There can be no doubt that Mikhail Gorbachev honestly believed there could be peace, especially between the east and west. But as Karl Marx once said, 'Men make their own history, but they do not make it as they choose.'[22] For soldiers just starting a career in the British Army, there would be no lasting peaceful era after the Berlin Wall came down.

CHAPTER 2

Early Days

Every soldier remembers their first day of basic training. Whether they joined in 1958, or 1988, entering the front gates of a training unit was an experience few would forget. At Aldershot, Bovington, Catterick, Chepstow, Lichfield, or Pirbright, each recruit would undergo a personal transformation. 'The Guards Depot was the biggest jolt to my life. Up until then I had a mum who washed and ironed everything, made my bed, fed me, and kept me clean. Well, I soon realised I had a lot to learn.' Many had been told by friends and relatives who were ex-soldiers what to expect. Some had tried to be as ready as they possibly could be, but nothing had prepared them for the visceral shock of day one.

'We were met at the station by a beast of a man dressed in this smart uniform. He was constantly bellowing at us, "Get on the bus", "shut your mouth", "sit still"; it was relentless.' After 35 years in uniform, Soldier B. still vividly remembers his first day when the instructor came into the room and told him he 'wouldn't last a week'. Owen C. remembers making the train journey from Gloucester to Dorset. 'Having arrived at Wool Station we were collected in a bus. It was our first taste of the Army, not some nice chap trying to get you to join in a careers office. Anyone and everyone was a target.'

Russian general Alexander Suvorov is the accepted source of the timeless military idiom 'Train hard, fight easy.' To the British Army it is an important phrase and highlights its policy with regards to preparing men for war. The system that turned young recruits – some just out of school, barely old enough to shave – into highly trained soldiers capable of going to war, was tried and tested. Based on discipline, a strict regimental uniformity, and a high level of fitness, basic training in the late 1980s had changed very little for decades. Some training depots' regimes were more intense than others and had a different focus.

Drill (especially at the Guards Depot) was the very first thing every new recruit was subjected to. It was and still is a huge part of Army ethos and the basis of all military discipline; its purpose is to instil an instinctive reaction to a familiar order. Drill also builds teamwork and cohesion among soldiers who come together as complete strangers. Almost every day, recruits are on the drill square getting barked at by instructors.

Having finally got into the Army at the third attempt, Doug K. arrived at Pirbright and became known in his platoon as the 'fat bloke with dodgy eyes'. Having failed the eye-exam portion of the medical, he kept coming back every six months to try again. On his third attempt, sitting in the doctor's office expecting to fail, the doctor smiled and said, 'They changed the rules, you passed!' This kind of persistence was what got many through basic training. His platoon started with 60 recruits, with only 38 passing out six months later. An attrition rate of between 40–50 per cent was acceptable as there were plenty of young school leavers looking to join up.

Although most were determined to finish, some either entertained the thought of quitting or struggled at one time or another. Conrad P. said, 'Training was horrendously difficult and I hated it ... thoughts of quitting became a daily occurrence but as individuals left and their pictures got taken off the board, the more determined I became to succeed.' Doug K. wasn't going to let his chance slip away either. 'Training was hard, very hard. Did I want to quit? Yes. But I just kept saying, one more day, one more day.' Angus T. joined up and soon found out that he had made the right decision. 'I absolutely loved basic training at the Guards Depot. I was the youngest in the platoon but I just loved it all. It was hard but bloody rewarding. I never once thought of quitting at all.'

Some found themselves physically unprepared for what they were about to face. Soldier G.'s basic training preparation included 'lager and far too many chips'. He arrived there 'about two stone overweight but was to leave a stone underweight and fit as a fiddle'. At the start of his basic training, Martin M. struggled physically. 'I just kept plugging away and eventually my fitness improved; in fact, I got obsessed with it and became a Physical Training Instructor.' Rich G. was a recruit at the Junior Leaders Regiment, Royal Armoured Corps. 'I enjoyed Bovington but wasn't a great recruit and never really excelled in training. But I never thought of quitting and knew it was what I wanted to do.'

One of the toughest courses to pass has always been at the Depot of the Parachute Regiment in Aldershot. Stuart B. showed the kind of determination and guts that has always epitomised those who wear the coveted maroon beret.

> I failed P Company the first time round (it was hard as a young lad) but there was no way it was going to beat me. I loved the training and learnt so much from scratch. Many of my instructors were Falkland veterans who were god-like ... At no time was I ever going to quit; it never entered my mind. 'Failure is not an option,' as they say.

What all recruits had in common was an immense pride at finishing what they had started. For Stuart B., 'Passing P Company, earning the "Maroon Machine" and obtaining my wings is probably my greatest achievement in life.' And for Soldier G., 'One of the proudest moments of my life was to receive the best recruit trophy.

As I marched out … I heard my Dad cheer and clap – a father/son moment never to be forgotten.'

For many, the bonds of friendship made in the first days of their Army careers during basic training would last a lifetime. Martin M. describes it perfectly. 'The best thing about being in the Army … the best, most supportive and consistently reliable mates you could have ever had. It's amazing, you chuck a load of teenagers from different social and geographic backgrounds together, make their life tough and miserable, and they end up having a great time together, managing to find humour in everything.'

***

The British Army has always taken great pride in the fact that its recruit training is difficult but its instructors are considered to be firm but fair. With the luxury of hindsight, some now look back with mixed views on their training, and in particular with regards to the actions of some of their instructors. After 22 years in the Army, looking back on his basic training, Owen C. says, 'There were various incidents that happened throughout my basic training which would certainly be cause for investigation in this day and age.' It is generally acknowledged that the vast majority of instructors were highly professional and only interested in making sure every recruit that passed through their establishment became a valuable asset to their regiment or corps. But from time to time an instructor tested the boundaries of what was acceptable and what was not. Doug K. completed his training at the Guards Depot and would later become an instructor there.

> If anywhere was meant to have a reputation for bullying this would be the place. But I did not find that to be the case. The instructors were very direct, very tough and forgave nothing but were the epitome of firm but fair. Did they lay hands on recruits? Yes. Would the way they worked have been accepted when I became an instructor? No. But it did not feel like bullying at all, perhaps it is linked to … what we thought was acceptable at the time.

There has always been the perception of a fine line existing between firm discipline and bullying. Where that line is now is a very different place from where it was in the late 1980s. Looking back we have to remember that we live in a different time and in a vastly changed society. The actions of instructors from that period are now viewed through a different lens.

Although there is no accurate record of numbers of complaints/incidents of bullying by instructors during this time,[1] it is safe to say that although it was rare it did happen. There was a reluctance by those bullied to approach an officer, and many of those who did complain were discharged recruits. This gave those in command a false impression that it never happened.

After completing basic training and enjoying their pass out parade in front of friends and family, most went on to complete specialised/trade training. If soldiers thought the worst was over because they were now 'qualified', then on arrival at their regiment or battalion, they were in for a rude awakening. Once again, they were about to find themselves back at the bottom of the food chain.

In his paper *Battling Bullying in the British Army 1987–2004*, James Wither says that although there were incidents of bullying that came from instructors or JNCOs, recruits and new arrivals at units in the British Army were 'more likely to be the victims of peer group bullying'.[2] Conrad P. confirms this. 'It was simply horrendous … in basic training instructors were governed to a certain degree, but when joining your battalion, your peers were not … There were simply no boundaries. You just had to make yourself popular somehow.' One soldier arrived at his regiment while his company was on leave. 'I lived in transit accommodation for a couple of weeks; it was a nightmare. Senior soldiers seemed to enjoy coming in off the piss and making your life hell, so I was glad when they came back off leave.'

Like most other service (and some civilian) institutions, the British Army had a history of unsanctioned initiation ceremonies that most new recruits had to undergo upon arrival at the new unit. They ranged from drinking some form of alcoholic concoction, to a barrack room 'court-martial' presided upon by a senior private soldier, to rituals that can only be described (both then and now) by those outside the barrack block as nothing more than criminal assault. 'When I arrived at the regiment initiations were the norm. Tied to a plastic chair while a bin is placed over you, a hose is inserted then turned on. Locked inside a metal locker and have it turned upside down.' At Knightsbridge in the Household Cavalry Mounted Regiment, initiations took on a very unique form. 'Tied to a saddle rack and covered with horse feed while a horse who was a known biter is allowed to nibble on you. Thrown into the horse trough with a wooden board over you, so you are fully submerged in water and left there until you could no longer breathe. All these were deemed as being character building.' When troopers went on their first Queen's Life Guard the occasion was normally marked with a very unique initiation, one that had gone on for many years. 'Most were hosed down and thrown into a pile of horse manure; some were even branded with a hot cap badge.'

Not all 'initiations' were one-off events, and some were nothing more than bullying. 'I do remember a couple of individuals who took it upon themselves to tour the accommodation block and rough up the new lads. This went on over a period of months until the next group of lads arrived from training.' Quite often new recruits were labelled as being 'gobby' and then singled out for extra treatment. The definition varied, but being gobby was often just speaking back to a senior soldier or sticking up for themselves, and often used as an excuse to justify someone's actions to a higher rank. And, of course when alcohol was added, some young recruits that were usually quiet and unassuming might not be able to hold their drink. 'We took part in several drinking games – a couple of the new guys got a bit cocky and received a good kicking. They then became the squadron whipping boys.' Doug K. describes a unique cure for those accused of being gobby. 'I did see one guy get crucified in the squadron block after he was being more than a bit gobby. They rigged double broom handles together and used black nasty [masking tape] to secure him to the handles. They then suspended him over the stair well from the top floor and left him to swing for a few hours.'

Not all bullying was physical; some young soldiers' lives were made a misery without them being touched. 'I was made to do other soldiers' duties … sent shopping for the platoon, given £5 but the bill was £15.' Rich G. said, 'I didn't encounter any physical bullying but was taken advantage of as I was a new guy. Mainly it was senior soldiers and some JNCOs borrowing money and kit and not returning it.'

Some soldiers avoided being bullied because they fought back. 'It's safe to say that most new guys got a rough ride for a while. And it was always the weak ones that were targeted; I fought back and generally got left alone. But I did wake up one night to find an NCO pissing on my bed while I was in it.' And some stayed together in large enough numbers to prevent their being targeted.

> We were a close and tight-knit group who looked out for each other and I had absolute confidence that if anything happened to any one of us there would have been four or five who would immediately back you up. But there were certain individuals who had a reputation of being bullies; people who used to strut around the block with a superior attitude and often with a retinue of weaselly minions in tow. I was never bullied.

Another soldier discovered a unique way to avoid barrack room bullies.

> The next morning, I was moving my kit across to my new room … the boxing team was being chosen in the bottom alcove. An NCO asked me if I knew my boxing weight (I was as skinny as a rake and 5'10" in those days). I said 'No,' so he said, 'Get on the scales.' I did and his next comment was, 'Right, you are now our company lightweight.' He then turned to everyone one else and said, 'Make sure no one touches him.' So, I was protected.

Quite often, after some soldiers had survived bullying over an extended period of time, they would then become the bully. 'The first six months in the battalion were the worst of my life… I honestly believe that I became a bully because of what happened to me.' Another soldier tried to justify his own actions.

> If we're being totally honest, not only did we receive rough treatment when we joined the regiment, we also gave it out to some degree later on when we became the senior soldiers. I know that many went way too far, and I was always for those people getting what they deserved. But for the most part my attitude was that if it didn't harm me, then it wasn't going to harm them either.

In 1987, the Army was rocked by a series of newspaper articles. Not only were the headlines in British tabloids and broadsheets, but they also appeared in Australian papers and even in the *New York Times*: 'British Army Stung by Tales of Brutality in Ranks'.[3] Detailing two incidents that took place in the Coldstream Guards and the King's Own Scottish Borderers that saw many arrested, court-martialled, imprisoned, and discharged, the article also claimed that initiations were not uncommon in the British Army. An Army spokesman acknowledged that the investigation was looking at 75 separate incidents.[4]

Most soldiers who took part in initiation ceremonies did so willingly and came through it unscathed, but some didn't. Even if the abuse or injury sustained during an initiation ceremony could be explained somehow as a way of toughening up new recruits, there was no explanation or excuse for some of the other bullying that took place.

> Over a four- to five-year period in the mid-80s I can remember three separate court-martials for basically the same thing. An old sweat would come back to the block after a night out, go into the room of a crow [recently arrived recruit], try to bully him into going out in the middle of the night to get him food that he had to pay for. When the lad refused, he'd gotten a beating. Two of the lads were beaten so bad there was blood up the walls and, on the ceiling, and one lad had his arm broken when the bullies dropped a car battery on his hand.

The incidents that took place in 1987 led to a major shake-up in the British Army. There were multiple court-martials, with at least one commanding officer removed from his command. The adjutant-general instigated a series of anti-bullying measures and outlawed all forms of unauthorized initiation ceremonies. Extracts from Queen's Regulations would be published at least annually in all unit and sub-unit routine orders.[5] Although these actions would not stop bullying or eradicate all reports of initiation ceremonies, it did send the message that this was not something they had to tolerate and that the Army now went to great lengths to confront it and take action when warranted.

In 2018, Soldier G. was interviewed about an incident that took place while he was serving. It shows how seriously the Army now takes any such allegations or claims.

> Five years after leaving the Army I didn't expect Royal Military Police to be sat on the other side of a desk asking questions … Apparently I was approached by a victim who claimed he'd complained about the person to me. It turned out we'd had a conversation in the mess in passing and I had given the guy the option to come and see me in my office later, but he never showed up. When a service complaint is made you now get a copy of all the statements and alleged incidents. I was quite upset [after reading them] because if I'd known the full extent of the bullying at the time, I would have certainly sought the perpetrator's discharge.

CHAPTER 3

The Short Peace

As the 1990s began, the momentous events of the previous year still loomed large. There was already talk of German reunification, and rumours began to circulate about massive troop reductions in Germany. But for any young soldier who had just joined up or recently finished basic training, nothing had changed. Their priorities were simple: 'Learn your job, keep your mouth shut, your head down, then get on with enjoying life.' Most were too young to worry (or care) about anything else; the events of the past year meant very little to them because they had no direct impact on their lives. Rich G. was finishing his training at Bovington. 'I was too young to understand the implications for the Army at this stage.' For those not stationed in Germany, life went on as normal. In Northern Ireland, for men like Stuart B. who was with 3 Para on a two-year tour in Belfast, nothing had changed; the bombings and murders continued unabated despite the collapse of the Soviet Union. 'It was a busy tour, so apart from watching it on the news it didn't affect me personally.' But for the 50,000 servicemen in Germany whose focus for decades had been on eastern Europe, the question was, what next?

Some soldiers still couldn't believe it had happened, with one noting that back in the 1980s, 'I [had] doubted if it [the Berlin Wall] would come down in my lifetime.' And for those who remembered the fear of a nuclear catastrophe at the height of the Cold War, 'My immediate thoughts were of relief ... could this be the end of the threat of war between East and West?'

David K. had been in Germany less than a month when the wall came down. His regiment was stationed in Wolfenbüttel on the East German border, and his was one of the closest units to the Iron Curtain. 'Within two days we were carrying out border patrols ... I was amazed by the amount of Soviet-built helicopters and military vehicles coming across the border from east to west.' Paul H. was stationed in Munster with the Grenadier Guards. Like many others he was 'not too sure about the future', especially with regards to the prospects of a reunified Germany, but he 'was pleased the Cold War was over'. In the short term it meant that the perceived threat from the east had evaporated. Soldier A. remarked, 'We were working on armoured vehicles to defend against an enemy that was no longer a threat. But none of us really understood the consequences; we just got on with our jobs.' There was a strange unease throughout the British Army of the Rhine (BAOR). Training continued; exercises and deployments on live-firing exercises to Canada that had been scheduled several years in advance went ahead as if the Russians were still the enemy. Soldier E. noted, 'It seemed to me that some in command still thought the Cold War was still happening; it was if nothing had happened.'

With all restrictions across the now-defunct Iron Curtain permanently lifted, it was not just one-way traffic of East Germans heading west. Many soldiers and their families took advantage of new travel destinations. The famous World War II POW camp at Colditz Castle was a favourite, as well as cities like Leipzig, Dresden, and Magdeburg. And although there were some restrictions regarding travel to Berlin, many soldiers jumped in their cars on a Friday afternoon and headed along the old Berlin corridor for the weekend. Some soldiers travelled much further afield.

> I can remember marking a soldier absent after a Monday morning first parade. When he came back about midday on Wednesday he ended up in trap one [jail cell] of the guardroom for the night and then went in front of the CO the next day. His excuse was that he had met a girl in a Berlin nightclub, got drunk, and then woke up in Poland. He claimed she had taken all his money and that it had taken him three days to get back to camp. The CO believed him and let him off with a warning – I didn't and gave him every crap job I could think of for a month.

Some members of David K.'s regiment took full advantage of their close proximity to East Germany. 'Many of the lads were crossing the border within days of the Iron Curtain falling, some coming back with exotic girlfriends, picked up from Magdeburg.' One of those having fun in the east was Simon J. 'This was one of the best times during my whole career … it started my love affair with Germany and its women. Today I am still married to one. I didn't go home for a year because I was having so much fun.'

For politicians coming to terms with the new reality, the changes they faced were immense. President Reagan, shocked by events of 1983 that had almost started World War III, had welcomed Russia's change of position under Gorbachev, but President Bush was less trusting. Some in the west believed that Gorbachev's reforms had been made out of necessity. Many, including President Bush, wondered if the Soviets really wanted peace, or just enough time to rebuild their forces.[1] If Bush was right and Gorbachev was putting in place some devious Stalinesque plan, then the United States and its allies who were already making large-scale defence cuts were making a catastrophic mistake, unwittingly leaving Europe undefended. Bush and Foreign Secretary James Baker arrived at the US–Soviet talks of February 1990 with these suspicions in mind. The Bush administration might not have trusted Gorbachev's intentions, but it was actually the Americans who would make empty promises. During the talks Baker suggested that if they (the Russians) cooperated over German reunification (which they were strongly against), then the United States would give 'iron-clad guarantees' that NATO would not expand 'one inch eastward'. Nothing was agreed in writing; however, transcripts show a deal had been made.[2]

Margaret Thatcher, who had been a key player in the demise of the Soviet Union, now found herself in a much-changed situation. Under immense pressure at home because of the Poll Tax, she also found herself locked out of talks with Gorbachev. The 'special relationship' she had enjoyed with Ronald Reagan was altogether different with George Bush. His Secretary of State did not see things the way his predecessor did. Britain was not considered an equal partner and so the United States began to align itself with continental European allies as opposed to London.

With the Berlin Wall down, the Warsaw Pact gone, and the Cold War officially over, many countries now scaled back on their military spending. Margaret Thatcher, who had increased defence spending to a peak in 1985 at 5.1 per cent of GDP,[3] was now under pressure to deliver the much-anticipated Peace Dividend. On 25 July 1990, the government issued a framework document, Options for Change,[4] announcing substantial cuts. For the Army the proposed cuts were drastic though expected. BAOR would be reduced by half, going from four divisions to two. Secretary of State for Defence Tom King made a statement in the House of Commons the day the framework document was released. 'The aim is smaller forces, better equipped, properly trained and housed, and well-motivated. They will need to be flexible and mobile and able to contribute both in NATO and, if necessary elsewhere … our proposals will bring savings and a reduction in the share of GDP taken by defence.'[5] Little did the Secretary of State know, just six days after his speech to Parliament 'elsewhere' would take on a whole new meaning, with the viability of the proposed cuts being tested on the Arabian peninsula.

As nations were trying to adjust to the new realities of a post-Cold War world, they were plunged into a crisis that would immediately test the new world order. On 2 August 1990, led by four Republican Guard divisions, Iraq's military forces invaded the neighbouring state of Kuwait. This planned incursion crossed the border in the early hours of the morning, catching Kuwait's defence forces completely off guard. Despite this they managed to arm and fuel several battalions of British-made Chieftain tanks and used them to destroy and severely damage many Iraqi tanks near the town of Al Jahra. Low on ammunition and eventually overwhelmed by sheer numbers, they were forced to flee south to Saudi Arabia.[6] By that evening, despite brave resistance in several pockets in and around Kuwait City, the Iraqi military controlled most of the country.

The Iran–Iraq War of 1980–88 had left Saddam Hussein's regime greatly weakened. Domestically, with 300,000 war dead, the conflict came to an unsatisfactory end after a protracted stalemate. This led to widespread dissatisfaction in a country where previous unpopular leaders had not survived long. Economically, the country faced enormous reconstruction costs and now had massive debts, owing billions to both Saudi Arabia and Kuwait, and politically, the collapse of the Soviet Union had threatened Iraq's strategic importance on the world stage. Saddam Hussein knew he had to act quickly and started to see his smaller, richer neighbours as easy prey and a way of solving many of his issues in one bold move. Invading Kuwait was a massive risk; he was gambling on the west being preoccupied with a collapsing Soviet Union, hoping the world would not pay attention to yet another regional conflict in the Middle East.

When news spread around the world there was overwhelming condemnation. An emergency session of the United Nations Security Council called for an 'immediate and unconditional' withdrawal. Margaret Thatcher said it was 'absolutely unacceptable'; George Bush described the incursion as 'a naked act of aggression'; and even Russia said it was suspending delivery of all weapons and equipment to its former ally.[7] Although Iraq's and Kuwait's assets were frozen, there had been no condemnation of the attack from any Arab nation, with even the slightest suggestion of a military intervention. Saddam felt emboldened, threatening to turn Kuwait into a 'graveyard' if anyone dared challenge him.[8]

Most British Army soldiers were aware of what had happened in Kuwait; it was all over the news though many (author included) did not take much notice. One soldier said, 'It was just another Arab-on-Arab conflict and I was sure it wouldn't involve us. How wrong was I?' Soldier M. was home on leave. 'My dad joked that this time next month I would be playing in the sand – he later said he regretted that joke.' Soldier B. heard the news as he was finishing a course. 'I didn't dwell on the political enormity of what Saddam had done, but militarily I knew the world would not and could not allow him to grab Kuwait and its oil fields.' He was right.

The invasion should not have come as a complete surprise. In hindsight, the signs were there. But for several days afterwards President Bush and his National Security Council (NSC) seemed to struggle with a response. The last United States Middle East military intervention had ended in disaster on 23 October 1983 with the deaths of 241 Marines in Beirut. And with the legacy of Vietnam still casting a dark shadow over the American psyche, many asked whether Kuwait was actually worth saving. Even Saddam questioned America's appetite for war. Speaking to US Ambassador to Iraq April Glaspie just one week before the invasion, the Iraqi president said, 'Yours is a society which cannot accept 10,000 dead in one battle.'[9]

After a chaotic NSC meeting on the morning of 2 August 1990, President Bush flew to Aspen, Colorado, to open a conference and attend a pre-arranged meeting with Margaret Thatcher. During that meeting the prime minister reminded the president that 'appeasement in the 1930s had led to war and Saddam would have the whole Gulf at his mercy – and 65 per cent of the world's oil supply with it – if his aggression were not quickly checked.'[10] After another NSC meeting on 3 August, President Bush left for Camp David. Records show that although the meeting was less chaotic, attendees remained unsure how to respond to the invasion.[11]

It is unknown whether it was the influence of the British prime minister or the failure of Arab leaders to persuade Saddam to withdraw, but by the time President Bush arrived back at the White House on the afternoon of Sunday 5 August, he appeared to be full of resolve. After walking from his helicopter he spoke with reporters. What he said left the world in no doubt of what was going to happen next. 'I view it very seriously, not just that but any threat to any other countries, as well as I view very seriously our determination to reverse out this aggression … this will not stand, this aggression against Kuwait.'[12]

As the weeks went by with no Iraqi withdrawal in sight, the prospects of an all-out war between Iraq and a broad coalition of nations led by the United States became more of a reality. At first, deployment of troops was carried out to counter a very real concern that Iraq might invade Saudi Arabia; the operation was known as *Desert Shield*. As the number of troops, tanks, and aircraft grew, the threat of an Iraqi invasion of Saudi Arabia lessened, and as the troop numbers approached a half-million, the assembled force started to look more like an offensive weapon. A string of United Nations Security Council resolutions called for Iraq to withdraw. It ultimately led to UNSCR 678 that called for a complete Iraqi withdrawal by 15 January 1991 or it would face forced removal.

Saddam tried to unite the Arab world by linking Kuwait to the wider Palestinian issue. He knew that getting Israel involved would fracture the US coalition. Saudi Arabia had taken the unlikely (and unpopular) decision to allow a large deployment of non-Arab troops on its soil – but it would never allow them to be used against brother Arabs if Israel were involved. Saddam knew this and went to great lengths to try to bring Israel into the conflict.

Over the next few months there was a steady build-up of British troops in the Saudi desert. Initially it was limited to air assets; two RAF squadrons of Tornado F3 interceptors were deployed to deter any Iraqi aircraft from straying too close. Then the 7th Armoured Brigade – the Desert Rats – were deployed with two Challenger tank regiments. A second brigade, the 4th Mechanised, followed when it was decided to send a full armoured division. Constant increases in the UK's commitment in equipment and men were to have a big effect on soldiers' lives, especially in Germany, regardless of whether they were deployed. As regiments and battalions were warned off for deployment, there was a frantic rush to ensure that each unit had the best and most up-to-date equipment available. One soldier remembers being on leave at the time.

> When we got back we were told to hand over our Mark III Challenger tanks to the Royal Scots Dragoon Guards. We were really pissed off. Just before leave we'd had a Colonel's tank inspection – they were immaculate. The tanks we got back from the RSDG, older Mark Is, were a mess. We then spent several months getting these tanks back in shape only to be told we had to spray them sand-coloured and they were shipped off too.

Like many soldiers not sent in the initial deployment, Soldier B. was disappointed. He said he felt like 'a glorified pit crew doing crappy jobs like changing fuel bags and track bashing'. Rich G. had just finished basic training and clearly remembers 'the constant prep and handover of vehicles to other units who were going, then taking on other vehicles to hand over again'. After leading a spray team on a whole squadron of Challenger tanks that were now sand-coloured, Martin M. was placed on CO's orders and told he was being promoted and sent to London on ceremonial duties. 'This was my chance to go to war, this was why I had joined in the first place, how dare they steal this from me … my protestations fell on very deaf ears. Apparently, I should have been grateful for the promotion; I wasn't. So off I went to Knightsbridge at the end of December, with my tail between my legs.' After arriving at his new unit, Neil S. was also going to be disappointed. He was ordered to 'paint an entire combat tractor with a 2-inch brush after a weekend misdemeanour', followed by being told that his unit would now go to the Falklands on a construction tour.

As the months went by and attempts to solve the crisis peacefully all failed, there was a real sense among soldiers that they might actually see combat. With the commitment of a full division, many more men were warned off that they would be deployed. Owen C. recalls learning the news while his squadron was busy carrying out Northern Ireland training. 'We were gathered together and told that as we had already started deployment training we were going to change tack slightly and were being deployed to the Gulf instead.' Paul H. was on a four-month military expedition in Brunei. Although he was thousands of miles away, he had a feeling he might be involved eventually. 'I knew we'd get recalled, they were calling everyone back to Oxford Barracks … we were on R&R in Hong Kong … late Nov '90 at HMS *Tamar* on the harbour front … we had been posted back to the battalion and would be leaving for Munster ASAP.' Pete R. was with the Coldstream Guards on public duties in London and about to go on Christmas leave. 'The CO gave a battalion briefing and said, "Enjoy your leave. I will eat my hat if we are involved in this." Halfway through leave we were called back and told we were going. The Quartermaster offered the CO salt and pepper with his hat.'

Throughout the crisis, President Bush, Prime Minister Thatcher, and her successor, John Major, remained resolute in the face of mounting pressure to avoid an armed conflict. Mikhail Gorbachev was in general agreement that Iraq could not stay in Kuwait, but he became increasingly vocal, wanting the US coalition to give Saddam a way out. When they met in Helsinki in September he gave the US president a stark warning after Bush had said that if Iraq was not removed, 'it will set a terrible precedent for the future'. He replied, 'But if he gets nothing at all, if he is backed into a corner, it will be more costly for us all. We need to give him some daylight.'[13] Bush knew that it might be costly. As a World War II pilot, he had seen the price war had exacted from his own generation. But he also knew what history had taught us all: Appeasing a dictator never works. He'd drawn a line in the sand – Iraq's army was leaving Kuwait and how they left would be up to Saddam.

One thing was clear: Politicians, military leaders, soldiers, and civilians alike all knew that forcefully removing Saddam's military forces from Kuwait could result in thousands of casualties. Iraq had over a million men in uniform; 66 divisions comprising thousands of Soviet-built tanks and artillery added up to the world's fourth-largest standing army.[14] Saddam had shown the world he was willing to use poison gas not only on his enemies but also on his own people. He had delivery systems (artillery, missiles, and aircraft) capable of hitting opposing troops in the region. With Saddam promising 'the mother of all battles',[15] Senate Majority Leader George Mitchell warned of massed casualties and deaths.[16] The cover of *Time* magazine, leading with the headline 'Are we ready for this?' above the picture of a soldier in his respirator,[17] left many questioning the wisdom of military intervention. For soldiers arriving 'in theatre' there was no doubt that casualties were expected. 'After we landed on the US base in Saudi Arabia, we drove past a long line of converted white buses that had red crosses on them – there were dozens of them.' As well as converting part of the airport at Riyadh into a 2,000-bed hospital, the military covertly shipped thousands of body bags to Saudi Arabia.[18]

Both British and American commanders were determined to minimise and avoid casualties wherever possible. General Norman Schwarzkopf, Commander of the United States Central Command and then leader of all Coalition forces during the operation, was reluctant to act before he had assembled overwhelming forces in the region. His British counterpart and de facto second-in-command, Lieutenant General Peter de la Billière, was of the same mind.[19]

Back in Germany and the UK, troops about to be deployed with the 4th Mechanised Brigade, or as battlefield casualty replacements, were also busy training. Just 48 hours after leaving Hong Kong, Paul H. was back with the Grenadier Guards in Germany on a freezing-cold range. 'We went from range to range, training stand to training stand … there were not enough hours in the day.' He also noticed a change in the mood of some of his fellow soldiers. 'There was a real serious tone … friends and commanders alike were very quiet. There was none of the usual banter.'

While the world was focused upon the escalating situation in the Middle East, East and West Germany became one nation, and Britain suddenly found itself with a new and relatively unknown prime minister. Soldiers I interviewed hardly remember either event; their focus had been elsewhere. 'Looking back, I'm quite ashamed that I don't recall either event, but for those couple of months before deploying to the Gulf, I was preoccupied. We were in Canada on exercise when the reunification happened, and at the ranges in Hohne getting ready for deployment to the Gulf when Maggie was knifed by her own party.'

It is fair to say that many countries had reservations and fears about a united Germany. The first half of the 20th century had been dominated by two global conflicts in which German militarism was a major factor. There was now a very real possibility of renewed German nationalism if countries blocked what only seemed natural to both East and West Germans. After the collapse of the GDR, the future of any united Germany would rest on the opinion of the four occupying powers – America, Russia, France, and Britain. President Bush supported reunification with Germany as a full NATO member, Margaret Thatcher reluctantly gave her support because she did not want to jeopardise Britain's 'special relationship' with Washington, and France was wary at first as it had suffered three German invasions since 1870. The promise of monetary integration and tighter European bonds persuaded French President François Mitterrand to give his support. In return, Germany would support France's wish for both countries to be at the centre of an ever-growing European union. Russia was the only one that would strongly object to a united Germany. With the collapse of the GDR, Russia had lost an ally, and the prospect of a united Germany being in NATO was deeply concerning to Moscow. German Foreign Minister Hans-Dietrich Genscher admitted, 'To think that the borders of NATO could be moved 300 kilometres eastward, via German unification, would be an illusion … no reasonable person could expect the Soviet Union to accept such an outcome.'[20] Russian acquiescence came after a combination of promises made by Bush and Baker that there would be no eastward expansion by NATO and the realisation that the Soviet Union didn't have the political will to intervene in East Germany. In the end there was an air of inevitability about German reunification. The collapse had happened so quickly that countries against German reunification had very little time to react. The only country to officially object to German reunification was Israel.[21]

Margaret Thatcher's approval rating had plummeted and she was now seen as being a drag on her party. Severely damaged by the Poll Tax, it would be her objection to European Monetary Union and Britain joining the European Exchange Rate Mechanism that would see her leadership challenged from within her own party. It was Geoffrey Howe's removal as Foreign Secretary, later resignation as deputy prime minister, and subsequent speech in the House of Commons that brought about a leadership battle.[22] She was challenged by Michael Heseltine, and although she won the first ballot, she did not have enough support to avoid a second. At first it appeared she would fight on, but after members of her own cabinet turned on her, advising her that she should go, and after the news that many MPs were planning to switch support to Heseltine for the second ballot, she resigned from office. On 27 November, John Major beat both Michael Heseltine and Douglas Hurd to became prime minister.

As the end of 1990 approached, soldiers in the desert started to sense that they were going to be used offensively. As well as the massive increase in troop numbers and equipment, there were other signs too. In mid-December, the decision was made to 'up-armour' all Challenger tanks and Warrior Armoured Personnel Carriers (APCs). This appeared to have been a last-minute decision and led to an enormous amount of work being carried out by crews aided by Royal Electrical and Mechanical

Engineers (REME). The Challenger was excellent in defensive situations; however, it was not designed as an offensive tank. Any armour deficiencies were thought to be on the front and sides of the hull. So, to this end, slab armour for the sides and explosive reactive armour for the front started to arrive in the desert. 'When we took over our tank, there were dozens of boxes stacked beside it. With REME help we got on with it and had it done in about a week. It was really easy to fit, just extremely heavy.' As well as extra armour, each tank was fitted with brackets that could hold two 50-gallon fuel drums, another hint of future intentions.

In early January, the British 1st Armoured Division came under the command of the US VII Corps and moved out into the western desert. It was felt by the British commanders that the highly mobile and well-supported division could be better employed in the open desert and a valuable asset within any offensive action.[23] It was now not a case of if but when. Eyes now turned to 15 January, the date the UN mandate would expire.

Just two hours after UNSCR 678 expired, Operation *Desert Shield* ended, and Operation *Desert Storm* began. Cruise missiles and F-117 Stealth bomber raids paralysed Iraqi command and control installations. Knocking out Iraq's air defence was the first priority. With air superiority the Coalition forces could severely reduce Iraq's ability to fight and defend its positions in Kuwait. The advent of 24-hour news coverage meant the world had a ringside seat as CNN news reporters in a Baghdad hotel room witnessed the start of the air campaign, while worried friends and families of soldiers back home sat glued to their television screens.

For troops in the desert it was a strange experience. Some describe feeling detached from it all, only hearing about it on the radio or reading about it in newspapers a few days later. Rich G. recalls the first night of the air campaign. 'I remember it being my commander's daughter's birthday ... and watching cruise missiles going over our position towards Iraqi forces.' During the next month, for troops far away from urban areas, the experience was the same. Soldier B. remembers seeing vapour trails of bombers going over to attack Iraqi positions. Paul H. recalls planes flying high above, then hearing 'the bombs exploding and the ground shake at times'. One armoured squadron was surprised when a Patriot missile unit deployed just behind their position during the night. They only found out they were there when they suddenly fired. 'The whole squadron thought we were under attack for a minute or two.'

If the air campaign was a surreal experience for troops deployed in the desert, the air campaign suddenly became very real for those in transit camps having just arrived at Al Jubail or those stationed in the Saudi capital, Riyadh. Most soldiers in and around the port of Al Jubail clearly remember the first few nights of the air campaign.

> We'd arrived at Blackadder Camp the day before the air war started: a transit encampment of hundreds of massive canvas tents that slept about 30 soldiers in each. We knew it was about to kick off because the British Forces Broadcasting Service announced that active service had been declared. About the second or third night of the air war in the early hours of the morning there

was a huge bang. We all woke up and immediately put on our respirators. We heard a siren go
off in the distance so everyone in my troop started to put on the rest of their NBC [Nuclear,
Biological, Chemical] gear as quickly as they could.

The loud explosion caused a similar panic throughout Al Jubail. It was the sonic
boom from two US aircraft returning from a bombing mission over Iraq. They crossed
over Al Jubail at 3.32 a.m. on the morning of 19 January at a speed of 805mph.[24]
Over the following week the sound of sirens wailing around Al Jubail was a nightly
occurrence. 'We got used to it after a few nights. I decided to put on my NBC suit
before going to sleep and kept my respirator close to hand. When the siren went
off, I just put on my respirator and went back to sleep.'

An early target for Coalition bombs were Saddam's Scud missile launchers;
planners knew they had to be hit before they could be launched at Israel. Although
many were destroyed the first night, it soon became evident that not all of them
had been taken out. The next night Iraq launched eight Scud missiles at Israel.
Four were aimed at the capital, Tel Aviv, and two at the port of Haifa. The Israelis
launched an immediate response. Dozens of aircraft were on their way to Iraq
before being recalled. General de la Billière said it was intense pressure from allies
that prevented the raid from reaching its target, which could have split the fragile
Coalition.[25] Finding any remaining missiles in the western desert was now a top
priority.

That same night, Riyadh was also fired upon. For the thousands of military
personnel and civilians in the Saudi capital, it was the start of a nerve-racking few
weeks. It was a prime target given the Coalition headquarters was situated in the city.
Of the 88 Scud missiles fired during the Gulf War, over 50 were aimed at Riyadh.
Gary R. was stationed at King Khalid International Airport (KKIA). One night he
was working on a C-130 aircraft when he heard the warning siren go off. He and
his team jumped on to their Noddy (towing vehicle) and trailers, then headed for
the safety of the nearest shelter, which was in the terminal.

Suddenly to my left I heard two massive explosions and saw streaks of light head upwards into
the sky. Moments later there was a bigger explosion right over our heads. The ground seemed to
shake and the night sky lit up. We eventually made it back to the shelter after abandoning the
Noddy outside the terminal. What we had witnessed were two American Patriot missiles being
fired and one of them taking out a Scud missile. The missile site was specifically positioned just
outside the airport perimeter to protect KKIA. We drove past the Patriot missile site the next
morning and gave them a round of applause.

The air campaign continued for another month. Soldiers waiting in the desert
were wondering if they would ever be used, and politicians, keen to get on with it
too, wanted to end the war quickly before Israel was drawn into the conflict. But
military commanders were determined not to launch a ground war before they were
ready. Commander of all Coalition forces, General Schwarzkopf was adamant that
he would not be rushed, threatening to resign if forced by politicians to start the

ground war early.[26] Even though there were risks in delaying the ground offensive and aircraft losses were incurred, the constant bombardment of Iraqi military targets was taking its toll.

The ground war began at 4.00 a.m. on 24 February 1991. As Coalition ships bombarded the Kuwaiti coastline in an attempt to convince Saddam's generals that a marine invasion was about to happen, two separate formations breached the border at the same time. In the east the 1st and 2nd US Marine Divisions cleared a way through dense minefields and started to fight their way towards Kuwait City. In the far west a joint force of units from the US XVIII Corps with French units started on a wide arc across the desert; the aim was to cut off the main highway between Baghdad and Basra. The early hours of ground operations went so well that the decision was made to move forward the deployment of VII Corps by 15 hours. Armoured bulldozers of the 1st Mechanized Infantry Division cleared 16 lanes through the minefields, and within two hours US cavalry units were securing a semi-circular screen 10 miles to the north.

The long wait was over for British soldiers of the 1st Armoured Division. On G-Day + 1, Challenger tanks, Warrior APCs, and thousands of support vehicles passed through the cleared lanes of the minefields and entered Iraq. Next to the breach was a huge sign that said, 'Welcome to Iraq, courtesy of the Big Red One'. After the initial breakthrough was achieved, the division turned to Iraqi positions. These positions were named after metals: Copper, Brass, Steel, Zinc, Platinum, and Tungsten. They didn't represent any particular geographic feature or point of interest other than they were simply circles drawn on a map around large concentrations of enemy forces. It was the divisional commanders' plan to attack each objective, take out enemy armour, then rapidly move on to the next one.

Attached to the division was a US National Guard artillery brigade. As well as providing more self-propelled guns, the division had at its disposal a regiment equipped with the Multiple Launch Rocket System (MLRS). This extra firepower was a spectacular sight to those nearby.

> It was a really dark night, full cloud cover and no moon. I was on stag [security duty or radio watch] in the early hours when all hell broke loose. Just a couple of clicks away what seemed like at least a dozen MLRS vehicles suddenly opened up. The rockets streaked up into the night sky and disappeared through the clouds. It lasted for several minutes then went quiet again. I felt sorry for the poor buggers who were on the end of that lot.

Each highly mobile M270 tracked vehicle was fitted with 12 launch pods firing a missile capable of delivering 644 bomblets the size of a hand-grenade. Known as 'grid killers' because of the ability of a single M270 launcher to saturate a 1-kilometre-square box, the weapon was ideally suited for the Iraqi desert. An entire position could be hit with no warning, showered with munitions just before being rolled over by armour and infantry.

Virtually no one had combat experience. Some soldiers had been under fire in Northern Ireland, with a handful of older NCOs and officers having fought in the Falklands War. But for the vast majority of men who were now crossing over into Iraq this was to be a baptism of fire. David K. was attached to the 16th/5th Lancers who were tasked with providing a reconnaissance squadron for the 4th Mechanised Brigade. 'We crossed the border early and I remember the weather being cold and dusty. There was a sandstorm and it was raining. I can't remember if I was shaking with the cold, excitement, fear, or all three, but I remember that I was shaking.'

Paul H. and his section were sat in the cramped confines of a Warrior. He recalls going through the breach then moving on to three separate objectives his company had been tasked to clear. 'I remember being scared before de-bussing from the Warrior, then hostilities, being tired, and loaded down with ammo, as well as feeling really stressed.'

One of the major worries before the ground war started was the reliability of armoured vehicles in desert conditions; sand was the major issue for the Challenger, Warrior, and Combat Vehicle Reconnaissance (Tracked) (CVR(T)) fleets. This fear led to increased maintenance standards and support given to keep the vehicles going. Even though just about every spare engine was sent to the Gulf, British commanders were still concerned about the reliability of their vehicles.[27] And as the division started the advance towards enemy positions, there were numerous breakdowns to contend with. After crossing the border, David K.'s Scimitar headed north with the rest of his squadron.

> We drove in convoy formation for an hour or so and as we started to shake out, my vehicle died … we recognised the symptoms of a fuel blockage all too well … I assisted the driver stripping the fuel filter and blowing it through. This did the trick but it kept happening. We seemed to have lost the squadron for about 12–15 hours.

Rich G.'s Challenger tank broke down not long after crossing the start line on the first night. 'I remember trying to change boost filters with the squadron in contact all around us. We spent most of the 100 hours being towed around by a REME armoured recovery vehicle.' Although 74 Challenger engines had to be changed, only one Challenger tank was out of action when offensive operations ended.[28]

After the first engagements, it soon became apparent to everyone that weeks of bombardment from the air had seriously reduced the fighting capability and morale of the Iraqi Army. Soldiers started to surrender by the hundreds, then thousands, until eventually entire units abandoned their tanks and armoured vehicles in an attempt to save their lives. Even if they had survived the allied air onslaught, Iraqi soldiers soon realised they were no match for Coalition forces. Owen C.'s squadron had advanced on to an objective during the first night. 'In the early hours as dawn was breaking we were moving forward; it was misty. The driver suddenly shouted that there was a tank in front of us.' The commander barked his fire order. Owen had a high-explosive round loaded from the night before instead of a preferred anti-tank projectile. At such close range it would not have mattered. 'I made the shield, and almost instantly we fired upon it. It was a T-55, and we saw it burning for a while afterwards before we moved on.'

Pete R.'s battalion had been taken off ceremonial duties in London and hastily moved to the Gulf. 'We were positioned just behind the lead troops and it was our job to round up prisoners and funnel them back to the POW camps.' With thousands of Iraqi soldiers surrendering, at times they had a difficult job dealing with such large numbers. 'Our dispatch rider went out one day on his own to Battalion Headquarters and came back with 150 prisoners. He said he rode over a hill into Iraqi soldiers; on seeing him they immediately dropped their weapons and put their hands up.' Owen C.'s squadron also had a close encounter with a large group of Iraqi soldiers keen to surrender. 'We were leaguered up to resupply when from behind a sand dune a group of soldiers appeared with their hands in the air. After a bit of a panic they were seated and covered by a guard … they had no food or water and very little proper equipment.' Soldier M. crewed an armoured ambulance throughout the war waiting to deal with casualties as and when they occurred. He saw lots of Iraqi prisoners including those that were wounded. 'We tended to their wounded and had one in the back of the ambulance for a day … we gave him morphine but he died where he lay of a gunshot wound to the abdomen. He was buried in an unmarked grave in the desert. RIP whoever he was.'

By the afternoon of G-Day + 2, everything had gone to plan. The Iraqi Army was being routed and surrendering in large numbers, and Coalition losses were extremely low. Then came the news many commanders had feared from the start: loss of life from a blue-on-blue. Also known as fratricide, the accidental killing of one's own forces was nothing new in combat and was always a risk, especially when there are inter-service units and forces from different nations working together. All Coalition vehicles displayed a large fluorescent panel on their upper surface as well as large black inverted Vs on the sides of the hull and turrets, although this did not stop fratricidal incidents from happening. Twenty American soldiers had already lost their lives this way,[29] and a major blue-on-blue involving Challenger tanks had been narrowly avoided during one of the first few engagements.

The 3rd Battalion, Royal Regiment of Fusiliers, had just cleared a position when two of its Warrior vehicles blew up and caught fire. At first it was thought that the vehicles had struck mines, so violent and unexpected were the explosions. But it soon became apparent from brigade and division air liaison officers that two A-10 Thunderbolt aircraft had reported attacking positions which corresponded to the locations of the destroyed Warriors. Nine soldiers were dead, and 11 more injured. Regardless of the deep anger and sorrow that lives had been needlessly lost, the campaign continued. The division had final objectives to take and needed to remain focused. Inquiries and recriminations would have to wait.

Phase line *Smash*, the codename for a line on the edge of the Wadi al-Batin beyond which the division could not exploit without permission from VII Corps, had been reached after just two days, when best estimates had predicted four. All objectives had been cleared of enemy forces and any remaining Iraqi soldiers had either surrendered or fled northwards. Everyone was exhausted; there had been little opportunity for sleep, as elements of the division had been in contact for the best part of three days and nights. Before being tasked to chase the remnants of the Iraqi Army, there was a lull as units were resupplied and crews managed to get a few hours' sleep. On the evening of G-Day + 3, the division was warned off to move rapidly to the east the next morning. The plan was to race towards a new objective named Cobalt (the main road from Basra to Kuwait) and cut off any Iraqi forces trying to retreat to the north. At 6.00 a.m., 28 February, 7th Brigade set off in the lead with the rest of the division following behind. Travelling at about 40km/h over rough terrain, lead units of the Queen's Royal Irish Hussars arrived at the road at 7.30 a.m. Just 30 minutes later, a suspension of offensive operations was announced.

As the division moved eastward that morning they saw first-hand what had happened to the Iraqi Army. Rich G., whose Challenger tank had broken down the first night of the ground offensive, had finally caught up with his unit. 'We joined the squadron on the last morning and the dash to cut off any retreating Iraqis from Kuwait. I remember seeing the carnage and destruction caused by the battle group. Also, how wretched the POWs were; I remember thinking how we had overestimated the Iraqi Army and their Soviet equipment.' Soldier M. also recalled what he saw. 'It was clear how much carnage Coalition forces had caused – burnt-out vehicles, many with charred bodies still inside, dead soldiers everywhere … many had started to decompose.' Most British soldiers advancing through the desert experienced the terrible aftermath of battle; most had seen the effects of modern weaponry. But it is fair to say that nothing could have prepared them for what they would see on the Basra–Kuwait road.

On the night of 26–27 February, a large convoy of vehicles had left Kuwait and headed along the main highway north towards Basra. The convoy was a mix of military and civilian vehicles: tanks, APCs, buses, fuel tankers, cars and trucks, vehicles of all kinds desperately fleeing Kuwait. Coalition commanders believed the Iraqi forces were attempting to leave with loot they had stolen – eyewitnesses in Kuwait confirmed as much.[30] Evidence of Iraqi soldiers' looting was everywhere. Six months after the war had ended, the United Nations supervised the return of 3,216 gold bars that were stolen from Kuwait. In 2017, five gold bars were found in the fuel tank of an Iraqi T-55 tank that was being refurbished in Northamptonshire.[31]

That night the front and rear of the convoy – about 1,400–2,000 vehicles – was hit with cluster bombs effectively blocking the road. Over the next 10 hours dozens of Coalition aircraft turned Highway 80 near the Mutla Ridge into what became known as the 'Highway of Death'. There are differing accounts as to how many people died there. Some reporters who arrived quickly on the scene suggest that of the estimated 10,000 people in the convoy at least 500–600 died; others say far fewer. It is now thought that after the first US Navy A-6E Intruder aircraft attacked the convoy, most occupants got out of their vehicles and fled into the desert with between 200 and 300 Iraqis left dying in or around their vehicles.

Photographs taken of the carnage on the highway would become the most iconic images of the war and became the basis of a discussion about what was the only questionable Coalition action of the war. For those who witnessed the aftermath, the sights and smells they experienced will never leave them. As images of the devastation were broadcast all over the world, President Bush quickly decided to bring the offensive to an end; what he (and his advisers) had seen clearly influenced their decision.

As well as seeing the devastation on the Basra–Kuwait road, troops arriving in and around Kuwait City were well aware of the misery Iraq's occupation had inflicted upon the Kuwaiti people and their small country. Before fleeing Kuwait, Iraqi soldiers had set fire to over 650 oil wells and damaged many more. The thick black smoke rose from the desert as far as the eye could see. It became so bad that on several occasions day became night.

Units were told to stay put in and around the area outside of the city in company and squadron formations. After making sure their weapons were cleaned and conducting basic vehicle maintenance, they finally got some much-needed rest. For some soldiers there was a sense of anti-climax. So complete was the manner of victory that most soldiers had not fired their weapons. Soldier B. said, 'Being told the war was over felt surreal.' Some troops that were tasked as Battlefield Casualty Replacements (BCRs) had spent most of the 100 hours of combat on tank transporters following behind the division as they swept through Iraqi positions. Angus T. was a BCR. 'The night before the ground war started, the colonel briefed us all and said he thought we'd be called up in the night as BCRs. We went to sleep, woke up, and before we knew it, it was all over. I was disheartened (I think we all were) … after all that build-up, we didn't get in to the fight.'

Although most soldiers spent the following days away from civilization, not seeing much but burning oil fires and desert, some got to see first-hand what had taken place in Kuwait city.

I was asked to go on a jolly in a Land Rover with two officers. They wanted to have a look around the outskirts of the city but were told they ought to take an armed soldier with them, so I sat in the back with my rifle. As we approached the city you could tell something was going on, there were large groups of people chanting and singing, waving the Kuwaiti flag. But there were also groups of armed men roaming around who were clearly looking for trouble. There had been widespread looting; it was as if the contents of every house had been taken out and thrown on the streets. We came across an RMP patrol who politely advised us to leave. They said that although most Kuwaitis were happy to see British and American soldiers, some of the

Kuwaiti population were turning on anyone that was not their own and that several innocent people had already been strung up. We followed their advice and left.

David K. was able to view the same chaos from above. 'I was fortunate enough to get a flight in a Sea King helicopter … flying over Kuwait City, we could clearly see bodies hanging from lamp posts, but were told to ignore them; it was an Arab problem being sorted by Arabs.'

While Coalition commanders held talks with senior Iraqi commanders regarding boundaries, demarcation lines, and the handover of POWs, soldiers stayed in their positions not knowing what was going on or when they would be going home. An incident involving unexploded ordnance being picked up off the battlefield and placed on a New Zealand C-130 as a souvenir prompted General de la Billière to issue strict orders. He warned his commanders of the dangers and sent strict instructions to ensure there would be no needless loss of life.[32] These instructions could not have permeated all the way down the chain of command, and if they did, some simply ignored them.

One of the biggest causes of casualties after the end of hostilities was from discarded or unexploded ordnance. British troops travelling across the desert did not fully comprehend the amount of unexploded submunitions from cluster bombs and MLRS rockets that were everywhere. Coalition aircraft and artillery dropped bombs or fired shells and missiles that contained over 50 million submunitions.[33] Delivered by aircraft, cluster bombs were used during the destruction of the convoy on the Basra–Kuwait road, and the MLRS was used with great effect to destroy hundreds of Iraqi positions in the desert. One MLRS rocket contained 644 M77 grenades (bomblets), which meant that from one three-vehicle salvo, 23,184 bomblets would land in the target area. In normal conditions an expected dud rate of 2 per cent translated to 400 undetonated bombs scattered in that area, and the soft-sand conditions would make the percentage of duds much higher.[34] The word soon came down not to touch anything found in the desert. Unfortunately, several did, and it ended very badly.

During the period after the cessation of hostilities 11 British servicemen lost their lives. Garry F. was travelling in a convoy heading south along the Basra–Kuwait road when he was badly injured. 'We were on our way back to Al Jubail after the ceasefire to collect personal belongings we'd left at the port. Most of us were asleep but were woken by the convoy stopping. A few of us jumped out of the trucks to take a pee when suddenly there was a loud bang; I then collapsed to the ground.' Garry was casevaced back to the UK with a large shrapnel wound. He had several operations to remove it. 'I was told afterwards it was a bomblet from a pod off a Coalition aircraft. An idiot who was also in the convoy picked it up. When he realised what it was he threw it away, but a small parachute deployed, primed the device, and it exploded on contact with the ground. We were all lucky not to be killed.'

The motorbikes that were given to units when they arrived in the desert became the cause of many accidents, too. Mainly ridden by soldiers with very little to no experience, some accidents were very serious. Pete R.'s company received a bike before they took up their role dealing with Iraqi POWs.

> Due to the struggle with communications, each company was allocated a motorbike to be used by a dispatch rider. Using no common sense at all, rather than pick someone who could actually ride a motorbike we were told to use the company clerks. Of course, ours had never ridden a bike in his life … later on he came off and ruptured his spleen.

Waiting to go home, bored soldiers sitting around close to an unlimited supply of ordnance was a dangerous situation. Paul H. recalls having a lot of fun after the ceasefire. As well as firing every flare that they could get their hands on, he remembers 'using plastic explosives to blow stuff up', and Rich G. remembers someone throwing a de-activated grenade into his driver's cab while he was in it. One of the things every sub-unit did after the war was dig a big firepit and burn anything they could get their hands on. 'Some idiot threw several rounds of Iraqi ammo into the fire without telling anyone. When it went off he was the only one laughing as we all hit the deck.'

Within a week of the ceasefire, troops started to move back south to Al Jubail. The vehicles were de-bombed (cleared of all explosive material) and left by the side of a road where they would be guarded until loaded on a ship and sent back to Germany. Angus T. was tasked with staying with his tanks, driving them to a staging area. 'Whilst driving back we went close to a POW camp. Next minute all these Land Rovers came out. They asked if we could divert our route as the POWs were going ballistic. They thought we were going there to kill them.' After a few days in the transit camps it was back to Germany or the UK.

Regiments were welcomed back at their barracks with bands playing and families smiling eagerly. But for most younger single soldiers who arrived back in Germany, it was very different. 'Returning to Germany was a bit of an anti-climax for me. I remember that there were families and a mounted dutyman waiting at camp. There was no one there for the single soldiers.' David K. returned to Wolfenbüttel with other QDG personnel who had been attached to the 16th/5th Lancers, two days after their A Squadron had arrived home. 'Having witnessed homecomings for Falkland War veterans, my return was very flat. By the time the rest of us who had been loaned out to other regiments had returned, the camp was like a ghost town.' Despite 'all the bells and whistles' of a homecoming, Soldier B.'s strongest memory of returning to camp was 'trudging back to the squadron block and an empty room'.

Most soldiers went straight on leave. Rich G. had been to war but was still not old enough to drink in a public house – he turned 18 while he was on leave. Angus T. drove back to the UK with another soldier from his squadron. With lots of soldiers on the cross-channel ferry there were many cheering at the sight of the White Cliffs of Dover. 'As we drove off the ferry, we were all honking our horns; people were cheering and waving everywhere.'

For some soldiers who had not been involved, there was a touch of envy, especially for those in regiments that did deploy, and many soldiers who had just left their regiments for postings elsewhere tried anything to get posted back. 'I was really disappointed to not be with my regiment at such a time; I was desperate to go with everyone else who I knew.' Soldier G. arrived at his regiment from trade training just a few days too late. He spent the next few months guarding an empty camp as part of the rear party.

> I was so disappointed … stagging on was no fun especially as most of the guys left behind weren't the best of soldiers … when the regiment returned I was green with envy. I remember the desert combats; tanned skin and the stories were fascinating … these men who had been to war were the people I wanted to be with. Smart, fit, professional soldiers with an air of confidence about them.

Martin M. had been promoted and sent on ceremonial duties just as his friends were preparing to go to war. News of his reluctance to be promoted and go through riding school rather than be deployed to the Gulf with his squadron had reached Knightsbridge. Instead of understanding his frustration, he was treated as if he'd committed some terrible sin.

> I bugged everyone that would listen on a daily basis to get me back to the regiment and out to the Gulf. But it didn't work, they weren't interested. Then a couple of weeks before the end of kit ride I'd had enough. Completely disillusioned and at a real emotional low, I signed off. With all their constant undermining and harassment, they'd won. I was dragged off my horse in ceremonial kit and marched into the CO's office.

After receiving the wrath of the commanding officer, adjutant, and regimental corporal major he was told he was being reduced in rank to lance corporal and returned to his regiment in Germany. 'No way, is that all I had to do? I should have done it five months earlier … I left the CO's office to a wave of abuse but with a big grin on my face.' He arrived back in Germany, went to his old squadron, and withdrew his papers to leave the Army. He was happy to be back with his friends, but there was still one ironic joke left to be played. 'Having done such a good job of spraying the tanks to go to the Gulf back in December, and having missed the entire war, I was put in charge of spraying them back to green again. Who said the Army doesn't have a sense of humour?'

After the Gulf War most people thought it would be back to business as usual for soldiers and their families. Some thought the whole Iraq–Kuwait thing was just a blip, an anomaly. The problem was that the full effects from the end of the Cold War were still only just beginning to be felt. The new normal was going to be the unpredictability of future conflicts like the Gulf War. As soldiers went home feeling a sense of accomplishment, there were some who were less optimistic. 'I was talking to one of our officers after the ceasefire. We were sat around a fire one night chatting about the future when he said something I will always remember: "Mark my words, lads, we'll be back here one day." How right he was.'

CHAPTER 4

Life after the Gulf War and Options for Change

After being on leave soldiers returned to their regiments and got back to their peace-time jobs. Most returned to empty barracks, their tanks and vehicles not making it back from the Gulf until June 1991. In the finest tradition of the British Army, units carried on as if nothing had happened, sending men on routine courses and preparing for training exercises. Despite the uncertainty that lay ahead with Options for Change, announced just six days before Iraq invaded Kuwait, the Army's mantra to 'carry on' regardless meant that for most young soldiers, what was happening outside their barrack walls hardly registered.

For some who had been in combat, coming back to a mundane regimental life was difficult. Owen C. says it was a struggle for many soldiers to go back to peace-time duties. 'We had to try and adjust to the old routines of camp life … there was a distinct attitude that we had proved ourselves in combat … being expected to carry out low-level troop training felt like a huge step down.' Many who returned to peace-time duties struggled with more than just the routine.

Paul H. started to see changes in some people he had served with in the Gulf. 'I don't think I changed that much, but some did. Not straight away, but over a long period of time.' In some cases soldiers viewed those struggling in the aftermath of the war with mistrust. Owen C. said he knew someone who left the Army, citing the Gulf War as the reason. He admitted, 'I thought he was on a bit of a scam at the time.' Another soldier now regrets his attitude towards a fellow soldier who was suffering. 'I actually laughed when I heard someone had broken down and cried because they kept thinking about Iraqi prisoners they'd seen. At the time, I thought he was pathetic – in hindsight, I'm not too proud of that now.' Owen C. thought the same; however, time has changed his opinion. 'Now I'm a bit older and wiser with access to a lot more information on PTSD and mental health, I believe people shouldn't be judged too quickly. You can have multiple people experience exactly the same event under the same conditions and all of them will deal with it in their own way.'

Even after vehicles had arrived back from Saudi Arabia and regiments were brought back up to operational strength, the legacy of the Gulf War still loomed large. Public support for the war had been strong throughout. Prime Minister John Major was able to win a 21-seat majority in the 1992 election despite a faltering economy on the back of his handling of the war, and in the United States, President Bush's approval rating soared to 82 per cent.[1] A British contingent marched in victory parades in both Washington, D.C. and New York before London held its more 'subdued welcome-home parade presided over by the Queen'.[2] But some started to feel that the support they had felt throughout was waning. Because the war had been such an overwhelming victory with so few casualties, some thought there was a public perception that it was not a real war and that soldiers who fought in it perhaps should not be held in the same regard as Falkland veterans or those who had served in Northern Ireland. One soldier recalls being back home.

> I was on leave in a pub when a guy I knew sarcastically asked if I'd been on a winter holiday. He prattled on about how they shouldn't bother issuing Gulf War medals because it had been so easy and we hadn't done much of a job as Saddam was still in power. I got really pissed off – all I could think of was the poor families of those who were killed. Just because there had been so few casualties didn't make it any less of a war.

Throughout 1991, despite losing a large percentage of his army, it became apparent that Saddam Hussein was killing his own people. In March, Shia Iraqis in the south and Kurds in the north simultaneously rebelled against the regime. After Kuwait was liberated, President Bush stoked the fires by calling for 'the Iraqi people to put Saddam aside',[3] but when they tried, they received no assistance from Coalition forces. Both rebellions were brutally crushed by Republican Guard units that had escaped Kuwait. There were those who started to question why Coalition forces had not 'finished the job' by moving on Baghdad. President Bush would later explain his reasoning:

> To occupy Iraq would shatter our coalition, turning the whole Arab world against us, and make a broken tyrant into a latter-day Arab hero ... it would have taken us way beyond the imprimatur of international law ... assigning young soldiers to a fruitless hunt for a securely entrenched dictator and condemning them to fight in what would be an unwinnable urban guerrilla war.[4]

Ending the war when he did, limiting Coalition troops to the aims of UNSCR 678, is still hotly debated. Most historians and political pundits agree that not allowing Coalition forces to move on Baghdad kept the fragile Coalition in place. And President Bush's statement provided a hauntingly prophetic warning to politicians who might consider the removal of Saddam Hussein in the future. But there were now many soldiers who saw what was happening and asked if it had been just a job half-done, wondering if they would be going back to finish it off sometime in the future.

Just a few months after the Gulf War ended, both British and American soldiers started to get ill. Thousands began to report sick with a range of different disorders including extreme fatigue, strange rashes, numbness, joint pain, sweating, fevers, memory loss, and kidney and chest infections. Some soldiers' condition became so bad they either left the Army early or were medically discharged. At first the condition was thought to be a psychosomatic illness, with claims that some were malingering, jumping on the bandwagon in the hope of a government handout after they left the Army.[5] As the number of soldiers who became ill increased every week, both in America and the United Kingdom, doctors and scientists tried to draw a correlation between the symptoms as well as find the cause.

Different theories were put forward in an attempt to explain what was causing the illness. Soldiers had been exposed to both chemical and biological agents; pyridostigmine bromide pills (NAPS) were taken to prevent the effects of nerve gases like sarin, and organophosphate pesticides like DEET were widely used. There were a number of harmful chemicals that could have been ingested from the oil fires, and there was another theory that the illness was caused by exposure to depleted uranium shells. Many also believed the raft of vaccinations that were given before the war were to blame; anthrax, whooping cough, the plague, and others were an uncomfortable experience. Pete R. had 'seven inoculations at the same time' but decided not to take the nerve agent pills at all. Another retired soldier recalled, 'I was amazed at the amount of vaccinations we were given.'

A number of studies were conducted where blood and x-rays were taken from veterans suffering ill health. But in all cases, they could not find any physical differences between them and a control group.[6] The random nature of the illness resulted in a great deal of scepticism at first. One soldier said, 'It would be interesting to see the stats for those cases reported after discharge compared to those who carried on and served for longer.' But as the numbers increased and details of the suffering that soldiers faced came to light, there was an acceptance that the illness was real, even in the absence of a diagnosis. Over the next two decades, it would have a devastating effect on thousands of soldiers and their families. Paul H. shared a room with a friend who is still suffering. 'He rang last year and told me he had to put the army behind him. He asked me as a friend to cut all ties and help him forget. I was in tears but honoured his request … I check on him via his brother.' In the 25 years since soldiers returned home, 'about 250,000 of the almost 700,000 involved in the Gulf War 1 theatre suffered from some version of the complex of symptoms' we now know as Gulf War Syndrome.[7]

In May 1992, the United Kingdom was painfully reminded of the darkest day of the Gulf War. A coroner's court jury in Oxford handed down a verdict of 'unlawful killing' in the inquest into the deaths of the nine soldiers who had died when two USAF A-10 aircraft had mistakenly attacked their Warrior APCs. Lawyers for the soldiers' families called for the two USAF pilots involved to face extradition to England and trial for manslaughter.[8] It was obvious from the outset that no matter how hard a coroner or grieving families pleaded, American authorities were not going to allow its pilots to be blamed by a jury in a foreign land or risk their security by having their names released to the public.

When asked, soldiers held a wide range of views on the jury's verdict and the culpability of the American pilots. All felt great sympathy for the families and mourned the loss of comrades, but most thought nothing positive would come out of charging the pilots with a crime. Pete R. said, 'Blue-on-blue happens in war; if people are found to be totally negligent then there may be a case to answer but generally during the fog of war anything can and does happen.'

Michelle W. was serving with 32 Field Hospital when the bodies of the soldiers were brought to their mortuary. Although she thinks the pilots should have been allowed to testify, she was not sure making their names public would have served any purpose. Paul H. witnessed the incident; his company of Grenadier Guards were attached to 3RRF.

> There should have been a proper inquiry. War is war, and mistakes happen, but this was just covered up. Those pilots were trigger happy … poorly trained in identifying British armoured vehicles. I would not want anyone prosecuted, but maybe if they admitted they were ill-trained in vehicle ID or possibly off route … this could have been avoided … it was a cover up.

The refusal of the US military to even name the pilots clearly shows how the American military protected its servicemen. Although there had been criticism of the US policy regarding the A-10 pilots, in the years to come, many British soldiers would be left wishing their government adopted the same policy, protecting them the same way their ally's did.

***

The one subject that kept senior officers in Regimental Headquarters fully occupied throughout 1991 and 1992 was Options for Change. There was a general consensus that the white paper written in 1990 and announced in Parliament just days before Iraq invaded Kuwait would be shelved or at least reconsidered in light of the Gulf War. But even while cavalry and infantry regiments whose history dated back over three centuries were preparing for battle, their very future was in jeopardy. The danger to their existence did not come from an enemy in uniform, but rather from those wearing pinstriped suits.

If the Gulf War had shown one thing, it was how unpredictable the world had become. Many were now asking if it was the right time for the country to make such deep cuts to its military. General de la Billière recorded that as he visited his troops on the eve of battle he was unable to understand the logic or timing of the cuts.[9] It was an opinion all soldiers agreed with. 'I couldn't believe after a war the thought was to reduce numbers.' Andrew C. was thinking the same. 'In the aftermath of the war I don't think anyone really thought the Army would be downsized.' Owen C. noticed that the 'Options for Change process didn't seem to pause (during the war) … we thought it might cause them to have a re-think but it just carried on gaining momentum.' Soldier D. said, 'I had no doubt it would happen … the Army was looking hard at reducing its size overall using whatever means they could.' Pete R. added, 'I did think they might have altered or at least held off on Options for Change. But at the time I was still gullible enough to believe that politicians were doing what was best for us.' And Dave M. put forward his own laconic viewpoint: 'It was bonkers!'

The practical implications of Options for Change for the British Army were revealed on the afternoon of Tuesday, 23 July 1991. At 3.31 p.m., as the Secretary of State for Defence Tom King rose from his seat in the House of Commons, soldiers in regiments throughout the Army were simultaneously briefed on the changes by their commanding officers.

> We were formed up in the gym; the whole regiment was crammed in. I was stood next to a bunch of officers and senior ranks who all thought they knew what the CO was going to say, despite him being the only one privy to what was in the sealed envelope. They were saying things like, 'that'll never happen' and 'over my dead body'. The look on their faces when the colonel gave us the news; it was if they'd seen a ghost.

The 'news' being announced in Parliament and relayed simultaneously to soldiers through commanding officers would fall like a hammer blow to some, but for others it would be greeted with a sigh of relief. In the Royal Armoured Corps only three regiments would remain unscathed: The Royal Scots Dragoon Guards, The Queen's Dragoon Guards, and the 9th/12th Royal Lancers. The infantry was to be reduced from 50 to 38 battalions over a five-year period, with many regiments losing second and third battalions. There also were reductions in the number of regiments in the Royal Artillery, Royal Engineers, and Royal Corps of Signals. Two new corps would be formed to encompass many existing organisations: the Adjutant General Corps and the Royal Logistics Corps. Household Division troops were not spared the axe but did receive some special treatment because of their unique position with regards to ceremonial duties. Even though the Army board had insisted that the Household Cavalry Mounted Regiment (HCMR) remained unchanged, two separate Household Cavalry service regiments (the Life Guards and Blues and Royals) would form a 'union' of one armoured reconnaissance regiment in Windsor, while keeping their separate identities. Although the Coldstream Guards, Grenadier Guards, and Scots Guards would all lose their second battalions, placed in suspended animation rather than being amalgamated, they would all have incremental companies that would be permanently based in or around London to carry out ceremonial duties.[10]

Soldiers did question the reasoning and logic of the cuts, but surprisingly most seemed to take the news of the amalgamations in their stride. A soldier recalls, 'We all knew that if they had their hearts set on a 20 per cent reduction we were likely to get the chop; they weren't going to please everyone.' This reasonable approach was not reciprocated by the many MPs that rose in response to Tom King after he had delivered his statement. Whether the anger was real, or just meant to placate constituents, is open to debate. Dave M. was with the Blues and Royals in Windsor when the announcement was made. 'There were a few who struggled to come to terms with the union … but on the whole I think because we knew so many people in each other's regiments it worked. But the one question we all asked was, how the hell did the 9th/12th Lancers get away with it?'

Even if soldiers appeared to have accepted the news of the amalgamations and cuts with more calm than some of their elected politicians, it was when these cuts were implemented and regiments started to amalgamate that reality began to sink in. Paul H. was not looking forward to the prospect of combining two battalions of Grenadier Guards into one. 'I hated it; the first and second battalions might as well have been completely different regiments. I did consider leaving or looking for a posting but hung in there as I wanted to at least be able to qualify for a half pension.' He says the move caused 'a lot of stress and moaning because so many missed out on promotion', and it seemed to some that there were too many 'Yes men' now in positions of responsibility. Another complaint regarding the amalgamations was that 'it was felt that in some instances one regiment seemed to swallow the other and things that had identified them for hundreds of years were lost forever.' Andrew C. had been in Northern Ireland when he returned to the newly formed Household Cavalry Regiment (HCR) in Windsor. 'On my return … the first thing I noticed was a feeling the senior regiment had more say … it was also going to be much harder to get promoted.' It wasn't just young soldiers who lamented the loss of opportunities. For those who wanted to continue serving after their 22 years ended, there would be very limited job openings. Long Service List appointments were being slashed, and holds on Late Entry officer commissioning were put in place for many regiments that were amalgamating.

Less than a month after the details of the sweeping cuts were announced, with barely enough time for the changes to have sunk in, events in Moscow would bring into question the common assumption held by politicians that the cuts were based upon – the premise that the Soviet threat no longer existed.[11] Policy makers were reminded just how volatile the new world order had become, and even though the attempted coup in Russia only lasted a few days, it was a massive wake-up call to those who thought the end of the Cold War would automatically usher in a period of peace and stability.

Mikhail Gorbachev had just started a much-needed holiday at his *dacha* in the Crimea. He had intended to return to Moscow on 20 August to sign the new union treaty which would have re-organised Soviet states into a confederation. Hard-line Communists within the government rejected the decentralization of power away from Moscow towards the republics; they saw it as a precursor to the end of the Soviet Union. On 18 August, a delegation arrived at Foros in the Crimea. They met with Gorbachev and demanded that he either declare a state of emergency or resign. When he refused, he was placed under house arrest and a *coup d'état* began. The attempted takeover was poorly organised and lacked the full support of the military, especially among junior officers and soldiers on the ground. After Boris Yeltsin made a speech on top of a Soviet tank in Moscow, the coup collapsed, the ringleaders were arrested, and Gorbachev returned to Moscow. Ironically, the coup did nothing but destabilise and precipitate the end of the Soviet Union, the very thing the hardliners were trying to prevent. The new union treaty proposed by Gorbachev could have persuaded Soviet states to join the confederation rather than declaring independence. Throughout the two days that the coup lasted, it seemed highly likely that the Soviet Union would be taken over by Communist hardliners with the reforms instigated by Gorbachev being reversed. For many leaders in the west who were actively engaged in arms reduction based on the premise that the Cold War was over, it was the nightmare scenario. A few nerves were rattled at the Ministry of Defence, too, and there was a renewed attempt by MPs from all parties to try to make the government think again.

Options for Change had marked a major shift in policy; no longer faced with a single threat, strategists now planned for an Army with a set of capabilities that could be applied to any potential threat in the new political environment.[12] But after the attempted coup in the Soviet Union, this move towards a capability-based rather than threats-based policy now came under fire. In an October debate in the House of Commons, former Conservative Minister Julian Amery asked the Defence Secretary a rhetorical question. 'Putting your hand on your heart, could you say, "Yes, we could cope with another Falkland operation, with another Gulf operation?" If you can't, you had better go back to the drawing board.'[13] Liberal Democrat defence spokesman Menzies Campbell was sure he knew who was behind making such massive cuts. 'The Ministry of Defence is being led by the nose by the Treasury towards reductions in Britain's armed forces which have no rational basis.'[14] Despite the unpredictability of the world, the Defence Secretary was not going to be swayed. Defence procurement minister Alan Clark clearly saw an opportunity to save money. He wrote, 'We are at one of those critical moments in defence policy that occur only once every 50 years.'[15]

As the months went by, the realisation began to dawn that many serving soldiers were going to lose their jobs, due to the need to compress soldiers from units being amalgamated or disbanded into existing units. In practical terms, it clearly meant most soldiers' prospects of promotion were going to slow down or even come to a halt for several years. 'We were told that our career paths wouldn't be affected because numbers would be lowered through "wastage." It used to amuse me that they threw that term around like they were describing a piece of meat.' Going from 153,000 to 120,000 in such a short period of time was always going to hurt, and no matter how it was dressed up, it was going to take more than volunteers and 'wastage'.

There would be many who did not want to leave but would find themselves being made redundant nonetheless.

Soldiers who had served more than 15 years were invited to apply for voluntary redundancy. The attractive package was a bigger lump sum than most soldiers could expect to receive after 22 years. It was attractive to those who felt that Options for Change and its subsequent upheavals had brought a premature end to promotion in their own career. For the Ministry of Defence, although the pay-outs were higher than those given for soldiers leaving after 22 years, it was still saving much more money in the long term because those taking redundancy would not necessarily be eligible for a full, lifetime pension.

As well as the thousands who applied for voluntary redundancy, there also were many who received letters stating that they might be subject to compulsory redundancy. Before 1993, very few serving in the military would have heard the term 'Manning Control'. But after that date the controversial policy would become well known. It allows the Army to terminate the service of soldiers at a certain manning control point (six, nine, or 12 years) to free up promotion log jams. If a soldier had not reached a certain rank, he could be dismissed under Queen's Regulations para 9.413 – 'Not required for a full Army career'. It was first used in the late 1950s as a way of reducing numbers when National Service ended. But the policy was suspended and not used again until 1993.

For soldiers who were excited at the prospect of leaving the Army with a lump sum, and those facing dismissal, it was a long and nervous wait. When the day arrived, soldiers were each told in person by their commanding officer. Dave M. knew there was a possibility he'd lose his job. He received notification that he was 'in the zone' under 'Phase Three Redundancy'. However, because there were so many volunteering, he was told 'not to worry'.

> I was summoned along with all the hopefuls to the CO's office. The first person came out smiling; the next two did not. Then it was my turn. I knew right away that I was out – the look on the face of the colonel told me all I needed to know. I was gutted and totally shocked. It was all a bit of a blur but I left the CO's office by the side door and was sent home. My wife was in tears and I felt like crying too.

After the shock of the news, he read the details of the letter and saw that he could appeal the decision.

> So, I wrote a letter, handed it in, and was then called for by the CO. He basically ripped up my redundancy letter and said, 'Leave this to me.' Anyway, I won the appeal, but they made me wait for ages before telling me. I was lucky to have the support of my wife; it was just as hard for her having to cope and live with me throughout the whole process.

He credits his commanding officer, whose support helped him through, something soldiers in other regiments and corps did not always get. 'I met some people from other units that had no idea that there was an appeals process and were gutted about having to leave. They all said they got very little support.'

By 1994, the redundancies had started to kick in, the effects there for everyone to see. To some they seemed very haphazard, devoid of any rationale that accounted for individual soldiers. Anonymous personnel making decisions at manning and record offices, using some arbitrary equation on which a soldier's future was decided, seemed out of touch with reality. Soldiers could see what was happening – those who were slightly behind their peers on what some administrators called the 'Power Curve' were cast aside even though they had exemplary service records and were perfectly capable of performing their jobs. And there were many who thought 'the wrong soldiers were taking redundancy, which meant the wrong people were getting promoted above their ability'. After his experience with compulsory redundancy, Dave M. is obviously critical of the whole process. 'No, they didn't get it right. They got rid of people who wanted to stay and kept people who wanted to leave, some of whom got out anyway.' Soldier G. thought two things went wrong after Options for Change. 'They allowed too many good people to leave through voluntary redundancy, then turned the recruiting tap off for nearly two years – it was catastrophic.' A year after the final round of redundancies, Owen C. found himself on his regimental recruiting team. He noticed that there was a perception that the Army no longer needed recruits. 'Because it [redundancy] was so well advertised, people's attitudes were that the Army didn't need anyone to join. This was not just youngsters but their parents, too. We had to try and explain that there was always a need for recruits. We all found out just how this impacted the Army a few years down the road.'

One of the major problems with the cuts was that there was no reciprocal decline in the Army's commitments. With troops being promised to the United Nations for deployment in the Balkans and emergency tours in Northern Ireland assumed by the infantry, many battalions were dangerously under-strength. This would lead to many infantry regiments deploying with additional troops brought in from non-infantry units. The redundancies had created an even worse manning shortage in some specialised trades. It was so bad that it led to the ridiculous situation of soldiers who had taken voluntary redundancy being asked by the MOD to sign back on a few weeks later. 'It was madness. One guy handed in his ID card, cashed his check, left to go home, then showed up again a few weeks later in uniform. I heard another soldier even got a signing-on bonus too.' S-Type (three-year) engagements used mainly for Territorial Army soldiers while serving with regular units were used as a short-term solution. Long-term manning problems caused by Options for Change and the subsequent redundancies would not be felt for a few years, but they would come at the worst possible moment. An ever-shrinking Army would be tasked with taking on more and more commitments, and in 1993, as well as the never-ending cycle of violence in Northern Ireland to contend with, the Army would be sent to help prevent sectarian atrocities in another country.

CHAPTER 5

Discrimination and Reform

Although the 1960s and 1970s had ushered in a more tolerant society, attitudes regarding an array of social issues were as hard in the 1980s as they had been in post-war Britain. Not only did Margaret Thatcher change the political map, but she also imposed upon the country her old-time social values centred around the family and spoke of what she termed the British public's fear that the country 'might be rather swamped by people with a different culture'.[1] These attitudes were reflected in the British Army of the late 1980s, in which female soldiers were restricted to administrative jobs and nursing, and homosexuals were barred from serving. In terms of cultural diversity (or lack thereof), the number of Black and Asian soldiers in the Army had been at about 1 per cent since the end of National Service in 1962. One soldier who joined the Army in 1985 said, 'When I first joined, not only was it illegal to be gay in the Army, but the whole attitude and environment was stereotypically masculine and homophobic.' Another soldier who joined two years later noted, 'You couldn't be gay, Blacks were not welcome, and I didn't see a women soldier for over a decade into my Army career.' This chapter discusses how the Army responded to its discrimination towards ethnic minority groups and the gay community during this period; the changing role of women in the Army is discussed in Chapter Nine.

***

In the year 1987/88, applications from ethnic minorities to join the military were just 1.6 per cent of all applications received.[2] Many of those soldiers were grouped into a few regiments whose recruiting areas were in and around London; some battalions of the Queen's Regiment and the Royal Green Jackets contained between 8 and 10 per cent Black soldiers. In January 1990, with the Army facing scrutiny over claims of widespread racial discrimination, Lord Arran, the Under Secretary of State for Defence, made a speech about racial discrimination in the armed forces. He said, 'I firmly don't believe there is an enormous amount of racial discrimination in the services ... the armed services have done all they can to stamp out racism.'[3] Evidence now shows that on both counts, Lord Arran was wrong.

In the 1960s, the War Office (now Ministry of Defence) excluded 'coloured' soldiers from Household Cavalry, Foot Guard, and Scottish regiments. They also kept in force an unofficial quota of 2 per cent on the recruiting of ethnic minorities. In 1966, Secretary of State for Defence Dennis Healey defended this policy in Parliament, saying, 'No coloured man has ever been turned away as a result.'[4] He was in favour of increasing the number of ethnic minority soldiers, especially in regiments of the Household Brigade, but soon realised he was fighting a losing battle. In his autobiography he describes the attitude of both officers and SNCOs during a visit to the Coldstream Guards. He was courteously received during his visit until he asked why there were no Black Coldstream Guards. In the Sergeants' Mess he received a harsh response, and in the Officers' Mess over lunch, the reaction was even more vitriolic.[5] Twenty years later, despite passage of the Race Relations Act 1976, which placed a duty on the armed forces not to discriminate against individuals because of their race, it appeared that nothing had changed.

In the mid-1980s Prince Charles made it known he wanted Black and Asian soldiers on ceremonial duty in the regiments of the Household Division. Soon after that, Guardsman Richard Stokes became the first Black man to serve in any Guards regiment; he lasted three years. Although he didn't file a formal complaint while he was serving in the Grenadier Guards, there is overwhelming evidence that he was racially abused. Similar stories have come from other Black guardsmen that followed after him, and other guardsmen have now come forward to confirm the appalling treatment he received. Paul H. said, 'The second battalion got a lad called Stokes, the first Black Grenadier. He had a crap time ... burnt bedding, lockers and equipment trashed, verbal abuse, black dolls set on fire and so on.' Another guardsman recalls, 'Racism was inherent in the guards' and remembers when, 'my whole company was ordered to spit in Stokes' direction.'[6] In 2006, two decades after he joined the Army, Richard Stokes spoke of his time with the Grenadier Guards.

> The first day I got to the camp in Northern Ireland I went into the Mess Hall. Of the three or four hundred guardsmen in there most of them just got up and walked out. The others threw bananas at me, stubbed their cigarettes out in my food, called me names – ni**er, coon. Before I left the army I was receiving hate mail from guardsmen in two other battalions on a regular basis.[7]

In the years since Guardsman Stokes joined the Grenadier Guards, there are now dozens of accounts of racism right across the Army. 'Bananas being thrown, abusive language ... there was only one person in the regiment that was wasn't white; he didn't last longer than a few months but in that time he received a lot of abuse.' Owen C. told me, 'There was a certain PTI who always insisted on calling the only coloured guy in our intake, "jungle bunny".'

Many recruits came from areas with small ethnic minority populations and arrived in the Army naive and with little experience of racial matters. One soldier remembers a discussion in a barrack block 'about how they would never allow Black soldiers in the regiment ... We were young and to be honest few of us had any exposure to other ethnic groups. Where I grew up I don't ever remember seeing a Black person while I was at school.'

Politicians and military commanders not only denied racial discrimination and abuse was taking place, but they also stated it was not condoned, with strict penalties against those that were caught. A soldier recalls a meeting he attended to discuss bullying and racism. 'A senior officer stood up and said that racial discrimination was a "barrack block problem" and that those in command at unit level should stamp it out. I remember thinking to myself that he was talking crap – racism was not just confined to the barrack block.' With the passage of time, retired soldiers now tell of systemic racial prejudice that was not just limited to junior ranks.

> Racial prejudice was prevalent throughout my service. One example of this was when I was working in Regimental Headquarters. I was summoned by the CO and told that as our PTI was about to retire I was to get hold of the Department of Physical Training at Division and tell them that his replacement was not to be someone looking for an easy ride as the CO was keen to maintain our high level of fitness. In due course I contacted DOPT, expressed the CO's comments and thought nothing more about it. About a month later I got a call from the Captain in charge of DOPT saying they had found the perfect replacement, Para trained, Commando qualified, but there was only one problem – he was Black. I asked the captain to hold whilst I spoke to the Adjutant who in turn spoke to the CO. Two minutes later I was told to say that we don't want him.

Back in 1969, then Secretary of State for Defence Dennis Healey witnessed the same entrenched attitudes and saw the writing on the wall. He knew that unless the Army addressed their prejudice there would be a public outcry.[8] Two and a half decades later, there was.

In 1994, the Commission for Racial Equality (CRE) began an inquiry under Section 49 (3) of the Race Relations Act 1976 into alleged racial discrimination within the Household Cavalry. Two years earlier, Corporal Jake Malcolm of the Royal Electrical and Mechanical Engineers had his posting changed from the Life Guards to the Royal Tank Regiment because he was Black. He filed an official complaint about his treatment and was eventually awarded compensation.[9] Although the focus of the report was the Household Cavalry, the CRE cited evidence of widespread racism throughout the armed forces.

Among some Household Cavalry soldiers there was pushback. 'At the time, I thought we were being used as scapegoats and all this had stemmed from the way the Grenadiers had treated Stokes.' There was also a perception that this particular incident was a REME problem that had nothing to do with the regiment. 'I remember the incident in Germany where a Black guy from the REME was turned away by the ASM [Artificer Sergeant Major]. I believe that this led to court action for the CO and the Adjutant even though they had nothing to do with it.' But on 9 May 1996, Labour MP for Leyton, Harry Cohen, read extracts of the report during a debate in the House of Commons that showed this perception was not true. 'The CRE concludes, that the Commanding Officer had, in effect, given an unlawful discriminatory instruction to the officer in command of the REME detachment.'[10] And it now appears that it was not the first time this had happened. One soldier remembers, 'A Sikh Royal Army Pay Corps NCO turned up at the gates – he lasted two hours before he was posted somewhere else.' Another soldier remembers a similar incident in Cyprus when 'a Black medic was posted to our squadron. He wasn't with us long – less than a day – he was swapped with a white medic from another unit up the road.'

After the report was released, the Commission for Racial Equality and the Ministry of Defence agreed upon 'a tight schedule for the Army to put its affairs in order'.[11] As well as the threat of a Non-Discrimination Notice, the Army agreed to a series of measures to root out racism and build an equal opportunities policy. Over the next two years while the threat of legal action was still a very real possibility, there was a concerted effort to build lasting relationships with ethnic minority communities through outreach programs to increase the number of ethnic minority recruits.

On 27 September 1999, in Strasbourg, Switzerland, the European Court of Human Rights (ECHR) ruled in favour of two ex-British servicemen who had brought a lawsuit against the British government. Both servicemen had been dismissed from the armed forces on the grounds of their homosexuality. The ECHR ruling said it was a 'grave interference'[12] into the private life of an individual, a right guaranteed under Article 8 of the European Convention of Human Rights. The importance of the ruling was not only that it made the government's stance on homosexuals in the armed forces untenable, but it is also important because the ECHR found in favour of the servicemen, overruling the British High Court and Court of Appeal, both of whom had previously ruled against them.

During the Thatcher premiership there was absolutely no talk of ever lifting a ban on homosexuals in the military. One example of her view on the subject was the inclusion of Section 28 of the Local Government Act 1988. This controversial clause stated that a local authority shall not 'promote the teaching in any maintained school of the acceptability of homosexuality as a pretended family relationship'.[13] Regardless, British society was changing. Before January 2000, it is estimated that although 80–90 per cent of service personnel were against homosexuals being allowed to serve in the armed forces,[14] 68 per cent of the civilian population were in favour of the ban being lifted.[15]

The Sexual Offences Act of 1967 had de-criminalized homosexuality in the United Kingdom. But in the Army it was still considered an offence for which you could be charged: 'Conduct to the prejudice of good order and military discipline contrary to Section 69 of the Army Act 1955.'[16] After 1986 it was no longer considered a military offence for service personnel; however, homosexuals were still barred from serving in the armed forces and, if discovered, were given an administrative discharge.[17]

From 1986 up until the ECHR ruling, if a soldier was accused of being a homosexual while serving, then that individual was usually interviewed by military police. If during the interview process the soldier admitted to being a homosexual, then they would be automatically discharged within a matter of days. Hundreds of well-trained service personnel, ranging from high-ranking officers to privates, were discharged this way. Between 1991 and 1994, 260 servicemen were discharged for being homosexuals.[18] The gay rights pressure group, Stonewall, said that a further 240 left the armed forces due to the unbearable conditions they faced, while others suggest the number was closer to 600. The cost of training these service personnel totalled around £50 million, only for them to be discharged.[19]

Many soldiers remembered the inconsistency with which the regulations were enforced.

> In 1987, during my basic training … a guy who was close to finishing his 12 months at Bovington was found with some photographs in his locker of him and his boyfriend on holiday. He was gone within hours, never to be seen again. Yet when I got to the regiment (expecting zero tolerance) … it was clear that there were homosexuals already serving.

Some soldiers did feel there was a double standard – a big difference between how gay men and gay women were treated. 'Homosexual men were not tolerated at all … but lesbians they seemed to turn a blind eye to.' There were also examples of how a soldier could 'work their ticket' by going to the doctor, telling him he was a homosexual, and receive an administrative discharge from the Army long before he was due to leave.

Although the ECHR ruling was not binding, allowing the British government the ability to opt out if it wished, Defence Secretary Lord Robertson decided that it was time to act and accepted that the ban was no longer legally sustainable. Despite objections from most of the service chiefs, the ban on homosexuals was lifted by the Labour government on 12 January 2000 when a new code of sexual conduct was introduced. The ruling now allowed homosexuals to serve, but the law that prohibited a 'homosexual act' was not repealed until it was included in the Armed Forces Bill of 2015–2016.

Despite most service chiefs and many retired generals speaking out, including General Sir Anthony Farrar-Hockley, who called it 'this ridiculous ruling',[20] many who were part of the 80–90 per cent before 2000 have since changed their minds. 'I've witnessed a radical change … many soldiers adopted a completely different attitude.' Another soldier said, 'I was dead against the ban being lifted. But if I'm honest, over the years I knew of several who I suspected were gay but never admitted it – in fact I think everyone knew. They were good friends and great soldiers, and as such never did anything to undermine discipline or morale.' Owen C. said, 'My attitude has changed over the years. I wouldn't say I was homophobic, but my opinion has evolved.'

Although there would be radical changes in both legislation and attitudes, in the late 1980s and throughout the 1990s, bigotry persisted. Soldier G., an instructor at an Army Training Regiment, described one such incident.

> In my section was a young recruit who had been on several visits to see the padre. I thought nothing of it … Then in about the eighth week of training I received a message from my platoon commander that the recruit was being discharged. I was furious because this lad was an enthusiastic and well-motived recruit who seemed to be doing well. My fury was also fuelled by the fact nobody would tell me why I was losing one of my best lads. I offered the guy a lift to the station and on the way down he told me he was leaving due to his homosexuality. He had joined the army to get away from the ignorance of the small community he lived in … I remember feeling disappointed because I truly thought a lot of this lad and thought he'd make a good soldier. After the dust had settled a few days later the recruits in my section wanted to know why he had left … in my naivety I thought they wouldn't be bothered … How wrong I was. Most of the soldiers in my section were fuming that they'd had to share a shower with this guy.

Even as a new code of conduct was being introduced after the ECHR ruling, several senior officers who were still in favour of the ban resigned because of it.[21] Up until the ECHR ruling the government's official position had been 'that overt homosexuality continues to be incompatible with service in the armed forces'.[22]

***

On 27 March 1998, in an open letter, Minister of State for the Armed Forces Dr John Reid announced that the CRE had dropped the threat of legal action against the Household Cavalry.

> When the CRE reviewed progress last March they took the view that, while the mechanistic processes were being addressed, there had not been enough progress to recruit more ethnic minority personnel or remove racist attitudes, where these exist. I am delighted to say that, with a further year behind us and, in particular, the changes the CRE have noted in the last six months in the resolve of the Armed Forces to put their house in order, the CRE have decided not to proceed with the enforcement of a Non-Discrimination Notice.[23]

After announcing that legal action would not now happen, both the MOD and Army signed an agreement with the CRE to continue the progress they had made and to overhaul its policy on race. Over the next decade numbers of ethnic minority soldiers would increase from 1,015 to over 7,500, going from 1.1 per cent of the total force to nearly 9 per cent.[24]

One of the main reasons the CRE agreed to stop legal action and saw a marked change in the six months before their announcement in March 1998 was due largely to the appointment of Major General Sir Evelyn Webb-Carter as Commander of the Household Division. First commissioned into the Grenadier Guards in 1964, he took over at Horse Guards in June 1997. He arrived at a time when the Household Division was plagued with accusations of racism that played out in the press, leaving the public with a perception that the Guards were proud to be exclusively white. He immediately asked for advice from the CRE and members of the Black community.

He also went out into ethnic minority areas like St Paul's in Bristol, Brixton in south London, Bradford, Birmingham, and Tiger Bay in South Wales.[25] He talked to community leaders, visited their temples and mosques, and was brutally honest with both his soldiers and with himself. 'The image was pretty bloody awful and if I was Black British I wouldn't have joined – I'd have thought the Army was dodgy and the Guards, you must be joking. I think I was probably racist in the past without realising it. I thought of Blacks as completely different.'[26]

As well as putting in a series of measures to make sure young men were being actively recruited from ethnic minority areas in cities like Birmingham and Manchester, he also 'made quite a thing' of letting all his officers and soldiers know that there was now no place for racism in the Household Division.

> Sometimes there is a slight intake of breath and some are better at it than others and I have to kick arse. But our tradition of discipline means that if I say something, that goes … Some people say I'm politically correct – I defy that. It's straight common sense. It's their army as much as it's ours. When I speak to some of the old comrades, the old and bold, there are mutterings and some think I've gone pinko. But I don't ask for their support, I demand it. If we don't do it, we'll be damned.[27]

The Household Division selected several SNCOs to be trained as recruiters. They had one objective in mind – to recruit soldiers for their regiment from ethnic minorities.

> I was the recruiter for the first Black man into my regiment. Some have never forgiven me for that … During my time there I had to work closely with the local CRE office and report to them on a regular basis. I fell afoul of them on one occasion for doing what I thought was the right thing. I had a potential candidate for the regiment. He was a young man with a degree who could have applied for officer entry but didn't want to. As part of my brief I explained to him … he'd be the first Black soldier in this regiment and asked him how he felt, and if he could cope? I looked at this as being honest and fair. I recorded it in my interview notes and he was confident he could handle it. But he wanted to be a paratrooper … so he enlisted in the Paras and I know he passed P Company first time. I was told by the CRE to never do that again. I ignored them as I felt it would have been unfair. After that I recruited a number of soldiers into the regiment both Black and Asian. Some did well, and some did not.

Although numbers of ethnic minority soldiers enlisting across the Army steadily increased, some die-hard attitudes from the past lingered. And although officers clamped down hard on racism, trying to convince the public that action was being taken, it was difficult because military justice was often unseen and slow. In 2000, while filming for the television series *New Model Army*, a Channel Four film crew were at the Household Cavalry Mounted Regiment in Knightsbridge and saw racist graffiti on a washroom wall. The show's producer said, 'We didn't go looking for racism when we set out on this series – it found us.'[28] The film crew could see that senior officers like General Webb-Carter were trying hard to change things but they knew it was a slow process. 'However much the policy changes at the top, however many equal opportunities lectures are given to the ranks, it will take at least another generation for racist attitudes to be squeezed out of the barrack room. And even then that's by no means guaranteed.'[29]

Some soldiers describe racial issues of a different kind. Rich G. was an instructor at an ATR when the first ethnic minority soldiers joined the Household Division. 'I didn't see any open prejudice towards them from instructors. I did see them given preferential treatment compared to their fellow recruits. They didn't have to meet the same standards as their peer group and were pushed through training.' Several NCOs had issues with a few ethnic minority soldiers after they arrived at their regiments. One soldier developed 'a bit of a reputation'.

> He was put on a pedestal and used a lot by the regiment for PR purposes but after a while he turned out to be quite lazy and ill disciplined. Once I was Orderly Corporal during an inspection and I was ordered to charge him for being in bad order. Just before we went in on orders he turned to me and said, 'Corporal, is this a Black thing?' I was furious; under no circumstances was it a Black thing on my part. As far as I was concerned I was just doing my job.

Another NCO had an issue with a soldier who seemed to be using his ethnicity in a different way.

> I had dealings with a member of my troop who insisted on wearing jewellery stating that it was symbolic to his religion ... he then asked for time off for the festival of light during a really busy time of the year. At Christmas when I didn't give him leave because he'd already had time off, he then complained saying his family celebrated Christmas. I was summoned with my leave records to explain my case. I highlighted the fact that he'd already had more time off than anyone, including me.

One of the common complaints centred around the fact that most ethnic minority soldiers had direct access to a warrant officer at divisional level who would in turn by-pass the chain of command and go directly to that soldier's commanding officer to address any race-related issues that came to his attention. It left some NCOs feeling like they had to walk on eggshells and may have led directly to ethnic minority soldiers being treated differently.

During the late 1990s, huge efforts were made to break the cycle of a passed-on culture in the barrack blocks, combined with a concerted effort to recruit more ethnic minority officers. One soldier noticed positive changes when he returned to his regiment after a posting. 'There were Black, Asian and Fijian guys in the squadron. We even had a couple of Black officers, one who still serves today. I always thought if you're going to change the mentality in the regiment then you need to start in the Officers' Mess. These guys all integrated well and never again did I see any racial prejudice.'

Twenty years after he had joined the Grenadier Guards as the first Black soldier in the Household Division, Richard Stokes was asked if he had any regrets about joining the Army. Despite all he had been through, and all he had endured, Stokes said he would do it all again.

I was unfortunate to experience what I did, but there's so much you can get out of the Army, there's such a career you can make, travel the world, you can pick up skills, you can learn what it's like to live in a team, and that's what I miss … it's the comradeship, being part of a team. Knowing what I know now about the ways in which the Army has changed, definitely I'd do it again.[30]

CHAPTER 6

Bosnia

I asked, 'When did you first become aware of what was happening in Bosnia?' Very few of the retired soldiers who helped me with this book could recall. They all remember when Saddam invaded Kuwait, or where they were on 9/11, but no one could put a finger on the first time that they were aware anything was happening in the Balkans. Shaun G. said he became aware of 'ethnic cleansing on the news' and 'we kind of knew from a very early date that the Army would be going in.' Another retired soldier said, 'The only reason I can remember it, is because I was about to book a holiday on the Adriatic Coast at Dubrovnik, but decided against it when I saw it getting shelled on the news.'

So many soldiers were traumatised by the war that it is not surprising no one remembered how it all started. After serving in Bosnia, Andrew T. struggled with mental illness for the rest of his Army career. A combat medic, he would later witness the horrors of war in both Iraq and Afghanistan; however, it was Bosnia that affected him the most. 'The Balkans still haunt me to this day.'

In the long history of the British Army, there was never a more convoluted conflict in which its soldiers found themselves. Soldiers that were sent as United Nations peacekeepers between 1992 and 1995 as part of the United Nations Protection Force often returned home more traumatised than if they had been fighting a war. The job they carried out was frustrating, dangerous, often heart breaking, and spread across large tracts of the former Yugoslavia. Their hands tied by restrictive rules of engagement trying to enforce a weak mandate, soldiers often found themselves defenceless and left to deal with the aftermath of ethnic cleansing, and genocide.

The complex situation was not accurately portrayed by mainstream media. Reporting painted an over-simplified picture of a war caused by ethnicity, with atrocities solely carried out by the Serbs. Although ethnicity was a factor, the major underlying cause of the conflict was nationalism, with atrocities being carried out by all sides. The Great Schism of 1054 had split the Catholic and Eastern Orthodox churches, and the rise of Islam in the Balkans came about during the 13th and 14th centuries through the expansion of the Ottoman Empire. The end result was that the Balkans became a melting pot of complex ethnic and religious tensions. Despite the numerous wars that ravaged the region, the various ethnic factions had lived together, side by side, in the same communities, in relative peace for decades.

Using an analogy from James Hawdon, Ph.D., regarding group violence and precipitating factors to help understand the complex relationship between ethnicity and nationalism in the Balkans, we can say that just as underbrush provides fuel for a forest fire, it is fuel, and not fire itself.[1] Ethnicity was the underbrush and nationalism was the fire that destroyed the entire forest.

Serbian nationalism was kept in check throughout the Cold War; however, after the death of Yugoslavia's president Josip Broz Tito in 1980, other republics started to harbour nationalistic aspirations too. Steeped in historical lore stretching as far back as the battle of Kosovo in 1389, and stoked by resentment of horrific events from the past, Serbian nationalism had always been there, awaiting the right time to provide the spark that would set the Balkans ablaze.

On 28 June 1914, Bosnian Serb Gavrilo Princip assassinated the Archduke Ferdinand, heir to the Habsburg Empire, and his wife Sophia, in Sarajevo. This single incident caused a chain-reaction of events that led to the start of World War I. Faced with an advancing enemy on two sides, the Serbian government and its army were forced to flee south to the Adriatic coast through Albania and were exiled on the island of Corfu. During the war and occupation, a quarter of Serbia's population died, including 60,000 Serbian civilians who were executed by German, Austro-Hungarian, and Bulgarian forces.[2]

During World War II, the Balkans were once again involved in heavy fighting. In April 1941, German, Italian, and Hungarian forces invaded and quickly overran Yugoslavia, a country still in its infancy, created after World War I. There were two main resistance groups that fought against the Axis army of occupation – Josip Broz Tito led the Communist Yugoslav partisans, and Draža Mihailović led the Serb nationalist movement, the Chetniks. Initially they both fought against the Axis armies, but by 1942, the Chetniks, who were supported by the Eastern Orthodox Church, had sided with the Axis powers in an attempt to form a Serb-dominated Yugoslavia when the war ended. After the invasion, Croatia, which was part of Yugoslavia, became an independent country under Axis control. A puppet state with support from the Catholic Church, Croatia adopted Nazi racist ideology, and with their militia, the Ustaše, committed unspeakable crimes.

Throughout the war, terrible atrocities were carried out by all sides, but the brutality of both the Ustaše and Chetniks was unsurpassed. Even the Nazis considered their methods extreme; a 1942 report sent to Heinrich Himmler from an SS officer stated, 'The Ustaše committed their deeds in a bestial manner not only against males of conscript age, but especially against helpless old people, women, and children.'[3] The brutality of the Ustaše was only matched by that of the Chetniks. In January 1942,

Chetnik forces massacred thousands of Muslims in Visegrád, Žepa, and Srebrenica,[4] where tragically, 53 years later, history would be repeated.

After the war, Tito made sure that he was even-handed when dealing with ethnic and nationalistic factions. Both Ustaše and Chetnik leaders, including Mihailović, were rounded up, tried, and executed. For the next 35 years Tito kept a tight lid on nationalism using a mix of iron-fisted rule and concessions to placate different groups. When Tito died in 1980, his influence was no longer there to stop decades of deep-seated hatred from tearing the country apart. Inside Yugoslavia there was turmoil, the economy took a nosedive, there were widespread strikes, and nationalist unrest was rife. The most prosperous republics, Croatia and Slovenia, pushed for a more decentralised government. After the fall of the Berlin Wall, Slobodan Milošević, who had climbed to power by promoting Serb nationalism throughout Yugoslavia, now positioned Serbia for a more centralised role. He wanted to keep the country together not because he shared Tito's wish for pan-Slavic unity, but because he wanted to realise the dream of earlier radicals for a Greater Serbia.

On 25 June 1991, while the eyes of the world were still focused on events in the Middle East and impending German reunification, Slovenia and Croatia declared independence. Milošević refused to let this happen without a fight. The Serb-controlled Yugoslav Army (JNA) moved to secure borders, airports, and centres of communication. In Slovenia, where the population was 90 per cent ethnic Slovenian, the people supported their government and were willing to fight for their independence. After a brief 10-day conflict, the JNA was defeated and abruptly left. In Croatia, where over 500,000 ethnic Serbs were against independence, the JNA and Serb rebels started what would become a protracted full-scale conflict. In the autumn of 1991, the town of Vukovar was set ablaze and the Adriatic town of Dubrovnik was severely damaged during heavy bombardment. In January 1992, former US Secretary of State Cyrus Vance negotiated a ceasefire. The Vance Plan, which offered no permanent political settlement, created four United Nations Protected Areas where 10,000 UN Protection Force (UNPROFOR) troops would keep the peace while a lasting settlement was negotiated.

In April 1992, Bosnia and Herzegovina also declared independence after ethnic Croats and Muslims held a referendum. For a time it looked as though a peace conference led by Lord Carrington would stop Bosnia from sliding into the abyss. But even after the three sides came to an agreement, the conference ended when Bosniak (Bosnian Muslim) leader Alija Izetbegović withdrew his signature, refusing to agree on any partition of the country. Worse still was the fact that the Bosnian Croat leader Mate Boban, and Radovan Karadžić for the Bosnian Serbs, both left the conference knowing any future peace deal would be based upon 'the ethnic principle for the reorganization of the republic'.[5] Unwittingly, the conference had opened a Pandora's box that would lead to ethnic cleansing and genocide.

With Macedonia proclaiming independence, the Federal Republic of Yugoslavia now only consisted of Serbia and Montenegro. Eighty thousand former soldiers were released from the JNA and allowed to keep their weapons. Most formed a new Bosnian Serb Army, the Army of the Republika Srpska (VRS). As well as recruiting Bosnian Serbs, the VRS also welcomed over 4,000 Orthodox Christian volunteers from other countries, including Russia, Bulgaria, and Greece. The swollen ranks of the VRS were now ready to go on the offensive.

As war spread throughout the country, on one side were Bosnia's Croats and Muslims, held together by a tenuous agreement; on the other, Bosnian Serbs. Serb forces took large tracts of Bosnia and laid siege to Sarajevo. The city's 350,000 residents were surrounded and struggled to survive; over 10,000 would be killed from sniper and artillery fire. By May 1992, the Serbs controlled three-quarters of Bosnia despite only making up less than a third of the total population. Throughout the summer hundreds of thousands of refugees fled the fighting, and large tracts of Bosnia were systematically ethnically cleansed.

Although the United Nations was involved in Croatia, and in June 1992, UNSCR 758 authorized UNPROFOR to be responsible for the protection of Sarajevo airport, the world seemed oblivious to what was happening in the Bosnian countryside. It was not until a photograph of an emaciated Muslim man in a Serbian camp appeared on the front page of *Time* magazine in August 1992 that the world would pay attention. While on a supervised visit, reporters stumbled upon Trnopolje Camp where thousands of Bosniak men and boys were imprisoned. 'No one anywhere can pretend any longer not to know what barbarity has engulfed the people of former Yugoslavia',[6] the article declared.

After the images of emaciated Muslim prisoners, reports of ethnic cleansing, and television coverage of the constant bombardment of Sarajevo broke across the globe, there was an acceptance by most of the global community that something had to be done. In the autumn of 1992, a series of UN Security Council Resolutions were passed to extend UNPROFOR's mandate to include Bosnia. Unlike Croatia the mandate for Bosnia was not to monitor a ceasefire, but rather to try to keep people alive until the fighting ended.

On 21 August 1992, a formal offer was made to the United Nations from the British government to send a mechanised infantry battalion, an armoured reconnaissance squadron, an engineer squadron, and a large logistical support element – 1,800 troops in total. By the time the offer was accepted, the British government had authorized the deployment, and the troops had shipped their equipment to the port of Split; it was the middle of November.

Under extremely tense conditions throughout central Bosnia, makeshift bases were quickly constructed and became operational. The first infantry battalion to be deployed to Bosnia was the 1st Battalion, the Cheshire Regiment, with Warrior Armoured Personnel Carriers (APCs). They established their Battalion Group HQ at a school in Vitez with three companies, the SHQ element of the 9th/12th Lancers, and three troops of Scimitar CVR(T)s. In Gornji Vakuf, located in an abandoned factory complex, were stationed another company of the Cheshire Regiment and a fourth troop of 9th/12th Lancers. The National Support Element HQ was situated at Tomislavgrad and consisted of support and logistical units. The Royal Engineer company built several mountain camps along the main supply routes (MSRs) from Split. Their primary task was keeping the MSRs open – an enormous accomplishment considering the mountainous terrain and treacherous weather conditions. Both routes (Triangle and Square) kept the logistic support and humanitarian aid flowing. All soldiers familiar with the MSRs considered this 'an amazing engineering feat'.

Despite promises from Prime Minister John Major that his government would not take any unacceptable risks with the lives of British troops, the situation that Lieutenant Colonel Bob Stewart, CO of the Cheshires, now found himself in was more violent than expected.[7] That autumn the situation deteriorated, with the bulk of aggression coming from Bosnian Serb forces. But early in the new year, the fragile Croat–Bosniak alliance started to crumble in Novi Travnik before turning into all-out conflict in Gornji Vakuf. On 12 January 1993, the first British soldier was killed. Lance Corporal Wayne Edwards, Cheshire Regiment, was hit by rifle fire while driving a Warrior APC in Gornji Vakuf.

Throughout the spring of 1993, UNPROFOR soldiers constantly found themselves fired upon from three sides. The media present in the war zone, always looking for a soundbite, turned Colonel Stewart into an unwitting celebrity. He did try to push the limits of the mandate and was outspoken at times, often upsetting both those in New York and Whitehall. But on 22 April 1993, the harsh reality of what his soldiers had been dealing with on a daily basis was on full display for the world to see.

The BBC correspondent Martin Bell, who became a good friend of the British commander, was with the Cheshires when they entered the village of Ahmići. What they saw there, they would never forget. Six days earlier, about 70 soldiers belonging to the Croatian Defence Council[8] advanced on both sides of the village. Mortar fire blocked the roads, preventing any escape, while soldiers threw grenades in through windows, and snipers shot people running out of their houses on to the streets. Men, women, and children were beaten, shot, or burnt alive in their own homes. Colonel Stewart's men buried a total of 103 people.[9] Addressing Parliament in January 2019, he spoke of his experience in Ahmići:

> I stopped to pick up what I thought was a black rubber ball. I put it in my hand, looked at it and then dropped it in horror. I had picked up the blackened, burnt hand of a baby. I was horrified and guilty. The day before I found a whole family – a father, a mother, a boy and a girl – lying where they had been shot. From the way the bodies had been arranged, it looked as though the little girl had been shot while holding her puppy. The bullet had killed them both.[10]

Martin Bell, a man who had experienced the horrors of war many times before, recorded a broadcast from the burnt-out shell of one of the houses, with the charred remains of the family on the ground all around him. His normally deliberate and steadfast tone now tinged with anger. 'It's hard to imagine, on our continent, and in our time, what people could do this.'[11] Writing later that year, Colonel Stewart was determined to see those who had committed these unspeakable atrocities stand trial.[12] Only six people were ever brought to justice by the International Criminal Tribunal for the Former Yugoslavia (ICTY); two of them, Dario Kordić and Tihomir Blaškić, were men Colonel Stewart had been forced to work with throughout his time in Bosnia. They denied to his face any Croatian involvement in the Ahmići massacre, and even claimed that as good Christians their men would never commit such crimes, and that it must have been the Serbs that had carried out the atrocities.[13] They were sentenced to 25 and nine years, respectively.

During the spring and early summer months of 1993, fighting throughout Bosnia had caused a humanitarian crisis, with towns such as Srebrenica being flooded with refugees. In May, on recommendations from a 'fact-finding mission', UNSCR 824 'demanded that all parties treat Srebrenica as a "safe area" which should be free from any armed attack or any other hostile act'.[14] The resolution also included Sarajevo, Tuzla, Žepa, Goražde, and Bihać. In June, the UN Security Council changed the mandate for its troops as well. 'The Council authorized UNPROFOR, acting in self-defence, to take necessary measures, including the use of force, in reply to bombardments against the safe areas or to armed incursion into them or in the event of any deliberate obstruction to the freedom of movement of UNPROFOR or of protected humanitarian convoys.'[15]

On paper these moves by the UN looked like ensuring the safety of refugees in the newly established protected areas and gave UNPROFOR troops some teeth. Yet, despite the changed mandate and the UN's wish to appear to have the capability to defend itself, the practical reality for troops on the ground was very different. Andrew T. describes an incident when UN soldiers observed a Serb tank engaging civilian targets. 'The commander wanted to engage, but the process went a bit like this – Commander on the ground to Unit HQ to Brigade HQ to UNPROFOR HQ to UN New York back to UNPROFOR HQ to Brigade HQ to Unit HQ finally to Commander on the ground – but the Serb tank was long gone.'

The conflict in Bosnia developed into a macabre stalemate, with all sides trying to play a game of political musical chairs. Realising that a peace plan would be forced upon them eventually, all sides were trying desperately to hold on to as much territory as possible, not being left without a chair when the music stopped. With ceasefires and local truces continually agreed upon only to be broken a short time later, UNPROFOR seemed overwhelmed and woefully undermanned. In June 1993, when its commander requested 34,000 more troops 'to obtain deterrence through strength', the UN Secretary-General opted for a 'light option, with a minimal troop reinforcement of around 7,600 ... and reaffirmed the use of air power in and around the declared safe areas'.[16] Future events would tragically prove that replacing boots on the ground with air power would not be enough to stop opposing forces from seizing a United Nations Protected Area.

In March 1994, the Secretary of State for Defence, Malcolm Rifkind, announced to Parliament that Britain was sending an additional 900-strong battalion group. The very next day the UN Security Council called on 'all parties in Bosnia and Herzegovina to cooperate with UNPROFOR in the consolidation of the ceasefire'.[17] The Duke of Wellington's Regiment was equipped with Saxon-wheeled APCs, and were supported by a squadron of Light Dragoons and elements from the Royal Signals and Royal Engineers. The air portability of the Light Dragoons CVR(T) vehicles was demonstrated when the entire squadron was airlifted from Germany to Split in C-130 aircraft, with the squadron operational in Bosnia just seven days after being told they were going to be deployed.[18]

For soldiers on the ground there was little time to involve themselves with politics or worry about 'the big picture'. They had a difficult job to do and most concentrated on just that. Each deployment fell into a routine, even though the hazards and problems they often faced were anything but. One soldier describes his arrival in Bosnia.

> We deployed in the middle of winter and took over from one of our own squadrons. The British UN camp was based in Gornji Vakuf; a strategic town in central Bosnia, the control of which was being fought over by the Muslim and Bosnian Croat armies. Also based out of this once-productive factory were infantry elements and support arms. The operational pattern of life for the squadron consisted of SHQ troop permanently based in camp; they also had the additional responsibility of manning a Rebroadcast site near Tito's fist, whilst the Sabre troops worked on a two-week Ops cycle.

If soldiers were tasked with carrying out village surveys, escorting aid convoys, or anything that involved travel away from bases, then there would be no way to avoid Bosnia's infamous roads. One of the major issues for troops responsible for patrolling the MSR were road traffic accidents and vehicles getting into difficulty. 'We were regularly required to recover, clear, and rescue broken-down vehicles and passengers that were woefully prepared for the hazardous journey.' As well as those who were supposed to be in the area, they also had the problem of 'battlefield tourists', soldiers and civilians working out of Split, travelling through the mountains, most totally unprepared for the road conditions. 'I think it was so they could say they were "up-country." These people were often ill-prepared with badly marked maps, poor comms, and outdated info.'

With all the troops, platoons, and other sub-units deployed on the ground were locally employed interpreters. Soldiers developed a respect for them, understanding that they had a dangerous but vitally important job to do. A misunderstanding caused by a poor translation at a vehicle checkpoint or wherever UNPROFOR troops came in contact with any of the opposing forces could prove deadly. For communities hit hard during the war, the money they earnt was often a lifeline for their families. But with it came great risk – after they'd finished working for the UN they would have to go back to their communities, where they often faced brutal reprisals. Six months after leaving Bosnia, Lt Col Bob Stewart and his men of the Cheshire Regiment were saddened at the news that one of their Serb interpreters, Dobrila Kolaba, had been killed in Vitez, murdered by a sniper. They flew their regimental flag at half-mast at their camp in Germany and sent a collection to help her parents in Novi Travnik.[19] Some interpreters not only understood the risks, but often had seen and experienced terrible violence.

> All the interpreters I had, we connected and empathized with, and they all had stories to tell. One pretty young lass who was on my wagon for an Ops cycle always wore a neck scarf. When we got to know her well she told us why she wore it. A friend she went to school with (Croat) made advances on her; when she resisted, he tried to cut her throat!

Some soldiers I interviewed felt a sense of guilt because they were restricted by the UN's insistence on impartiality, not being able to help the local population more. Shaun G., another soldier who said that his experience in Bosnia 'affected him the most', was there in 1994, and 'felt useless and totally ineffective' while he wore the UN's blue beret. Angus T., who was there a year later, disagreed. 'We did a hell of a lot. We even had friends and families from home sending stuff out for us to distribute.' And while there were many soldiers that went beyond what they were supposed to do in an attempt to try to help those worst affected, some took it further, disregarding the UN mandate entirely. 'It was forbidden to help the civilian population as it could be deemed as taking sides and we had to be impartial … morally it's something you just can't do. So we generally ignored that rule and did what we could. We were human and so were they.' Despite his misgivings about the UN's attitude regarding helping the civilian population, Shaun G. was another who did what he could despite the rules.

> On one of our regular patrol routes was this old Muslim man who was at least 80 years old. We always stopped to check he was okay because he had absolutely nothing. We gave him everything we could spare, helping him as much as we could. He was a gifted craftsman who made all sorts of wooden things to sell. At the end of the tour he was so appreciative he gave everyone who had helped him a wooden crucifix.

Getting shot at or threatened at gunpoint was a regular occurrence for UN soldiers. Several soldiers recall stories of being hit by small-arms fire while out on patrol. But the restrictive UN rules of engagement in force insisted that UNPROFOR troops could only 'return fire if we were fired upon directly and we could positively identify the firer/firing position'. Angus T. remembers being fired upon in Prozor. 'The police fired at us from their station and we couldn't do anything about it.' And Shaun G.

recalls getting shot at. 'Because no one in our patrol had been hit, we just had to take cover and wait for the firing to stop. It was frustrating to say the least.'

Even though soldiers tried to keep an impartial view, their experiences while out on patrol or when dealing with all sides left them with differing opinions. 'The few Serbs I met were arrogant and contemptuous with an air of superiority. It was mainly a Croat/Muslim area … some of the stories I was told confirmed that all factions were equally cruel but the Muslims were always the underdogs and if I'm honest I felt more pity for them.' Shaun G. spent a lot of time travelling around different areas of Bosnia. He encountered hundreds of local people from all sides. 'The civilians were pretty much the same; it was the soldiers who had the biggest differences. The Serb soldiers were very aggressive and tried to be overbearing towards us.'

Some soldiers' pre-conceived opinions changed as the tour went on. 'I hated the Serbs as I could see what was happening to the population on my side of the line. I was indifferent to the Croats but having been caught up in a convoy heading to Krajina, and a gun put to my head through the ambulance window, I grew to dislike them as well.' The level of violence that all sides were capable of left an indelible mark. 'Some were good and some were pure evil. The way they talked about each other was quite disturbing … how can you wake up one morning and kill or maim your neighbour after years of living next to each other? There's religion for you.'

By the spring of 1995, Serb dominance was waning in Bosnia, with the balance of power shifting in favour of Croatian and Bosniak forces who, for now, brought together through necessity and political expediency, appeared to have settled their differences. The Bosnian Serbs were left completely isolated – Serbia had closed the border and cut off all ties in an attempt to make the Bosnian Serbs accept the latest peace proposal. But there were ominous signs. The Bosnian Serbs would prove to be extremely vicious when cornered. And just when it appeared they were about to be forced to the negotiating table once again, they became even more determined to keep hold of all their gained territory in the east, ridding itself of non-Serb inhabitants in the three eastern enclaves still controlled by the UN.

In March 1995, Bosnian Serb commander General Ratko Mladić met with UNPROFOR Commander General Rupert Smith. During the meeting Mladić made it clear that his forces intended to take Goražde, Žepa, and Srebrenica. 'Mladić took out the map and with a bit of paper, he drew a scratch over each of the three enclaves.'[20] With the history of what had taken place since 1992, there can be no doubt that Mladić intended to make the Muslim inhabitants of the three eastern enclaves 'vanish completely'.[21]

It was now obvious that UN peacekeepers were unable to hold some of the designated protected areas. General Smith would later comment about the safe areas and the UN mandate being changed for that task without sufficient support or appropriate rules of engagement. 'This was demonstrably the case with the "safe areas" in Bosnia, where the idea was to deter further incursions into those enclaves but the forces to achieve that were inadequate.'[22] Smith wanted a peaceful end to the conflict but understood that the UN needed to be taken seriously. As UNPROFOR commander he was the impetus behind the idea of a Rapid Reaction Force (RRF) in Bosnia. After the hostage taking in May 1995, General Smith formed a battle group in case hostages needed to be rescued. Although the UN prevented any offensive action, the idea of an RRF gathered momentum and it was agreed that such a force should be deployed.[23] Units that were warned off to be involved in this new force were given 48 hours' notice to move to Vitez. They were told they would be preparing to take on a new role – peacekeeping was about to become peace enforcement. 'The British Battle Group (BG) was commanded by the 1st Battalion, Devon and Dorset Regiment. We ceased all Ops cycle activities and deployed as a squadron.'

Initially the RRF operated outside of the UN's mandate. Because there was a difference of opinion between some leading nations and senior UN officials regarding the role any UN Security Council-authorised RRF would play, a month lapsed between the formation of the force and it being approved. UNSCR 998 was passed on 26 June 1995, authorising an RRF of up to 12,500 additional troops. The officially sanctioned RRF would comprise Task Force Alpha and Bravo. Alpha was a joint British/Dutch force consisting of 1st Battalion, the Devon and Dorset Regiment, a CVR(T) squadron from the Household Cavalry Regiment, 12 105mm Royal Artillery guns, and 186 Dutch soldiers. Task Force Bravo was a French brigade based near Tomislavgrad. The 24th Air Mobile Brigade was flown into Croatia in July but was not deployed in Bosnia. As the crisis in the safe areas was starting to unfold, and it appeared that both Srebrenica and Žepa were lost, the French in particular were keen to use the RRF. They 'proposed using force to protect the eastern safe area of Goražde and to open a supply route to the besieged city of Sarajevo'.[24] Whatever the RRF would later be tasked with was still unknown, but its formation and deployment came too late to do anything about Srebrenica.

What took place during 11–22 July 1995, in and around Srebrenica, was the worst crime to happen on European soil since World War II. The deliberate separation of over 8,000 Bosniak men and boys and their subsequent murder was declared a genocide. Since then there have been many recriminations, claims and counter-claims regarding Srebrenica. The ICTY in the Hague and courts in Bosnia and Serbia convicted an array of soldiers and political leaders.

Survivors and victims' relatives have brought legal actions against the government of the Netherlands, whose soldiers were responsible for protecting the Srebrenica UNPA. Dutch soldiers have faced numerous accusations,[25] included standing by while women were raped and removing men and boys from the Dutchbat compound who were then murdered by Serbs.[26] Eventually the judicial system of the Netherlands found its own government liable for more than 300 deaths.[27]

There were also claims that both the US and UK knew of Serb plans a month before it happened, and that CIA operatives watched the genocide taking place live via satellite. A US State Department official was quoted by *The Guardian* reporters Florence Hartmann and Ed Vulliamy, 'All US partners were immediately informed.'[28] Despite the warning nothing was done to stop the slaughter.

What unfolded in Srebrenica and the surrounding area was a horrific crime. The murders that took place are beyond description and of immense complexity. They have taken years to fully comprehend and are beyond the scope of this book. However, it would be remiss of me not to highlight one simple fact – no politician, diplomat, or UN official resigned.

Srebrenica shook the world's conscience, but even as UN officials started to fully comprehend the enormity of what had happened, it was still unable to pull together enough force to end the conflict. In the eyes of the world the UN was toothless and had given a perfect demonstration of how not to conduct a military intervention, losing the confidence of those who needed its protection the most.[29] In 1993, the UN commander in Bosnia declared to the people of Srebrenica, 'You are now under the protection of the United Nations. I will never abandon you.'[30] It would take a heavy finger being placed on the scales of justice to finally end three years of brutal internecine fighting.

In November 1992, President George H. W. Bush had lost his attempt to be elected for a second term to the White House. Despite having a huge approval rating after the Gulf War, a slowing economy and the six words 'read my lips, no new taxes' paved the way for Democratic candidate Bill Clinton to become the 42nd President of the United States of America.

Domestically, things were going badly – after two years of Democrat-controlled government, they lost control of Congress to the Republicans. It wasn't much better on the world stage for the two-term Arkansas governor. In Somalia, American soldiers' dead bodies had been dragged through the streets of its capital, Mogadishu, and as leader of the world's sole remaining superpower, Clinton had been criticised for a lack of action in both Rwanda and the Balkans where it was now known genocide had taken place. By 1995, Bosnia was a thorny issue for Clinton. He was now facing a tough re-election battle against Republican candidate Senator Bob Dole, who had frequently accused the president of inaction. Clinton needed to bring the conflict in Bosnia to a swift and decisive conclusion or he, too, like President Bush, would be a one-term president.

The Serb offensive on the UN-protected areas had posed a serious threat to Croatia. On 22 July, Croatian President Franjo Tudjman and Bosnian President Alija Izetbegović agreed to launch a combined offensive against the Serbs. Bosnian Croatians and Bosniaks were also prepared to join the operation. On 3 August, Croatia launched Operation *Storm* and reclaimed most of its pre-war territory. In Bosnia the VRS was pushed off almost 20 per cent of land it had taken in earlier campaigns. Over 150,000 Bosnian Serbs fled from Bihać and other towns. There was little sympathy for the Serbs, so the brutal tactics and ethnic cleansing employed by both Croat and Bosnian Croat/Muslim forces went unnoticed by the western press who, after Srebrenica, saw the Serbs as the sole aggressors. After just three days, Operation *Storm*, having achieved all its aims, was brought to a swift end. Now all President Clinton needed to do was get Bosnian Serbs to agree to a ceasefire and come to the negotiating table.

On 28 August 1995, a mortar round hit the Markale market in Sarajevo, killing 43 people. The United States quickly blamed the Serbs; two days later NATO launched Operation *Deliberate Force*. The speed at which airstrikes against the VRS began should have come as no surprise. NATO had planned the campaign in detail on the back of earlier strikes, and on 28 July, had already agreed 'to launch extensive airstrikes under the authority of existing Security Council resolutions in the event of a Bosnian Serb attack against Goražde'.[31]

Just hours before the first airstrikes, UNPROFOR troops were quietly moved away from isolated positions where they might be kidnapped and used as human shields. Before allowing the attack to begin, General Rupert Smith ordered the remaining troops still in Goražde to evacuate the enclave. In a phone call to Mladić on 29 August, General Smith informed him that evidence suggested that the mortar rounds had been fired by his troops. Mladić then threatened British troops in Goražde, so the general abruptly ended the call.[32] Mladić, who had previously called General Smith the 'blue lamb',[33] was obviously unaware that the last soldiers in Goražde had been spirited away during the night, and he was about to find out that even a lamb can sometimes have very sharp teeth.

As the airstrikes were taking place, the RRF was deployed to Mount Igman, a mountain plateau of immense strategic importance that dominated Sarajevo, where UN artillery would be used against Serb air defences, artillery, and armour. The remainder of the RRF would not only hold the mountain while the artillery was being used in conjunction with air support, but it also was tasked with securing the route into Sarajevo so that the siege could be lifted. Soldier B. was part of Task Force Alpha. 'We were tasked with clearing and securing a route up to Mount Igman in order that the Royal Artillery's 105mm guns could safely travel up the trail. My troop was tasked to secure, man, and mark the route through a town. Because I had an interpreter with me I secured the main crossing in the centre of the town.'

While soldiers with Task Force Alpha were deployed to Mount Igman, Andrew T. and colleagues from 4th Field Ambulance provided a small medical section in the town of Konjic. Their job was to be ready to evacuate casualties from Mount Igman and respond to the numerous RTAs that regularly happened on the MSR.

> I was on the first deployment to Konjic. We were to relieve the guys from 3AFA as it was the end of their tour … after our arrival we met a few guys who had that stare. They were dirty and thin. We had a very short handover then they were gone. They couldn't leave quick enough. The last words I heard were, 'Stay low, stay alive.' No further explanation was given. Well the weather was great, the place was quiet … we spent three or four days sunbathing, playing volleyball and doing radio stags.

One morning Andrew had just finished radio watch, made himself a hot drink, and was standing next to the entrance of their bunker. Everyone else was still asleep in the back of the ambulances or in their tented accommodation.

> I remember hearing a distant thump, thought nothing more of it, then my whole world turned upside down. I remember all the air being sucked from around me, and being thrown to the floor … BOOM, dirt and stones rained down on me, the ambulances rocked from side to side. I tried to scream out, but my mouth had gone dry. I spat and managed to shout 'Incoming.' Artillery and mortar rounds started dropping randomly. The scream of an incoming round is something I will never forget. I crawled further into the bunker entrance, curled into a ball and put my hands over my ears. Moments later a few others joined me. And then silence.

He and his comrades survived, but that was just the start of a daily shelling ordeal that their position was subjected to. He recalled another close call with artillery on his way back from transporting a casualty to Split. 'The ambulance sped through the deserted streets. I recall watching as a shell hit an apartment building, sending debris into the road.' Being subjected to daily artillery and mortar fire was already starting to have an effect.

> I have to admit we had become a bit feral … military discipline was maintained, but as a group of people we had become a bit wayward. Within a few weeks, I wasn't taking cover during bombardments anymore … instead we would sit on deckchairs on top of our bunker. We'd blast out Vietnam-era music and watch the town being shelled, scoring the hits.

By 14 September, the NATO action in conjunction with negotiations led to Milošević applying pressure on the Bosnian Serbs to accept a ceasefire, and on 20 September, the UN and NATO commanders declared that the aims of the military mission had been achieved.[34] The Serb offensive that had begun in July had gone spectacularly wrong. Not only were the Serbs vilified with images of suspected mass graves being broadcast throughout the world, but the balance of power in Bosnia had shifted against them. Backed into a corner, Karadžić now agreed to negotiate a deal that would give Bosnian Serbs half of Bosnia. Milošević desperately wanted the oil embargo on Serbia lifted, and Croatia wanted eastern Slavonia, so it was also willing to compromise on Bosnia.

The changed situation on the battlefield, use of limited ground forces (RRF), and tireless efforts to bring about a mutual agreement, combined with NATO air power, led to the Dayton Accords. After a 60-day ceasefire had been agreed, all sides then met in Dayton, Ohio, to negotiate a permanent settlement. The war officially ended on 21 November, with the signing of the Dayton Peace Agreement, before the final version was signed in Paris on 14 December 1995.

Even though all sides seemed 'militarily spent', having fought a brutal civil war for three and a half years, any NATO force put in place had to be robust enough to guarantee that the peace so hard won in Dayton would now hold. The troops needed a mandate that would allow them to use the force available to keep the peace if necessary. A large proportion of the troops of the Implementation Force (IFOR) came from troops already under UN command in Bosnia. The white vehicles were painted back to their original colours, off came the blue beret, and tactical command was transferred from the UN to NATO.

For the first 12 months, IFOR's job was to implement the Dayton Accords. Once all troops in Bosnia were in place, IFOR consisted of 54,000 soldiers from 38 countries. Not only was the number of troops larger than ever deployed with UNPROFOR, but the firepower at its disposal was much greater, too. The American 1st Armoured Division entered Bosnia with Abrams M1 tanks and Bradley AFVs supported from the air by Apache attack helicopters. To reach its area of responsibility, the division's engineers built a 600-metre pontoon bridge across the River Sava.[35] If the Bosnian Serbs had thought about resisting the terms of the Dayton Accords, then this show of overwhelming firepower and military capability now entering their country made them think again. The British contingent seriously beefed up its ability to enforce the peace with the deployment of Challenger tanks from Germany. On 20 December 1996, IFOR became SFOR (NATO Stablisation Force). The role of the Stabilisation Force was similar to that of IFOR in that the aim was to deter hostilities and stabilise the peace. But it also had a greater role in helping with 'nation building activities' in a 'secure environment ... without further need for NATO-led military forces'.[36] SFOR was in place for eight years until 2 December 2004, when its responsibilities were taken over by the European Union Force (EUFOR).

NATO's intervention in Bosnia was unparalleled, and according to United Nations Senior Political Affairs Officer Susan Allee it was to set a new precedent. 'It was the first time that NATO had got together to undertake an action that was not defensive in nature ... it enabled it to go on and do something similar in Kosovo and it is also the foundation of what it is doing in Afghanistan. It changed the whole way of thinking of the potential of that force in global affairs.'[37]

Owen C. arrived in Bosnia as part of IFOR and then transitioned to SFOR. His squadron was based in Banja Luka with a responsibility to ensure all military forces still in Bosnia were complying with the Dayton Accords. 'A lot of the time was spent conducting inspections and patrols ... we did have a number of incidents where an attempt was made to move vehicles without permission ... the incidents were reported; various commanders didn't like our intervention ... we had to confiscate a lot of equipment because they tried to move vehicles or didn't catalogue equipment correctly.'

Trying to bring law and order to a country awash with weapons was not going to be easy. Having lived through one of the worst civil wars Europe had ever seen, Bosnians were genuinely scared to give up their weapons, fearing they would be left unable to defend themselves. One soldier saw the abundance of weapons available first hand. 'Foot patrols were sent out around the local markets where there were stalls selling weapons, ammunition and even grenades.' Many civilians hid their weapons and ammunition; some were found, but it is not difficult to imagine that there are thousands upon thousands of weapons and large quantities of ammunition and explosives that remain hidden today.

We carried out patrols right up into the mountains where they had very little contact and had a lot of ammunition … some were reluctant to give it up. One day we went to a village where in one house they had hand grenades above the fireplace that had been painted by kids. We also had a car pull up and hand over two boxes of rifle grenades.

Andrew T.'s second tour to Bosnia was in the winter of 1997–98, with SFOR, and contrasted completely to his experience of Bosnia with UNPROFOR.

I was at a static medical centre [Banja Luka] as opposed to being mobile. I lived in a comfortable Corrimec [modular container building], had hot showers, a laundry … we had a cookhouse and bar. The medical centre was well equipped. We even had Sky TV plumbed in … To relieve the boredom we went on patrols with the RMP, both foot and mobile.

Despite the relative comfort Andrew T. now enjoyed, a population that had access to an unlimited supply of arms and munitions still posed a danger.

On New Year's Eve I was walking to the toilet when I was once again blown to the floor by an explosion. Opposite us was a detachment of SAS who deployed immediately. They brought back a rocket-launcher they'd recovered from a drunk farmer who thought it would be a good idea to fire it into the camp. The twat nearly killed me. The SAS guys gave me the rocket-launcher as a souvenir.

In Bosnia's towns and villages that had seen the worst of the fighting, it seemed like all fighting-age males had either been killed in combat, murdered, or simply vanished. Throughout the fighting in the Balkans, it was not unusual for people to just disappear. Towards the end of the war, when it became obvious that the international community would hold some kind of war crimes tribunal, the need to dispose of evidence became a priority. Many murders were covered up by burying bodies on top of existing graves. Soldier P. told me, 'They would go down as far as the coffin, then put the body on top and cover it up, making sure to leave the grave as they found it. That person then simply disappeared.'

Wherever British Army units were based throughout Bosnia, most helped the local population any way they could. Projects included helping rebuild schools, hospitals, playgrounds – anything to help locals get back on their feet again. Owen C. had been in Banja Luka for his first tour and now found himself in the Croat/Bosniak town of Jajce.

This tour was very different … I don't know whether this was due to it being a Croat/Muslim area rather than Serbian or attitudes had changed over time. Our focus was definitely on the local population rather than overseeing barracks and military movements … people were looking for handouts still but we now had to try and get them to start doing things for themselves to get the local economy moving again.

His troop also carried out foot patrols into towns and villages where people liked to stop and talk to them.

The attitude towards us was very friendly and I think that they were trying to get back to their old way of life … there were still those that had a hatred for other ethnic groups but they were quite positive that things were changing. The one thing that did stand out on both tours, there was a lot of hatred directed at the United States. I don't know if it was due to their bombing campaigns or their dealings with them on the ground? It was always one of the first questions we were asked, 'Are you Americans?'

Jules H. and his troop befriended a young boy (about five years old in 1997) who lived in a small village near the northern town of Bosanska Gradiška.

> Sayid was my mate, he had absolutely nothing. He lived in a garage with his mum. His dad had been killed. We used to give him ice cream and throw him in the bath. My wife who was a teacher sent books and pens and all sorts of things. He was incredibly bright. By the time we left he spoke better English than us.

Jules told me he often thinks about Sayid, wondering if he survived and where he is now.

Although the security situation had improved since the Dayton Accords, there were still incidents that could have quickly escalated had it not been for the presence of NATO troops. There was an internal power struggle throughout 1997 between Bosnian Serbs who remained loyal to Radovan Karadžić and the new president of Republika Srpska, Biljana Plavšić. Karadžić had been indicted by the ICTY and was on the run. Plavšić, who had been just as much a hard-liner as Karadžić during the war, had undergone a rather pragmatic political transformation and was now cooperating with the international community. In August 1997, NATO intelligence assets learned of a plot to overthrow her. Police still loyal to Karadžić had stored large numbers of weapons and explosives in the Banja Luka police station. UN police monitors arrived to inspect the building and were turned away by Bosnian Serb police. British and Czech troops then seized the building, where they found enough weapons and ammunition for a 2,000-strong force.[38]

It was not the first time that Biljana Plavšić had been under threat. Earlier in the year, Angus T.'s squadron had been called upon to assist. 'There was intelligence that a local female politician was about to get murdered, so a troop from our squadron was crashed out to put a ring of steel around her house. They had just minutes to get there ... this action undoubtedly saved her life.' Angus was also involved in an incident when fragmentation grenades were thrown over the perimeter fence into the Wood Factory camp.

> I was walking past the main entrance in our accommodation block to go to the Ops Room, when I heard an explosion in the vehicle park. Instinct took over, I grabbed one of the guard's weapons and went to investigate. Unbeknown to me another NCO was following. As I entered the vehicle park a second explosion went off that took me off my feet. I got up and saw several people run behind the vehicles to a hole in the back of the sheds – they had pulled off a few planks to get in. We both gave a warning for them to stop and when they didn't we fired.

Because the vehicles were tightly packed, they had a poor line of sight, so no one was hit. One person was caught running away outside the camp but was later released. Angus and his squadron flew home shortly afterwards, and because of increasing security issues at the Wood Factory, the squadron was moved to another camp in Banja Luka. Angus and the other NCO would later receive a Commander's Commendation.

As well as dealing with heightened security around the 1997 Bosnian elections, Rich G.'s squadron also took over an area that had previously been the responsibility of the American forces east of the newly opened Banja Luka airport.

> It was unruly … they had let the area go, did no patrolling and seemed to have let the locals run riot. The area was a challenge and took up a lot of manpower to get it under some sort of control. We had an IED detonated close to the troop house and several instances of rounds being fired close to or over the house.

It was not only political crimes that took place. To get by in the aftermath of the civil war a large percentage of the population resorted to buying and selling anything they could get their hands on regardless of where the goods had come from. 'What was evident at the time is that certain individuals were after the aid that was coming into Bosnia to sell on the black market.' Paul H. saw lots of crime and corruption. 'You'd see expensive German cars parked outside a tiny war-torn house. It was obvious that the car had been stolen.'

As the ICTY got under way in the Hague and more indictments were brought against those who had committed the worst atrocities during the civil war, troops on the ground in Bosnia were told to be on the lookout for war criminals. Radovan Karadžić, and his military commander, Ratko Mladić, had both been indicted to appear in the Hague but remained on the run for years. After she was saved by NATO forces and then voted out of office in 1998, Biljana Plavšić was also indicted for war crimes. She made a plea deal to avoid charges of genocide and was sentenced to 11 years in a Swedish prison. There were accusations that some war criminals were being sheltered by the Serb government and that Karadžić had struck a deal as part of the Dayton Peace Agreement.[39] When Conrad P. arrived in Bosnia in 2002, with the Welsh Guards Recce platoon, they were tasked as divisional reconnaissance.

> We were told that our mission was to find Karadžić and Mladić. We had a highly skilled platoon with a group of really good soldiers very keen to take on this mission. But we were given very little direction from division and absolutely no intel. We only carried out a couple of OPs and drank Becks beer by the gallon in Banja Luka … it was a complete waste of six months of my life.

Both Karadžić and Mladić were eventually captured and tried by the ICTY, and they are now serving life sentences in the Netherlands.

Mines were an ever-present risk and the cause of many casualties and damage to equipment. It's estimated that as many as 6 million mines may have been deployed during the civil war,[40] with many minefields unmarked and unrecorded by those who laid them. 'They were everywhere; I saw them lying on the ground, strapped to trees, anti-tank, anti-personnel – a horrific weapon. Standard SOP was NEVER leave a hard surface. When I came back home it was weeks before I felt safe walking on grass.' Shortly after IFOR deployed to Bosnia, the British Army suffered its first casualties as part of the NATO force. On 28 January 1996, three British soldiers died when their APC was destroyed by a mine.[41]

For crews of the lightly armoured CVR(T)s, Russian-made anti-tank mines were a deadly threat. During a tour in 1995, Soldier B. was part of a troop tasked with proving a potential route through the mountains. 'The troop plan was to work in sections and "recce" two routes either side of a large peak that crossed previously contested conflict lines … I remember hearing a contact report from the other section saying they'd suffered a mine strike and taken casualties.' Soldier B.'s section quickly raced to the location of the mine strike. On arrival they found the injured crew members had been rescued from the Scimitar and were being treated.

> Whilst no injuries were life threatening, two crew members were serious enough to warrant being medevaced back to the UK … the Scimitar was a total write-off but it had been robust enough to survive an AT mine and save the crew. Unfortunately the vehicle was not recoverable from the mountainside so we spent a day and a half stripping all we could from the wreck whilst the Royal Engineers cleared the mine threat.

David K. was in a Scimitar southeast of Bihać when it suffered a mine strike on the outside of its track. Although he and his crew were not hurt, the incident was to have a tragic outcome.

> Luckily the charge moved away and outwards from the Scimitar due to the camber of the track. Communications were difficult, however we managed to raise the 12m mast and sent a Minestrike report. We were told to stay on the vehicle, not attempt a self-evacuation and wait for the EOD [Explosive Ordnance Disposal] to arrive. We were stranded for 11 hours until a Czech EOD team arrived. It transpired that a Canadian EOD team was en route when it was involved in an RTA killing two of their soldiers. Although we were extremely lucky not to lose any of our own, it was difficult to deal with the knowledge that two soldiers died attempting to rescue us.

For anyone that served in the Balkans, especially those with UNPROFOR before the Dayton Accords in 1995, the total devastation that years of war had upon the country and its people would leave a lasting mark. Those who witnessed the genocide and ethnic cleansing felt helpless, and not being able to intervene caused endless torment. When I asked Andrew T. about his lasting memories of Bosnia, he said, 'The people, the hatred, the desperation, the destruction, feelings of helplessness and fear. Guilt we couldn't do more, distrust of politicians, friendship, pride and unity. It never goes away and I think about it every day. Those who were there know and those who weren't have no idea.'

Despite the world's media bearing witness, back in the United Kingdom it appeared that the full extent of what had happened or what soldiers had endured was never fully understood by the public. 'When I got home I was shocked at the sanitised coverage the media was showing. From watching the news it was obvious that no one fully understood what soldiers on the ground were going through or had to deal with on a daily basis.'

The public's perception of the Balkans conflict would change, however, with one television drama serial. *Warriors* was televised by the BBC on 20 and 21 November 1999. The two-part four-hour drama told the story of Colonel Stewart's Cheshire Regiment in Bosnia. The Ministry of Defence and senior Army officers were quick to point out before it was aired that it was 'a work of fiction'.[42] Their comments were obviously aimed at trying to lessen the effect the show 'might have on recruitment and on the families of soldiers still serving in Bosnia and Kosovo'.[43] But Peter Kominsky, the show's director, had done his homework. With the MOD's blessing he had interviewed over 90 soldiers who had served in and around Vitez and talked with many family members after soldiers had returned. Even though the filmmakers had crammed six months of incidents that happened to an entire battalion group into four hours of television from the viewpoint of just a single platoon, the film was met with praise by members of the regiment.[44] The drama also received widespread critical acclaim and had a profound effect upon the public. There was now an underlying consensus of public opinion that the government should not put British troops in that situation again.

CHAPTER 7

Northern Ireland and the Good Friday Agreement

By the time most of this generation of soldiers arrived in Northern Ireland on their first tour, the conflict known as 'the Troubles' had been ongoing for nearly two decades. Soldiers serving in Northern Ireland during the late 1980s/90s found themselves in the middle of another bitter ethno-nationalistic conflict, the roots of which date back 800 years. But this time it was not the Balkans, or the Middle East; it was happening in the United Kingdom, just a short flight across the Irish Sea, where the brutality and hatred were equally bad.

Following the Norman invasion of 1066, the English monarchy ruled Ireland from 'The Pale', a thin strip of land on the east coast surrounding Dublin where English overlords asserted control. After the Reformation, Ireland's reluctance to follow England and turn away from the Roman Catholic Church led to several bloody rebellions and wars. In an attempt to force Ireland to renounce allegiance to the Pope, Scottish and English settlers were sent to several Irish provinces, one of which was the earldom of Ulster. Implementation of the repressive Penal Laws that sought to restrict the rights of anyone who did not conform to the Anglican Church of Ireland resulted in more rebellion within the Catholic population. After the English Civil War was won, Oliver Cromwell's army brutally subjugated Ireland in an attempt to break up the threat from English Royalists and Irish Catholics who had formed an alliance of convenience. By 1653, half the Irish population had either died or been exiled, and any land worth farming that remained in Catholic landowners' possession was taken for Protestant settlers. In 1688, after King James II was replaced on the throne during the 'Glorious Revolution' by William of Orange, Ireland would become the site of more fighting between Catholics and Protestants. Irish Catholics rallied to James, while Protestant landowners supported William. On 1 July 1690, at the battle of the Boyne, James was routed and the history of 'The Orange Order' was born.

In 1798, the Republican movement United Irishmen staged another rebellion. Inspired by the French and American revolutions, their attempt to oust British rule once again foundered and was mercilessly crushed. In response to the rebellion, the

1800 Acts of Union meant Ireland would now become part of the United Kingdom of Great Britain and Ireland.

No two events in Irish history do more to ignite passions than that of the Potato Famine and the Easter Rising. Both furthered the Republican cause and both were made worse by British political and military leaders. There are long-standing debates regarding each event, but there can be no argument about their importance and influence upon the history of Ireland.

During the 19th century, Catholic tenant farmers became dependent on growing a single crop. After the introduction of the potato to the gardens of landed gentry around Dublin, it caught on and was used throughout Ireland to feed both humans and cattle. By 1850, because of potato blight, over a million people had died from starvation and disease and a further million had emigrated to the United States. Laissez-faire politics from London and harsh landlords made the problem much worse. The suffering caused by the famine and subsequent evictions left an enduring mark on the psyche of Irish Catholics. Between 1841 and 1851 there was a 25 per cent drop in the population.[1]

Home Rule became the dominant political issue in Irish politics after 1870 – government of its own people decentralised from Westminster. 'Rome Rule', as the Unionists called it, had been opposed by them from the start. They feared and objected to a Catholic-ruled united Ireland, touting economic decline and an end to their own cultural identity. It had been debated, agreed upon, then defeated twice in the Houses of Commons and Lords before finally gaining Royal Assent in 1912. Unionists reacted strongly by forming the Ulster Volunteers, promising to use force to ensure union with Britain was upheld, with the Irish Volunteers formed in response to ensure Home Rule was enforced. By the time the Third Home Rule Bill became law in 1914, it was soon suspended because of the outbreak of war. The sad irony is that if Home Rule had been instigated before the start of World War I, it is quite possible the history of Ireland in the 20th century could have been very different.

In April 1916, a rebellion organised by the Irish Republican Brotherhood occurred in Dublin and several towns in southern Ireland. With Britain heavily committed to fighting Germany and its allies, and with no sign of Home Rule being enforced while the war continued, some Republican leaders thought the time was right to establish an independent Irish Republic. The Easter Rising was crushed after just six days of fighting that cost 485 lives. After it was over, public opinion in Ireland was not on the side of the rebellion. With so many young Irishmen fighting against Germany, and with Home Rule signed into law, many questioned the need for rebellion. After the rebels were captured in Dublin's wrecked city centre, crowds gathered and jeered as they were marched away to prison. But the heavy-handed British response to the Easter Rising would change all that. General Sir John Maxwell was appointed military governor and given the responsibility of dealing with the rebels. Thousands were arrested (most had not been involved) and were interned in prison camps. A total of 183 civilians were tried by Field General Court Martial without defence counsel, 90 were sentenced to death, with 15 executed between 3 and 12 May 1916.[2] The brutality of Maxwell's ham-fisted attempt to crush the Republican cause had the opposite effect. As the executions continued and word of Army atrocities in Dublin spread throughout the country, the Irish public started to support the martyred rebels. Several of those executed were not even involved, and rebel leader James Connolly was so badly injured that he could not stand to face the firing squad. Despite doctors giving him only a day or two to live, he was carried into the courtyard of Kilmainham Gaol on a stretcher, tied to a chair, and shot. General Maxwell's actions handed Republicans a victory after they had been decisively defeated.

At the end of World War I, two and a half years after the Easter Rising, the separatist party, Sinn Fein, won the 1918 election with a majority of seats in the Irish Parliament. Cries for an Irish Republic turned into bloody guerrilla warfare. The Irish Republican Army, under the leadership of Michael Collins, routinely murdered soldiers and British intelligence officers and ambushed British Army and police patrols. These acts were always followed by equally brutal reprisals, including the Royal Irish Constabulary opening fire on the crowd at a Gaelic football match at Crooke Park on 21 November 1920, and the centre of Cork being set ablaze a month later.

Looking to resolve what the British ruling classes had long called the 'Irish Question', Parliament's answer was to partition North and South into separate devolved regions of the United Kingdom. After a ceasefire brought an end to most of the violence, the Anglo-Irish Treaty of 1921 saw the formation of the Irish Free State. In accordance with terms of the Fourth Home Rule Act of 1920, the Northern Ireland Parliament exercised its right to 'opt out' of joining the Free State, staying part of the United Kingdom instead. After the Anglo-Irish Agreement and formation of the Irish Free State there followed a bloody civil war between the British-backed pro-treaty government and the anti-treaty IRA. The pro-treaty forces won the seven-month conflict, due mainly to their greater firepower, much of which was provided by the British government.

In 1922, a boundary commission was set up to decide where the North/South border should be. As some areas of Fermanagh and Tyrone were Nationalist strongholds and had voted for Sinn Fein, it seemed logical that they should be part of the Irish Free State. The commission realised this, had the power to recommend such an action, and seemed willing to reduce the number of counties that would make up the North. Instead of a meandering border of 282 miles, they could have shortened it to 231 miles to create 12 pockets of population who would be affected by any change. Eight would move from North to South, and four from South to North. But after the chaos of the civil war in the South, the idea was not followed through by the new government in Dublin, especially after the proposals of the commission were leaked to the press.[3] It was a missed opportunity.

Although Northern Ireland was fairly peaceful, by the late 1960s there was a deep, underlying animosity on both sides. The Unionists felt threatened by Catholics with large families that were quickly changing the demography of many counties and towns. They saw all Catholics as the same, hell-bent on having Ulster ruled by Dublin, so they treated them like second-class citizens. Catholics who had for years felt victimised now sought change through a civil rights movement and demanded the reform of the Protestant-dominated Royal Ulster Constabulary (RUC).

As the civil rights movement grew, Catholic protesters came under increasing attack from Unionist organisations and Loyalist paramilitary groups that resulted in several Catholics being killed. In 1968, during the first organised civil rights march, the RUC were seen to stand by and watch as marchers were attacked. In an attempt to stop the violence, a planned march in Londonderry a month later was banned. But when marchers ignored the ban RUC officers beat them in the streets, in front of the world's media, leaving over a hundred people injured. This led to widespread rioting and barricades built in an attempt to keep the police out of Catholic areas.

The pattern of protest and violence was repeated throughout 1968 and 1969, culminating in what became known as the battle of the Bogside. On 12 August 1969, the Apprentice Boys of Derry marched along the edge of the Catholic Bogside, commemorating the relief of the Siege of Derry. Although this was an annual march, it was seen by many as a deliberate insult to the Catholic population[4] at a time when the situation in Northern Ireland was already extremely volatile. Verbal abuse and taunts turned into missiles and petrol bombs. The RUC attempted to enter the Bogside but were stopped by hundreds of nationalists. Petrol bombs were thrown off the Rossville flats, with dozens of RUC officers injured.[5] The fighting, which lasted for two days, spread to Belfast and other areas where IRA members openly fought Loyalists after they had attacked Nationalist businesses and homes. The RUC had lost control and now their heavy-handed tactics were receiving condemnation from south of the border. Taoiseach Jack Lynch called for a United Nations peacekeeping force, set up refugee camps along the border, and even considered a possible intervention by the Irish Army.[6] On 14 August, after a request from the Northern Ireland government at Stormont, British Army troops were sent to Belfast and Londonderry to assist the RUC to restore law and order.

Deploying British troops to the streets of Northern Ireland brought an end to the riots. They were greeted warmly by Catholics who saw them as impartial, expecting to be protected from the excesses of the RUC. But soldiers being handed cups of tea while on patrol in Catholic areas did not last long. In early 1970, when the British Army started to patrol with the RUC, the niceties of their welcome soon ended. The situation was also being exploited by the IRA.[7] The relationship between British Army soldiers and Catholics deteriorated so quickly that within the space of a few months they were seen by Nationalists as an army of occupation.

No one event in the history of Northern Ireland stands out more than Bloody Sunday. Regardless of your opinion, your belief, or your political persuasion, what took place on Sunday, 30 January 1972, was tragic and has left an indelible mark on both Northern Ireland and the British Army. The consequences of that day are still being felt today, not just by the families of the victims who are still seeking justice, but also by soldiers who were there, some living in fear that they might be indicted of a crime almost a half-century later.

There were many factors at play that had a direct influence on the events of that day. The IRA had stepped up its attacks and started sniping at security forces using demonstrations, protests, and marches as cover. The morning before Bloody Sunday a young officer succumbed to wounds he received at the hands of an IRA sniper just two days before.[8] Soldiers that were on the streets on Bloody Sunday were on edge and at a heightened state of readiness.

When the British Army deployed to the streets of Northern Ireland in support of the RUC, they were not adequately trained or equipped to deal with the situation they were to face. Soldiers of that era were trained for war against the Soviet Union. Crowd control tactics that had been used in Aden, Palestine, and Cyprus were from the colonial past and based upon the concept in British Law of 'Reading the Riot Act'.

The Northern Ireland government put pressure on London to introduce internment without trial as a tool with which known terrorists could be taken off the streets. Although it had been used in the past during a spell of violence in the 1950s, the introduction of internment was to do nothing but throw petrol onto an already raging fire. Dublin would never agree to help, so all that happened was when arrests were being made, the real terrorists would simply slip across the border where they were immune from arrest because they not been charged with a crime. The reaction from the Nationalist community was obvious – riots, shootings, and bombings. Barricades using burnt-out cars and buses were built to create 'no go areas' where people likely to be arrested next could be hidden. Of the 350 who were detained in the early raids, none were Protestants,[9] and most were not even Republican activists at the time. General Sir Mike Jackson was a captain in the Parachute Regiment in Northern Ireland when internment began. He was part of the first dawn raids and held the same general belief among the British Army that internment was counterproductive. 'The round-up might catch a few of them but most would escape the net. Meanwhile, many innocent people would be interned. The outrage at such injustice would undermine our attempts to isolate the men of violence. Internment was a blunt weapon which served to exacerbate rather than ameliorate the situation.'[10]

On Sunday, 30 January 1972, a banned civil rights march against internment took place in Londonderry. At the end of the day, 13 lay dead with a 14th dying of his wounds a few months later. What happened that day has been written about in depth and been the subject of two inquiries and a Police Service of Northern Ireland (PSNI) investigation that led to a single soldier being charged 48 years later.

Looking back with the comfort of hindsight it is easy to blame soldiers of the Parachute Regiment. The Saville Report, and even Prime Minister David Cameron, described their actions as 'unjustified and unjustifiable', saying that soldiers of Support Company, 1 Para, had lost 'self-control, forgetting or ignoring their instructions and training and with a serious and wide spread loss of fire control'.[11] But the picture now painted by the PSNI, Republicans, Nationalists, the world's media, and various cultural icons through songs and books about the event, is not a complete one. The 12-year-long, 5,000-page, 10-volume, £200 million Saville Report, released 38 years afterwards, clearly lays blame at the feet of the soldiers. But no one condemning those soldiers will ever fully understand what they were going through – none had been where they were or had patrolled those streets at that time and been under that kind of pressure.

Innocent people tragically died that day, of that there is no doubt. But not everyone involved in the banned march had peaceful intentions. Although the Saville Report 'finds that, on balance, the first shot in the vicinity of the march was fired by the British Army',[12] it also says, 'two official IRA men had gone to a pre-arranged sniping position and shots had been fired by Republican paramilitaries that were not merely in response to the British soldiers opening fire.'[13] Whether soldiers fired first or were reacting to being fired upon will probably remain unknown. However, there is little doubt that once again Republican terrorists had used an organised protest as cover. Martin McGuinness (later Deputy First Minister of Northern Ireland) was present that day, 'probably armed with a Thompson sub-machine gun'.[14] General Jackson was Adjutant of 1 Para on Bloody Sunday. He writes, 'A little later, there was a shot which holed a drain pipe close to the building in which we were standing … from this point we had every reason to believe that at least one individual out there had a weapon and that therefore we might come under fire again.'[15]

General Sir Michael Rose is convinced that it was the IRA who opened fire first on Bloody Sunday. He was a platoon commander with a Coldstream Guards patrol looking down on the Bogside when he heard the distinctive sound of a Thompson machine gun being fired in the vicinity of the Rossville Flats. His platoon had been fired at by an IRA terrorist with a Thompson machine gun a couple of weeks before, so he and his men recognised the distinctive 'thump, thump, thump … of a chunky low-velocity weapon'.[16] He went further when giving evidence to the Saville Inquiry. 'It was the IRA who started the firing with the Thompson machine gun – and, inflammatory though it may sound, I believe they started firing with the express intention of causing civilian deaths.'[17] This is backed by evidence that some of the victims were struck by low-velocity ammunition which the British Army did not use on this occasion.[18]

The one thing that can be said about Bloody Sunday with absolute certainty is that if the IRA had goaded the British Army into a trap, opening fire on protesters so that it would turn into a bloodbath, then it had worked. Not only did it turn public opinion both at home and abroad against the British Army, but it also gave the Republican movement its greatest ever surge in recruitment. In 2014, Martin McGuinness said, 'The greatest recruiting agent for the IRA in my city was the Parachute Regiment. When they shot 14 people dead on the streets of Derry, people joined the IRA in droves.'[19]

After Bloody Sunday the violence continued year after year. By the end of the 1980s, people on the mainland and in Northern Ireland seemed numb to it all, suffering from a kind of collective PTSD. Even civilians in London would duck and cover on hearing the slightest loud bang or disturbance. Every murder or bombing was followed by the scripted outcry from either the Loyalist or Republican side, no matter whether it was the Protestants or Catholics that had been attacked. It would soon dissipate until there was another one. There were several attempts to bring an end to the violence, with numerous ceasefires and agreements that tried to break the stalemate. But each ceasefire was broken with the vicious cycle of sectarian violence being repeated once more.

Both Republican and Loyalist paramilitary groups, entrenched in their own extreme ideology, carried out terrible atrocities for their cause. But it was the IRA that seemed to be able to monopolise the headlines, mainly due to its activities on the UK mainland and elsewhere. On 27 August 1979, as well as killing 18 soldiers of the Parachute Regiment in two remote-controlled explosions at Warrenpoint, they also murdered Lord Louis Mountbatten and three others by detonating a bomb on his boat. In July 1982, they attacked the Queen's Life Guard at Knightsbridge in London, killing four members of the Blues and Royals and nine horses. The same day they attacked another defenceless target by murdering seven Royal Green Jacket musicians, planting a bomb under a Regent's Park bandstand that exploded while they played. They also attacked off-duty soldiers in the UK and Germany, often killing innocent people in the process. In 1989, six-month-old Nivruti Mahesh was killed alongside her father, a Royal Air Force corporal, at a gas station in West Germany, and a year later two Australian tourists were shot dead in the Netherlands when they were mistaken for British servicemen. In 1984 and in 1991, they attacked the very heart of the British government itself when they exploded a bomb at the Grand Hotel in Brighton during the Conservative Party conference, and carried out an audacious mortar attack on Downing Street.

Soldiers arriving in Northern Ireland in the late 1980s or early 1990s did so after what had been a very violent and bloody few years. One incident was to leave a psychological mark on all soldiers no matter where they served. On Saturday, 19 March 1988, two Royal Signals corporals, Derek Wood and David Howes, were brutally murdered in broad daylight. The two plain-clothed soldiers, in a civilian car, mistakenly drove into the funeral procession of an IRA member. Three days earlier, Loyalist Michael Stone had attacked a funeral procession and killed three people. Believing they were Loyalists, dozens of people surrounded and attacked the car. Corporal Woods drew his pistol and fired shots in the air but did not fire at his attackers. The soldiers were dragged from the car, taken to waste ground, stripped, beaten, and murdered. The incident was caught on camera and shown around the world. Two men were sentenced to life for the murders but were released in 1998 under the terms of the Good Friday Agreement (GFA). Soldiers who saw it happen live on television said they were affected by it.

> I remember being home for the weekend when it happened. I was sat on our couch watching them being butchered on the BBC News. I was so angry I couldn't contain myself. I was swearing and shouting, vowing to get revenge if ever I got the chance. I suddenly noticed my mum was in tears – she didn't say as much, but I knew she was thinking that it could have been me lying there.

Another soldier also said that the terrible murders might influence his future actions if he found himself in the same situation. 'I swore that I would never let that happen to me. I wouldn't be shooting in the air; I'd take as many of the bastards with me as I could before saving the last bullet for myself.' And for one soldier who did find himself in a similar situation in the centre of a small town in Bosnia, the brutal murders of Derek Wood and David Howes remained very fresh in his mind.

> We were all sat in crew positions, opened up when a large crowd started to gather. Whilst the crowd's mood was not particularly hostile neither was it pleasant because the crowd was now somewhere in the region of 500 … It turned out that the local militia units had taken a number of casualties and the townsfolk were honouring their fallen, carrying them through the town to be buried … I got the driver to close down and start up … the operator made his weapon ready and I had cocked the machine gun on the cupola. I kept having flashback visions of the news clips of the two Royal Signals corporals in Northern Ireland who had been dragged out of their car and brutally murdered by a funeral crowd. I was determined that was not going to happen to us. The funeral procession passed by within 6ft of the vehicle, and whilst things became pretty tense it moved away through the town without incident.

Stuart B. passed out of Depot Para in January 1989, then went on leave for a few weeks before joining his battalion who were preparing for a tour of Belfast.

> Our platoon at the Depot had been split between 2 and 3 Para with all the lads under 18 going to 2 Para and the older lads going to 3 Para. I had turned 18 in the summer of '88 and wanted to go to 3 Para so felt lucky. We flew out to Belfast in late January 1989 with B Company who were the advance company to start the handover … All the lads from our Depot platoon were to carry out our NI training and the battalion acceptance cadre before the rest of the battalion flew out.

3rd Battalion, Parachute Regiment, was undertaking a two-year tour based out of Holywood Camp on the outskirts of Belfast overlooking the Harbour airport. 'I was full of nervous excitement. The camp, including married quarters, was inside the wire which was very different from Aldershot. It was all new to me.' Once all the training had taken place, Stuart joined 1 Platoon, A Company.

Joining your first platoon is a very nerve-racking experience. Obviously wanting to make the right impression but still aware that you are Joe Crow and there to be bested by the senior toms. The platoon was full of experienced lads, Falklands vets from Lance Corporal to Platoon Sergeant … The last intake of new lads the platoon had received was a year before so they were well settled by then. We were the brew boys, and we knew it.

The battalion carried out company rotations of the Quick Reaction Force covering West Belfast from Woodburn Police Station, at North Howard Street Mill, covering the IRA stronghold of the Falls Road and Divis flats area, and out-of-area support to other units as and when it was requested.

For a young paratrooper like Stuart B. it was a baptism of fire. 3 Para had a very busy tour, losing five men, all of whom came from Stuart's company; four came from his platoon. The costliest incident of the tour happened on 18 November 1989, when three paratroopers from Stuart's platoon were killed by a remote-controlled bomb planted in a derelict cottage; it exploded as their mobile patrol passed by in Mayobridge. In a very understated but resilient way, he said, 'It hit us all hard.'

Joyriders were a perennial problem in the urban areas of Northern Ireland. Young people, often under the influence of alcohol or drugs, or who had been sniffing glue, would steal cars and drive them at high speeds on the streets of Belfast and Londonderry. In any other city of the UK this was a reckless and dangerous act in itself. In Northern Ireland, where you had security forces patrolling the streets with live ammunition, it could be tantamount to suicide.

On 30 September 1989, 17-year-old Martin Peake and 18-year-old Karen Reilly were killed by soldiers of 3 Para when the car they had stolen drove through a checkpoint at high speed on Glen Road in West Belfast. After the incident there was widespread condemnation of the shooting within all sections of the Nationalist community. For several years there had been claims that the British Army was conducting a 'shoot to kill' policy against joyriders.[20] In 1993, Private Lee Clegg was sentenced to life imprisonment for the murder of Karen Reilly, and Private Barry Aindow was sentenced to seven years for attempted murder.[21] Clegg had fired four shots, three into the front windscreen and one into the side, after the car had struck a member of the patrol. At the trial, an RUC officer testified that 'no soldier had been struck and that the soldiers had invented a story to justify opening fire'.[22]

In 1995, Sir Patrick Mayhew, Northern Ireland Secretary, released Clegg on license two years into his sentence. He appealed twice, and on the second attempt Lord Justice Robert Carswell overturned his conviction with a retrial ordered. In 1999, he was found not guilty with the last charges against him finally quashed in 2000. Barry Aindow had his sentence reduced on appeal and left the Army when he was released from prison.[23]

The Lee Clegg incident highlighted the polarisation of opinion in Northern Ireland. Republicans and Nationalists applauded the sentence that the judge of the Diplock Court handed down, then criticised the Diplock Court system after he was acquitted.[1] They also renewed their accusations of shoot-to-kill, rehashing an older argument that if incidents like this 'had occurred in any other town in Europe, the car would have been immobilised rather than the passengers being shot.'[24] On the other side of the argument, Unionists, Loyalists, and the security forces saw Clegg's conviction as a miscarriage of justice and that Clegg and his colleagues were only carrying out their duty in a very difficult and dangerous situation.

There is also another factor that was never reported by the media or is never mentioned by the Nationalist community, who constantly complained that Clegg should not have been released. Every paratrooper that was on the streets of Belfast or Londonderry during that tour viewed joyriders as deadly weapons, and despite the lack of coverage in the media, they were justified in this view. Just three months into their tour, on 25 March 1989, Private Robert Spikins of A Company, 3 Para, was killed by a joyrider on the Falls Road.

> Spike was in 2 Platoon … out of North Howard Street Mill. He was patrolling down the Falls Road when a joyrider knocked him over. He was carried 200 metres down the road on the bonnet of the car before being thrown off. He died from the injuries he sustained in the hit and run. The car drove off and the driver was never found.

Unsurprisingly, this death would have had a huge influence on every member of 3 Para and could explain why soldiers would not hesitate to open fire on vehicles crashing through vehicle checkpoints. Stuart B., however, would disagree with this point of view.

> It was the first death in the battalion on the tour and we all felt it. Obviously the A Company lads and especially 2 Platoon felt a little aggrieved to say the least. But it didn't affect the way we worked or our professional attitude as we always expected to lose blokes during tours to Northern Ireland. It just brought it home when it happened. We knew this shit was for real.

Having lost four soldiers from his platoon, Stuart B., would leave Belfast with a healthy scepticism of some fellow security forces that they were there to assist. He was on patrol the night of the Lee Clegg joyrider incident, and he is quite clear with regards to what happened.

> There are many differing opinions on the incident but those of us who were there know what happened. I would never trust the RUC again. These feelings were confirmed during a later tour when a Special Branch Officer admitted to me that they knew who carried out the attack at Mayobridge but for obvious reasons couldn't act on their information. To say I was angry is an understatement!

Since the deployment of troops to Northern Ireland in 1969, for soldiers patrolling city streets or country roads, the deadliest and most unnerving threat came from

---

1   Diplock Courts were for the trial of specified serious crimes in Northern Ireland without a jury. They were instigated after Lord Diplock's 1972 report to Parliament outlining the problem of jury intimidation and witness tampering in Northern Ireland.

snipers. As every soldier left the sanctuary of a camp or police station on patrol, there was always a nagging doubt, knowing that at any moment he could come into the crosshairs of a sniper's sight. Even with a flak jacket and helmet, the psychological effect on a soldier that a sniper presented was formidable. During the 1970s and 1980s, snipers accounted for about 180 murders of members of the security forces. In the 1990s, in South Armagh, an IRA team perfected sniper operations with deadly results. Between March 1990 and March 1997 there were 24 recorded attacks by this one sniper team; nine were killed and one wounded.[25]

Although the IRA was highly successful with its use of sniper teams, they did have setbacks too. In July 1992, while patrolling in County Fermanagh, a soldier leading a patrol saw something out of place. 'At first I didn't know what I was looking at; it just seemed a bit odd. A signpost at a bus stop was pointing sideways as if something had hit it, but something about it didn't look right.' He followed the direction it was pointing and it led him to a concealed Barrett sniper rifle that was loaded and ready to fire.

In March 1997, Conrad P. was based at Forkhill Security Base with his company of Welsh Guards. This was his first time to South Armagh but his third tour of Northern Ireland. Like Stuart B., Conrad first arrived in Ulster as a young man. 'I was initially told that I couldn't go and would be staying with the rear party. But I begged both the CSM and OC to go, pointing out that although I was under 18 at the time, by the time the battalion deployed I would be 18 years and one month old.' His second tour was for two years at Ballykelly in Londonderry, then in March 1997 he found himself in South Armagh. When he first arrived in West Belfast, a young 18-year-old, he had no idea about the causes of the violence, the history of the Troubles, or the current political situation. 'I was 18, naive, and I didn't really care … I just wanted to earn my spurs with the battalion by deploying.' Now, looking back on his time and experiences in the province, he told me, 'My Ireland tours were the best time in my Army career.'

On the night of 27 March 1997, as he prepared to take his patrol out the front gate at Forkhill, he was now fully aware of what was going on in both South Armagh and the rest of Northern Ireland. 'I understood the political situation but it never really bothered me either way … The IRA were the enemy.' The sniper team in South Armagh that had been so successful over the past few years had been lost and had gone to ground. 'Firefox', the codeword for no movement in South Armagh, had been in place for some time. Conrad's patrol was the first to go out after 'Firefox' had been lifted. Realistically, the only way for the security forces to reacquire the IRA sniper team and have a chance of capturing them was if and when they attacked again. 'I honestly believe that we were being used as bait. The Company Commander came out with us which was unusual but tells you all you need to know about the man. He wasn't going to send his men out knowing they were trying to flush out the sniper team without being there and taking the same risk himself.'

The gates were opened at 11.40 p.m. Conrad and his men were well aware of the situation, so they sprinted out and took cover. The RUC officers (who never ran) calmly walked out. 'I crouched down by a lamppost just outside the gate. Suddenly there was a loud explosion – the RUC officer who was stood next to me collapsed to the ground. At first I thought it was a bomb in the lamppost because it was so loud, but soon we realised that it was a sniper from a house across the valley.' The RUC officer had been hit by a Barrett .50 calibre rifle. He was struck in the hip. The bullet split his Maglite in two before exiting his leg, then striking the tarmac.[26] Having narrowly avoided losing his leg, the officer survived the attack, which turned out to be the last one carried out by this sniper team. Earlier that evening a family had been taken hostage while the terrorists used a dog kennel to hide in while they targeted the front gates of the security base. After the single-shot attack, the IRA men fled back across the border.

The firing point was quickly identified and searched by the battalion's search multiple who found the footprint of a trainer that forensics would later match to one of the snipers. The tactic, known as the tethered goat option,[27] had worked. Just nine days after the Forkhill sniper attack, suspected IRA members Bernard McGinn, Michael Caraher, James Ardle, and Martin Mines, were arrested. Barrett and AKM rifles with over 50 rounds of ammunition were recovered at the scene.[28]

***

Long before the beginning of the Troubles in 1969, the Republican cause was strongly supported from within North America. Through organizations like the Irish Northern Aid Committee (NORAID), the IRA received funds which they used to purchase weapons. Although the US government went through the motions of classing Irish Republicans as terrorists and convicting several IRA members in the United States, it appeared to most British soldiers that they did not chase them with the same zeal as they would Middle Eastern terrorists. This was an aspect of the 'special relationship' that left a very bitter taste in the mouths of some British soldiers. 'Seeing a NORAID collection box on the bar of an Irish pub in New York was very upsetting. These bastards had contributed to the death of two of my friends.'

As well as receiving thousands of Armalite, Smith and Wesson, Colt, and Browning American-made weapons, the IRA was supplied throughout the 1980s by Muammar Gaddafi. As well as AK-47s, RPG7 rocket launchers, and several surface-to-air missiles, the IRA was given one ton of a Czechoslovakian-made explosive called Semtex.

Just before Christmas on 21 December 1988, terrorists planted a bomb onboard Pan Am 103, a Boeing 747 bound for New York. The same explosives being used to kill and maim British soldiers in Northern Ireland were used to kill 190 American citizens. In all, 259 passengers and crew, and 11 people on the ground died in the Scottish border town of Lockerbie where the wreckage came down. Soldier A.

vividly remembers the crash. 'I had just come home on leave for Christmas, was sat in the front room of my parents' house watching television when the news came in that a plane had crashed on top of a town in Scotland. We lived under the flight path out of Heathrow and realised that it could have been us.' The bomb had been set to go off while the Pan Am Jumbo Jet *Clipper Maid of the Seas* was over the Atlantic Ocean, but because it had been delayed by an hour it came down over a large swath of southern Scotland. This was vital in the ensuing investigation that was led by both Scottish police and the Federal Bureau of Investigation. Because the aircraft had not come down in the ocean, investigators were able to eventually tie the atrocity to Libya and one of its intelligence officers.

It was not until 31 January 2001, after the biggest criminal inquiry in British history, that Abdelbaset al-Megrahi was sentenced to life imprisonment. That same day the *New York Times* ran an article called 'Long before verdict, Lockerbie changed airport security'.[29] In it, the writer correctly points to the instigation of 'dumb questioning' of passengers by check-in agents regarding their luggage and whether they had packed it themselves. New and improved X-ray machines screened all luggage, computerised tracking that matched passengers with their baggage was installed, there were tighter restrictions on sensitive areas within airports, and most luggage was examined by sniffer machines or trained dogs.[30] What the article didn't mention is that most of these measures only applied to external flights and airports. This did not really affect Britain, as the vast majority of flights in and out of the country were international. But in the United States, with thousands of internal flights daily, security was not as tight as leaving or entering the country. Just seven months after the Lockerbie verdict, this gap in airport security would be tragically exploited.

***

During the 1990s, background manoeuvring that involved the British and Irish governments led to the real chance of a political solution. In 1994, both Republican and Loyalist groups declared a ceasefire. The period leading up to it had seen an escalation in tit-for-tat atrocities, so most thought the ceasefire would be short-lived. In 1995, the chance of a lasting peace was given a boost by the appointment of former United States Senator George Mitchell as US Special Envoy for Northern Ireland. Mitchell showed a deep interest and understanding, and got both the UK and Irish governments to agree to him leading an International Commission on the disarming of paramilitary groups. The ceasefire was broken on 9 February 1996, when the IRA detonated a massive bomb in the Canary Wharf complex in East London, killing two people and causing millions of pounds in damage at the heart of London's revitalised docklands. The IRA had broken the ceasefire in protest of the British government's insistence that before Sinn Fein were admitted to talks, the IRA must decommission its weapons.

Later that year, in a move that stunned all sides, Sinn Fein agreed to sign the 'Mitchell Principles' and were admitted to talks.[31] This unexpected U-turn by the political arm of the IRA caught many by surprise. It led to resignations by hardliners, with some pledging to continue the armed struggle. On 15 June, five days after all-party negotiations had begun at Stormont (without Sinn Fein), the IRA detonated a truck bomb in Manchester that was three times bigger than the Canary Wharf bomb. Despite a 90-minute warning, the explosion ripped out the heart of the city, causing £600 million in damage.[32] The violence continued throughout the summer, but after Sinn Fein had agreed to Senator Mitchell's six pre-requisites to peace talks, mounting pressure was exerted upon even the most militant Republicans. In October 1996, the *Irish News* (a Belfast-based newspaper) published the results of an opinion poll. It showed that 94 per cent of those polled (70 per cent of Sinn Fein supporters) wanted the IRA to call an immediate ceasefire.[33]

One of the reasons why Gerry Adams and the Sinn Fein leadership had agreed to the 'Mitchell Principles' was because they could clearly see that the political map in Westminster was about to change. A Conservative government was never going to allow Sinn Fein to enter to any peace talks until the IRA started to decommission its weapons. It would have been political suicide for the party of Margaret Thatcher to cave on this point. But if the Conservatives were no longer in power, any new government might not be so insistent. If Adams and other Sinn Fein leaders could be seen as leading the IRA towards peace without them having to give up their weapons right away, then maybe he could placate both sides.

John Major, who had become prime minister during the Gulf War, was now leading a Conservative government that had all but lost its majority despite winning a fourth consecutive election in 1992. After Black Wednesday, Britain's ignominious departure from the European Exchange Rate Mechanism, John Major and the Conservative Party never fully recovered. The Labour Party, under the leadership of Tony Blair, had moved to the centre of British politics, seemingly discarding its socialist past. By 1996, a series of by-elections had left the beleaguered prime minister without a working majority. With his government's five-year term coming to an end, he called a General Election for the spring of 1997.

John Major had described the possibility of sitting down with Gerry Adams as stomach churning,[34] but documents now show that he had secret talks with Adams as early as 1992. After all parties had eventually agreed to the 'Downing Street Declaration' of 1993, Adams continued to strike a balance between keeping Republican hawks in the IRA happy, as well as boosting his own credentials as an accepted politician. By 1995, Adams was well aware of the Labour Party's lead in the polls, so he made a calculated gamble that he could get a better deal from Tony Blair. On 2 May 1997, New Labour won the general election by a landslide. A record majority of 179 seats would keep Labour in power for 13 years and Tony Blair as prime minister for a decade. For Gerry Adams and Sinn Fein, it was the result they were looking for and presented them with a real opportunity.

Less than two years after Tony Blair became prime minister, with great fanfare and acclaim at home and around the world, the Good Friday Agreement was signed, with the official ceremony taking place on 10 April 1998, in Belfast. In attendance was US President Bill Clinton, who had thrown his full weight behind the peace process after he had secured a second term in office. The agreement consisted of two related documents: The first concerned the future of a devolved Northern Ireland, and a second document covered the relationship between the United Kingdom and Ireland. The wide-ranging agreement covered security, the status of Northern Ireland, decommissioning, police reform, and the normalisation of Northern Ireland. The DUP rejected the GFA, and the 'Real IRA' swore to continue the struggle. Despite Republican terrorists murdering 29 civilians in the Omagh bombing of August that year, it appeared the agreement might just be strong enough to hold.

Although most soldiers were happy the Troubles seemed to have ended, very few thought it would last. Michael P., a veteran of four tours to Northern Ireland with the Irish Guards, was sceptical. 'The GFA was a good idea but it is being used like a tool by all political parties when it suits them.' Conrad P. was ambivalent to events surrounding the GFA, saying, 'I didn't give a damn about it, not a second thought … Even after the removal of troops and dismantling of barracks it's natural to think the Troubles are over, but everyone knows they're not.' He then went on to explain, 'Personally, I don't think it will ever change. There are too many hardened folk educating their children … so it's a never ending cycle.'

As part of the Good Friday Agreement there was to be an early release of prisoners serving sentences in relation to crimes committed by paramilitary groups, as long as the prisoner's respective group maintained the ceasefire. For soldiers who had lost friends and colleagues at the hands of terrorists, the early release scheme was a real blow. In 1999, when the sniper team captured after the Forkhill attack were convicted and sentenced to prison terms ranging from 20 years to life, they knew it would not actually be that long. When they left the dock to start their sentences they laughed and joked. 'See you in 18 months,' one of them shouted.[35] Like many others who were disgusted at the release of murderers, Conrad P., who had narrowly avoided a sniper's bullet, felt that 'it was a real kick in the teeth'. If this wasn't bad enough, then later revelations concerning backroom deals would get much worse. 'No one really thought the peace would last … but in order to get the agreement signed, those negotiating on behalf of the British government had sold their souls to the devil.'

The Good Friday Agreement prisoner early release scheme resulted in up to 500 convicted terrorists released, but it did not include an amnesty for crimes that had not yet been prosecuted. In May 2013, John Downey was arrested as he entered the United Kingdom and charged with murders relating to the 1982 Hyde Park bombing. During his trial, 'he produced a letter stating that he was not wanted by the Police Service of Northern Ireland or any other police force.'[36] The judge ruled that the letter was legal and said Downey could not be prosecuted. The subsequent outcry and political scandal has not only been a huge setback to the Northern Ireland government, but it also led to a government inquiry and left a serious blemish to the reputation of Tony Blair.

After the Good Friday Agreement was signed, the subject of what to do with so-called 'On the runs' was difficult to solve. Blair wanted a formal scheme, but it was opposed by Sinn Fein and the SDLP as it would have included British soldiers. In order to solve the problem the prime minister asked Gerry Adams to provide a list of names to be considered. In all, 288 names were submitted, with 156 receiving a 'letter of comfort'. A hundred of the recipients were implicated in 300 murder cases.[37] The whole dirty scheme, meant to keep Sinn Fein within the peace process and the IRA ceasefire intact, was supposed to have been kept secret but became public knowledge during the Downey trial. The fact that Downey's letter was sent in error shows the whole sorry mess was a 'catastrophic mistake' by the PSNI.[38]

As part of the Hallett Inquiry after the Downey trial collapse, many new documents came to light. One such document was a memo from Secretary of State for Northern Ireland John Reid, drafted to Prime Minister Tony Blair regarding 'OTRs'. He acknowledged that 'an amnesty scheme is bound to be controversial' and although he personally had 'enormous difficulty' with the question of the security forces facing prosecution, he was persuaded that both the Army and the police should be held to a higher standard.[39] Written in May 2001, it is clear evidence that the Labour government had no intention of protecting soldiers who had served in Northern Ireland; keeping Sinn Fein and the IRA quiet was more important than British Army soldiers and RUC policemen. 'The legislation should exclude members of the security forces from the amnesty arrangements.'[40] The memo also shows Reid's fear of the public reaction to any drafted bill, when he wrote, 'We should not underestimate the difficulty of holding this line in Parliament in the face of the inevitable press campaign.'[41] This 'difficulty' surfaced in 2005, when an attempt to pass a bill regarding OTRs was rejected by all sides. Unionists wanted no part of it if Republicans were pardoned, and Nationalists refused to be involved if it included security forces. Ulster Unionist leader Sir Reg Empey said the legislation 'should be scrapped … this distasteful side deal which should have never seen the light of day in the first place must now be consigned to the dustbin where it belongs, never to be resurrected.'[42] This is the reason why no bill was passed, and the whole sordid affair that was 'questionably legal' and had 'distorted the process of justice'[43] was kept secret until Downey produced his comfort letter in court 13 years later.

If the underhand deal that left soldiers and policemen unprotected from future prosecution while terrorists received 'comfort letters' was not bad enough, then worse to come was the establishment of the Historical Enquiries Team (HET) in 2005. A unit within the newly formed PSNI, the HET was tasked with investigating 3,269 unsolved murders that occurred between 1968 and 1998. Although very few outstanding murder cases were against security forces, and with the HET criticised for inconsistency when investigating against the police or Army,[44] there was still a feeling among the public and veterans that former soldiers were being unfairly targeted. In 2014, the HET was wound up with a smaller Historical Investigations Unit being formed as part of the 2014 Stormont House Agreement. In April 2019, it was estimated by the Ministry of Defence that as many as 200 former soldiers and policemen were still facing legal action.[45]

Soldiers are unanimous in their support of former soldiers and demand the government halt what they call a Republican-inspired witch hunt.

> With murderers released after the Good Friday Agreement, and the rest given get out of jail free cards, soldiers and policemen are now easy targets. I believe in the rule of law but if a soldier had no case to answer 40 years ago, what gives the PSNI the right to investigate, charge, and harass what are now old men, on what is essentially hearsay. It's an absolute disgrace to the country, that ex-soldiers are being hung out to dry.

Paul H., who served two tours in Northern Ireland with the Grenadier Guards, said, 'All terrorists and soldiers who committed crimes should be treated according to the law. It's very different if they were ordered or made a mistake, but I don't agree with terrorists being released early from prison or soldiers being used as scape goats.'

There was not a single soldier whom I interviewed who did not think the Good Friday Agreement was a good thing, but they also agree that it was used as a political tool, especially by Sinn Fein, as and when it suited. And they are not afraid to say so.

> As for the comfort letters; what a joke. Murder is murder no matter how you cut it. Then to try soldiers nearly 50 years after the fact is ridiculous while there are known murderers from both sides walking the streets safe in the knowledge that they cannot be touched … they need to be dragged into court to pay for their crimes … if that happened you would see the end of trials against former soldiers.

CHAPTER 8

Overstretch and the Home Front

Throughout the 1990s, bases in Germany started to close, with units moving back to the UK. For many it meant a new posting, somewhere different to experience. Training for a new role and moving away from German garrison towns was something to look forward to for many soldiers. Rich G. was pleased to be going back to the UK and on to CVR(T). 'I was happy as I wasn't that keen on MBT life.' Soldier G. thought the same. 'I was well up for moving back to the UK … due to not really enjoying the social life in Germany. Also the slow pace of working with tanks didn't flick my switch.'

While the move was appealing for most, some wanted to stay in Germany. The Queen's Dragoon Guards (QDG), who took over from the Life Guards in Sennelager, were under strength because they were moving from a CVR(T) to an MBT establishment, so they were looking for Life Guards to stay behind and make up their numbers. Some stayed on in the short term, returning to the UK throughout 1992–93 as the QDG were brought up to strength, although many transferred. Robert C. had joined the Life Guards in 1988 and moved to Germany with the regiment in 1990. He loved Germany and was more than happy to stay there. Another reason he was not keen to return to Windsor was because he had been on two JNCO cadre courses and had still not been promoted. With the shrinking manpower requirements in Windsor he felt his career would be better served staying in Germany with the QDG. 'It didn't seem likely that I was going to get promoted anytime soon if I went back to Windsor.'

During this time many soldiers opted for a change to their career paths by transferring within the Army. Andrew C. said, 'I applied for a transfer to the Intelligence Corps due to the changes, and what I thought to be a lack of opportunities.' David K. was now a lance corporal in The Queen's Dragoon Guards. He had originally applied to join the Royal Military Police but ended up opting for his second choice.

> I initially enjoyed my time with the QDG; however, having converted to Main Battle Tanks in 1992, promotion and courses slowed right down. Therefore I requested to transfer. This was

declined and I was posted back to Home HQ in Cardiff as part of the Regimental Recruitment Team, in a hope of persuading me to stay. It worked to an extent, until I was recalled to train for an Op BANNER tour. Whilst in Belfast, I met two RMP NCOs and my interest in the RMP was reignited ... In early 2000, having returned early from Kosovo due to my father's death, a clerk on rear party assisted in my application, which miraculously went through without a hitch. I started training at Roussillon Barracks, Chichester, in April 2000, just as QDG were returning from Kosovo.

Paul H. felt trapped as a Grenadier Guardsman in his newly combined battalion where he felt like he was regarded as 'dead wood'. A few years after the formation of the Adjutant General Corps, he would transfer to the AGC where his experience would see him quickly rise through the ranks.

Others who did not transfer to new regiments explored new opportunities on their own. In the Army there were many ways to add to your military resumé, and volunteering to go on P Company, hoping to qualify to wear the coveted para wings, was just one. Rich G. and Jules H. were among many Household Cavalry soldiers that went on to P Company. 'I always had a desire to challenge and push myself – that's why I did P Company.' Jules H. said, 'Because I arrived at the regiment the day after it departed for the Gulf and I was left on the rear party with all the waifs and strays ... I felt like I needed to prove myself.' This would start a long affiliation with airborne forces for both of them.

***

As the situation in the Balkans worsened, the British Army started to feel the full effects of Options for Change. As manpower was being reduced and British involvement in the former Yugoslavia grew, life became increasingly chaotic. Soldiers could see what was happening; since the cuts were announced, everyone knew what was coming. 'It was like watching a train crash and being helpless to do anything about it.' There were widespread calls for the cuts to be looked at again, if not cancelled altogether. But they were ignored; the government was determined to plough ahead so the Treasury would get its long-awaited peace dividend. In time-honoured fashion, the British Army did what it has always done – obeyed orders and got on with its job.

The government acted as if there was not a problem despite the Select Committee for Defence ringing alarm bells in its 1992–93 report.

> The additional emergency tour tasks assumed by the infantry since the beginning of 1992, in Northern Ireland and Bosnia, have led to an unacceptable contraction of the emergency tour interval for infantry units, with serious consequences for individual service personnel and their families as well as for the Army's capacity to prepare for and carry out its primary wartime roles.[1]

The committee was not only warning the government that the British Army was facing problems right now; they also warned that it was not likely to get any better in the foreseeable future. 'Symptomatic of the pressures which the Army is likely to face on a constant basis in a future characterised by international instability and uncertainty ... the mismatch of the Army's resources and commitments looks set to continue.'[2]

On 3 February 1993, Defence Secretary Malcolm Rifkind accepted there was a problem and attempted to rectify the issue. In what he called 'small but sensible adjustments',[3] he cancelled the amalgamation of the Cheshire and Staffordshire regiments and the Royal Scots with the King's Own Scottish Borderers, adding '5,000 additional men and women for the front line units of the field Army'.[4] Despite his bandage approach to stem the bleeding, overstretch continued to be a major problem.

For some infantry and most CVR(T) cavalry regiments, the frequency with which tours to Northern Ireland and Bosnia came around was alarmingly quick. A few soldiers in affected regiments volunteered to do back-to-back tours, while many soldiers had a turnaround of less than six months. 'The unit that took over from us in Bosnia was looking for NCOs to stay with them ... having had our R&R cancelled and my daughter only two weeks old when I deployed, it wasn't for me.' Like many others who had left the Army and who were still on the reserve, Andrew C. was approached about joining back up. 'I was asked if I wanted to go back for a tour of Bosnia around 1997. I had left at the end of 1993 and was a reservist at the time.' Andrew T. said that between 1992 and 1995 he came across several soldiers in his unit who had completed four tours in the former Yugoslavia. During his SFOR tour 'there was an RMP Territorial who had been in theatre a year.' David K. couldn't understand why regiments like the QDG who had recently been on CVR(T) and had for many years been a reconnaissance regiment could not deploy to Bosnia, leaving their MBTs in the hangars for six months. The Russian threat had gone, and they were not being used. 'As we hadn't long re-rolled from recce, it was felt amongst the regiment that we could deploy, thus alleviating some of the back-to-back tours carried out by the Light Dragoons and others.'

Infantry regiments who were woefully undermanned were now looking to other regiments for help. Many were being supplemented with platoons from non-infantry regiments for six-month tours in Northern Ireland. In 1992, having just arrived in Windsor from Germany, Jules H. volunteered to be in a HCR platoon attached to the Scots Guards. That same year the Select Committee on Defence said, 'The increased use of non-infantry units in the infantry role to meet emergency tour commitments will threaten the effectiveness of those units in their primary roles.'[5] In 1994, Angus T. and other members of the HCR were due to be deployed for a tour with the Grenadier Guards. 'Just before we were due to leave, the platoon was stood down after the Director of Infantry pulled the plug. He told his battalions that they were no longer to be augmented by non-infantry soldiers.'

The ever-increasing British commitment to UNPROFOR saw some very short-notice deployments where several different Royal Armoured Corps regiments were thrown together to form one unit. In June 1995, while conducting rear party duties in Windsor, the HCR's HQ Squadron was given seven days to move to Bosnia to support the 9th/12th Lancers. With two sabre squadrons and Regimental Headquarters already deployed, and a third squadron just returned, getting enough men together to deploy in just a week was a tall order. Dave M. was involved in the process of giving soldiers the bad news.

> I was called in as I was one of the Heads of Department … we started by filling in the Orbat with as many people as possible who had been on the rear party, but a substantial number of posts could only be filled by people who had just got back and were on leave … so we hit the phones and were the most unpopular people in Windsor.

The deployment was advertised Army-wide, calling for volunteers to replace those who might have to do back-to-back tours. As well as regular soldiers, Territorial soldiers were now being allowed to serve in the regular Army where they were needed. They would sign S-type (three-year) engagements. 'As volunteers arrived in Windsor, after a brief handover, the Household Cavalry soldier was allowed to go home and continue their leave.' Despite this there were several soldiers that were carrying out either back-to-back tours or were returning within six months.

***

While the Army was under severe manning pressure and commitments built up, the accountants in Whitehall were still looking for more ways to cut costs. The *Defence Costs Study* of 1994 did not grab the headlines as Options for Change did, but the proposals in it were wide-reaching and had implications for soldiers in the years to come. The bill reduced staffing levels and recommended major restructuring in many areas designed to give 'estimated net annual savings of £750 million'.[6] Known as 'Frontline First', the *Defence Costs Study* not only restructured Joint Headquarters and Land Command, but it also did the same with procurement (collating everyone under one roof at Abbey Wood), financial management, the MOD Estate, recruitment services, defence medical services (shutting military hospitals), and the MOD police. The only good news to come from the bill was that another 259 Challenger 2 Main Battle Tanks would be ordered on top of those already in production.[7]

One of the major effects of the bill was a civilianisation of many military positions. The MOD's objective was to civilianise posts and so release soldiers for the front line wherever it made operational and economic sense.[8] For the most part civilians were cheaper to train and stayed in their jobs longer than soldiers. So as long as standards did not slip, then it made sense to Whitehall bureaucrats.

The MOD had been encouraged by the earlier privatisation of the catering sector.[9] However, appearances can be deceptive, and it was obvious the MOD had not asked soldiers who had to eat the food what they thought of the change. Although there have always been light-hearted jokes about the Army Catering Corps, soldiers would soon miss military chefs. In 2016, the situation had become so bad that some soldiers were threatened with legal action by civilian contractors after photographs of mouldy and disgusting food appeared in a newspaper.[10] In 2005, a 'pay as you go' system was put in place allowing soldiers to choose which meals they attended. Michael P. recalls, '"Pay as you go" was a complete failure … my QM got the chief chef of the civilian company to explain why the size of the portions got smaller and the prices increased, plus the standard got lower … I know a lot of guys who just went out and got takeaway … the government will never admit they got it wrong.'

Michael P. was also critical of other civilianised projects, saying, 'Like the recruiting farce … what do civilians that have never served a day in uniform know about life in the Army and the job it entails?' Dave M. brought up an example of the problem of replacing soldiers with civilians when it comes to deploying to a war zone. 'We had a Sergeant Chef who had to do back-to-back tours. The chef that was supposed to be coming with us got pregnant. With lots of civilian chefs there is no slack in the system as they don't do tours.' The reason any company looks to win a military contract is not out of some noble sense of duty or pride at being selected to serve their country; it is down to one thing – making as much of a profit as possible. But Martin M. points to the one potential benefit for some soldiers. 'A positive from this civilianisation of military jobs is that it provides work for ex-soldiers. Not only do many of the jobs require specific military skills, some companies actively recruit ex-service personnel. For many who leave the services with no transferable skills this is a major boost to their employment prospects in civvy street.'

The closure of military hospitals is a subject that provokes anger with Michelle W., who spent 22 years in the Queen Alexandra's Royal Army Nursing Corps. She believes that it is hospital closures that caused her corps to start to lose its identity.

> The Army really took a nosedive for me when the military hospitals started to close and they added military wings to civilian hospitals … Civvy nurses didn't want us there, and we didn't want to be there with a civvy bed manager breathing down our necks to kick patients out so they could find a bed for the next one … Call me old fashioned but I liked Matron and CO's rounds (although I'm sure I moaned about it at the time) … our hospital wards were never closed down due to MRSA contamination as our hygiene and cross infection protocols were second to none … I was very proud of our hospitals.

Soldier B. points out that having service personnel in civilian hospitals became a major issue when soldiers arrived injured from Iraq and Afghanistan and were put in general wards. 'Soldiers were placed amongst people who had no idea what they had endured and in the worst cases on wards where people were openly anti-war and opposed to British soldiers.'

The election of Tony Blair and his 'New Labour' government might have in years past had many in the Army and Ministry of Defence scurrying for cover. There had been a general perception for many years that if you were a soldier, then you should vote for the Conservative Party. But this view changed at the end of the Cold War, especially after the publication of Options for Change. 'I had always voted for the

Tories until 1997, when I voted for Labour (the first and last time). After all, there was no way Tony Blair could cut the military any more than the Conservatives had.' Defence spending during Blair's decade in power as a percentage of GDP remained at about 2.5 per cent. But in real terms, the figure spent on defence increased dramatically, peaking at over £45 billion in 2011.[11] One reason the percentage of GDP remained unchanged despite increased spending was that the money for the Iraq and Afghanistan wars was taken from the country's Treasury Reserve, not from the core defence budget.[12]

A year after coming to power, the new government published its policy document, *Strategic Defence Review*. Designed to enhance the United Kingdom's military capabilities, the document said that the British armed forces should be able to mount a military effort on a similar scale to that of the Gulf War. Defence Minister George Robertson said, 'The review is radical, reflecting a changing world in which the confrontation of the Cold War has been replaced by a complex mixture of uncertainty and instability.'[13] The world had already seen major upheavals and changes in the Balkans and the Middle East, but it is unlikely that the government could have foreseen quite how unstable and complex the world was about to become.

For the Army, the implications of SDR would be structural changes, but its overall strength actually increased by over 3,000. The reorganisation was based upon having two deployable divisions: 1st (UK) Armoured Division and 3rd (UK) Mechanised Division. The Joint Rapid Reaction Force (JRRF) was established to provide the deployment of a brigade-sized force at short notice with the newly formed 16 Air Assault Brigade, specialising in airborne operations, being at the vanguard of any rapid response.

The Royal Armoured Corps (RAC) were reorganised from eight Type 38 into six Type 58 regiments. This meant each division had three regiments equipped with 58 Challenger 2 tanks. The major change for soldiers in the RAC was the move to a new method of maintaining armoured vehicles known as 'whole fleet management' (WFM). Each tank regiment would have just 30 Challenger 2 tanks within their barracks for peace-time training purposes. These 30 tanks would meet the need for the JRRF's high readiness, with the remaining tanks being delivered for larger-scale training and deployment. This new method would allow regiments to concentrate on training rather than tank park maintenance and servicing.[14]

This marked a fundamental change for the RAC; the system of a crew assigned to vehicles full time had been in place for decades, with many retired tankies complaining that it would lead to a poorer standard of maintenance. But to modern-day soldiers the benefits (on paper at least) were obvious. Some retired soldiers I talked to were adamantly against the new system. David K. is one of them.

> WFM is simply a money saving exercise. Nothing else. Where commanders claim it will free up soldiers to undertake other meaningful training, it has the reverse effect in so much that soldiers' skills on the vehicle fade. Where WFM spans a number of regiments, there are always

arguments about the state of the vehicles when they were handed over. Regiments have lost pride in their vehicles as they no longer own them.

Doug K. was equally critical.

> As a young trooper I had my own vehicle to look after and take pride in. I knew its strengths and weaknesses. Life in barracks was focused on having your vehicle in the best possible condition … We still managed to fit in other training but the tank park was where we spent most of our time in barracks … With WFM the troopers have nothing to take pride in. They get a vehicle dropped off and often it is pot luck as to how it will perform.

Others were less scathing. Soldier G. thought 'the original idea was sound but as usual it wasn't backed up with finance and infrastructure', and Soldier B. considered it a sensible idea for an aging CVR(T) fleet.

> [Considering] the wear and tear the vehicles have endured over 50 years' service and subsequent campaign demands of both Iraq and Afghanistan it was probably the best thing … for years now, there has also been a finite number of major assemblies such as engines, gearboxes, and final drives because consecutive governments refused to invest money in a platform that was due to go out of service. This is ironic considering that CVR(T) is still in service.

Dave M. left the Army just before WFM was introduced. 'I never thought it was a good idea … I can't see how you can become familiar with the vehicles if you only get your hands on them on an exercise.' But he did concede that the system must be working because his regiment successfully conducted multiple operational tours to Iraq and Afghanistan using the whole fleet management system.

***

As well as struggling at times to cover ever-increasing deployments while trying to maintain a high standard of readiness, the Army was often called upon in unique ways that only added to its growing number of commitments. Throughout their careers, soldiers sometimes found themselves being deployed to help with the civil authorities. Whether it was industrial action taken by firemen, an outbreak of foot-and-mouth disease in the countryside, or a fire at Windsor Castle, it seemed that the Army was always being called upon to assist.

In 2001, the British countryside was devastated by an outbreak of foot-and-mouth disease. The epizootic would have huge implications for the United Kingdom's agriculture and tourist industries, costing the country an estimated £8 billion and resulting in the slaughter of over six million sheep, cattle, and pigs.[15] For those living in the countryside there was no escaping the disaster that befell their communities; public rights of way were temporarily suspended, there were disinfectant mats and sprays everywhere, and the smell of burning carcasses hung in the air. For many soldiers there were gruesome and grizzly tasks ahead as the Army was called upon to help.

Soldier B. was posted to the Territorial Army at the time. In February 2001, as the first cases of the disease were being discovered, he was sent to work with HQ 42 (NW) Brigade in Carlisle.

Because the size and severity of the crisis kept growing, the job kept evolving. Working independently and alone (one man and a Land Rover), initially it was ensuring that those farmers identified as having contaminated livestock were quarantined, implement disinfection measures and then arrange for the slaughter and disposal of the animals. I saw and had to deal with all sorts of reactions to this tragic news. I had some farmers get very angry, very quickly, with some threatening violence; ironically these were easier to deal with than those who simply collapsed in on themselves and fell apart. Needless to say it was emotional either way.

Throughout the summer as the crisis deepened, soldiers on the ground had to deal with the media scrum that followed the tragedy. Arriving at a farm that he had recently culled, Soldier B. noticed the farmer leaning on his gate. He pulled over just as a television news vehicle arrived. With the crew was a well-known national news anchor.

He spoke to the farmer who told him about the culling. He wanted to pass the camera to the farmer to get some shocking footage of the carcasses from inside the sheds. I intervened at this point and said the only way a camera was being passed over the gate was after I had fully immersed it in the large bucket of disinfectant set aside for this purpose. You can imagine the anchor and his cameraman's response to this, given it was a professional TV camera worth tens of thousands of pounds. We got into a bit of an argument but I made it absolutely clear that anything being passed over to the farmer would be thoroughly submerged … he became animated and asked if I knew who he was. My response was, 'I've never heard of you.' Clearly I had, but I wasn't going to give the prick the satisfaction. I said, 'Instead of acting like a petulant child, if you have any issues, follow me to Brigade HQ where I'm sure the press officer would be happy to speak with you.' Arriving back in camp, the Brigadier (who I knew) saw me and asked how it was going out on the ground. I mentioned the news team and the issues I was having, so he summoned the news anchor into his office. The last time I saw him he was leaving the Brigadier's office, hugely deflated with his tail between his legs.

Dealing with the media was an amusing distraction to what had become an extremely gruesome and upsetting task.

Disinfecting dead, bloated cattle and sheep, the vets were massively stretched and often asked for assistance, loading carcasses onto trucks for disposal and then unloading at designated pyres. Many truck drivers refused to come in contact with the carcasses and refused to pull the tarps over their loads so many times I had to climb up and scramble over the bodies in order to do it. Witnessing cows being separated from their calves; the noise as they were corralled into a small pen and seeing the panic in their eyes as those around them were being despatched where they stood. No-one can tell me that these weren't sentient animals, aware of what was happening. All in all a pretty shitty few weeks doing stuff I'd rather have not, but in a weird way I'm glad I did. You see people emotionally stripped bare and I dealt with issues that certainly developed my emotional intelligence … I discovered things about myself I was hitherto unaware [of], and the whole experience made me stronger.

Paul H. was now posted to 40th Regiment, Royal Artillery, and during the foot-and-mouth outbreak his unit was in North Yorkshire.

We were used for logistics, liaison, security of farms, and enforcing the infected areas. It was very sad at times, truck-loads of slaughtered farm animals going to be burned, farmers in despair, and huge areas completely desolated. We worked very hard; 16–18-hour days with minimal support and very little information. It really was not a good thing to be part of.

Soldier E. was in the southwest of England. His job involved helping units conduct training exercises on Defence Estate training areas.

> As the outbreak got worse I suddenly realised that we were out of a job for the foreseeable future. All the training areas were closed down with regiments cancelling all exercises. A part of my job was to build close working relationships with local farmers and landowners. The foot-and-mouth outbreak was devastating; to see people's lives destroyed this way was heartbreaking. But the thing I remember most about that summer, is the smell of burning cattle.

Throughout 2001, while all training areas remained closed because soldiers were helping the authorities, very little military training took place in the United Kingdom. In hindsight, knowing what was about to happen later that year, the outbreak could not have come at a worse time.

In 2002, as the Army was busy preparing to deploy troops to the Kuwaiti desert, it was called upon to prepare for a potential national firemen's strike. Operation *Fresco* would see 19,000 servicemen[16] deployed to provide a replacement fire-fighting capability should negotiations between the government and the Fire Brigade's Union (FBU) break down. With local authorities offering a four per cent pay increase, and the FBU asking for 40, it seemed that industrial action was a forgone conclusion. The last time the Home Office's fleet of ancient 'Green Goddesses' (Bedford fire pumps held in reserve) had been used was in 1977. The first 48-hour strike took place in November 2002. After that there were frequent multiple-day strikes until the dispute was settled in June 2003, when the FBU settled for a 16 per cent raise in their basic wage.

Just a year after being heavily involved in the foot-and-mouth outbreak, Paul H. and the soldiers of 40th Regiment, Royal Artillery, found themselves 'rushed in to a very basic training regime' to become firemen. As more firemen went on strike, the area his regiment had to cover expanded. 'We started off with a Green Goddess but eventually got a Dennis fire engine.' He describes the whole experience as being really hard work, with long shifts and limited support. 'It was eye-opening at times – getting stones thrown at you whilst helping to put out fires.'

Shaun G. was a Green Goddess driver during the firemen's strike. His unit was stationed in a TA centre in North London, and he was one of the first to be called out on the first night of the strike.

> I remember it was a rainy night and there was a lot of press about trying to find a story. We made the journey to the site of the call-out with blue lights flashing and a police escort. On the journey my GG broke down on the side of the road … very quickly it drew a crowd, some of which were reporters for London news networks, I eventually got the vehicle going and we made it to the fire with a number of news crews following us … as the strike went on we had a habit of driving past the real fire stations giving the striking fire-fighters a bit of friendly grief, calling them some choice words … they complained to the relevant powers and an order came

out that we were not allowed to be rude to them. We followed this order to the letter, 'No more shouting rude words,' we were told. Instead we just gave them certain silent hand gestures.

Stuart B. and his platoon were busy preparing for the invasion of Iraq; the last thing they needed was to be in Borehamwood covering for striking firemen.

> We were visited by the station commander from the local fire station who seemed surprised by our hostility until we explained that we had better things to do with Iraq looming. I remember him saying, 'See how you feel after you have done our job for a few weeks and see if you think we are worth a pay rise.' Well I can tell you now, obviously we would all like a pay rise, better working conditions and I would never disagree with someone trying to make a better life for themselves. But it was a piece of piss, and their job compared to ours was a walk in the park, and no, I didn't think they were worth the pay rise.

On Friday, 20 November 1992, at 11.15 a.m., a fire broke out in the Queen's Private Chapel at Windsor Castle. Within an hour there were 35 fire-engines with 200 firefighters from five different fire brigades in attendance. With smoke billowing into the sky, the Household Cavalry Regiment, a mile away at Combermere Barracks, received a call for help. Over 100 officers and soldiers were quickly transported to the castle.

Soldier B. was conducting CVR(T) driver training. As he came off the M4 motorway to head back to barracks, he saw flames and smoke coming from the castle.

> My immediate thought was an IRA bombing which obviously turned out to be wrong. Pulling into camp I was told to park up on the square and join my squadron who were all outside the block with helmets, belts and water bottles. We were then whipped up to the castle. The task I was allocated was emptying all the truck loads of rescued treasures and artefacts and storing them in a building within the estate. Each truck (which had been requisitioned by the police straight from the M4 traffic) had a policeman in attendance to prevent pilfering.

Shaun G. was on the Regimental Police Staff at the time. He had arranged for someone to stand in for him after he finished on the front gate at noon, as he had planned on going home for the weekend.

> Whilst on the 10–12 stag I noticed a large amount of black smoke coming from the town centre area but I didn't give it another thought … As my stag came to an end the person covering for me was in the guardroom so the Provost 3 bar said I could go. I ran to the squadron block, quickly got changed and threw some washing in my backpack then legged it back round to the guardroom where I was going to sign out. When I got to the guardroom there was a SNCO waiting; he told me to go back to the block, get changed, and report back in five minutes. We were going to the castle to assist as there was a fire raging. I wasn't happy but had very little choice … we were loaded into the back of a horse box and transported up to the castle where we were set to work on a number of tasks. These ranged from emptying out the library, moving lots of artwork and about forty of us had to carry a massive carpet. We were working in an area quite close to the fire and the heat was unbearable at times. I remember seeing the Queen there a number of times and she seemed truly upset that her home was in this state. Eventually we returned to camp in the early hours of the morning. The guy who covered for me on the RP staff knocked off at 6 p.m. with an extra £50 in his pocket and probably had a much better Friday night than I did.

I was one of the many Household Cavalrymen trying to get home for the weekend when I was told to get changed, get on a truck, and head to the castle. Over the years since the fire I have heard many stories told about what went on that afternoon and evening. Some are true as I witnessed them myself, and some have morphed into the realms of the unbelievable. Two things remain vivid in my memory. The sight of Her Majesty the Queen with a head scarf, wearing a green coat, standing among all the recovered artefacts, watching her home burn down. It was quite upsetting. And secondly, I have always wondered how none of those priceless artefacts did not end up disappearing in the fire, or in the back of a Land Rover.

***

One aspect of military life that changed over time for soldiers was Compulsory Drug Testing (CDT). Introduced in May 1995, the CDT team were an independent unit of the Royal Military Police that descended upon regiments with virtually no warning, testing everyone available who was subject to service law.[17] Commanding officers were given 48 hours' notice of the test date but were warned against making their soldiers aware. Their instructions were clear: 'Key individuals may be briefed on a strictly need-to-know basis … any planned test suspected of compromise will be aborted.'[18] Soldiers who provided a positive urine specimen were normally discharged. If a commanding officer wanted to retain a soldier under exceptional circumstances, he could order a test using a hair sample which would point to longer-term drug abuse. Most soldiers thought the introduction of random drug testing was a good idea and point to the fact that although they thought the number of soldiers using drugs was small, it was becoming an issue.

> In the early '90s, all officers and SNCOs had to sit through an RMP presentation on drugs. The officer out front asked a question at the start, 'Hands up if you have ever tried drugs?' Obviously no one did. He said, 'Statistics show that about half of you are lying.' It certainly brought home the point to me that although I had never seen any, they were being used a lot more than I realised.

Unlike some of their SNCOs and officers, soldiers who were living in barrack blocks knew what was happening. 'Drugs were ever present in the mid-'90s, but never openly. A good friend of mine tested positive on one of the very first CDTs; I was really shocked.' Robert C. said, 'Before CDT, many of the guys were going to all-night raves in Hannover. You could see that some were still on something when they got back to camp.' Rich G. admits that he was very naive about drugs, having never encountered them before he joined up. 'It was going on in my peer group, not openly but things being said, innuendo, and the rave scene that some of the guys were involved with. I think that drug testing was a very good thing and curbed what could have gotten out of control, if left unchecked. I know a number of guys who were caught and discharged.'

Simon J. thinks the introduction of random drug testing has worked. 'It caught out a lot of regiments, especially those near big towns and cities. The problem was there before 1995, just in smaller numbers. We had one bad experience in Germany when eight of our soldiers were found to be under the influence and thrown out.' Soldier G. also saw evidence of drug taking in Germany before random testing. 'After CDT, it still goes on and is reported in the newspapers, but I do believe that they all get caught in the end.' He also points out that it was not just young men and women. 'Two experienced SNCOs were caught … both had done 18 years in the Army and threw away a pension.'

Conrad P. thinks that soldiers in the Army are a product of the society it serves. 'In 1984, drugs were not popular, really. We just drank beer by the gallon. In 2008, prior to leaving the Army, I knew drugs were popular in society, so it just filtered into the Army with new recruits. Drug testing has worked without a doubt and was much needed; however, you'll always have the same issues that society does.' And Soldier C. points out that rather than changing habits after they joined up, soldiers in the CDT era were now learning to work around it.

> I didn't have much exposure to drugs in my career, but it appears that the young lads of today take drugs recreationally all the time. They roll the dice with CDTs … they know that for a couple of weeks after a test they are safe to do what they want. They are clearly not addicts, but more informed of what stays in the system for how long and what they can get away with … the CDT is not a deterrent.

It is now clear that soldiers were becoming better educated, learning that traces of cocaine and heroin only last in urine samples for two or three days after use, unlike traces of cannabis that last for two to three weeks. This newfound knowledge helps explain a dangerous increase in the use of Class A drugs. According to the Royal United Services Institute, 'In 2003, cannabis accounted for 50 per cent of all CDT positive tests, whereas cocaine was 22 per cent. By 2006, around 50 per cent of all positive tests registered cocaine use, with cannabis around 30 per cent.'[19]

Some soldiers found other ways of beating the system, too. Soldier J. found himself in his adjutant's office with two Royal Military Policemen who had come to arrest one of his soldiers for drug use.

> One of my lads lost his wallet after a night out. It had been found and handed in with a baggy of marijuana in it. The two RMP corporals stupidly left him alone with me for a few seconds. 'Have you smoked any of that recently?' I whispered. 'No, boss,' he said, 'it's my girlfriend's.' I quickly told him to deny everything, say it was planted and give a urine sample. They tried to pressure him to confess to using drugs but he did what I said and flatly denied ever using drugs before. They took the sample which came back negative, and he got off with a warning. He was a good lad, so I felt no guilt at trying to prevent him from getting booted out for smoking a joint or two.

The Royal Military Police (RMP) were not immune to being tested themselves. David K. was an RMP staff sergeant about to leave the Army when, 'Bizarrely, as my career was drawing to an end, I became aware of a large group (10+) of RMP soldiers in my unit who were taking drugs. The Chain of Command was informed and CDT tests were increased. However, only three actually failed the test.'

In 2017, a number of newspaper articles alleged that the Army was softening its stance, allowing young soldiers and recruits a second chance.[20] A year later, in an apparent response to this, Defence Secretary Gavin Williamson announced a strict zero-tolerance drugs policy that mandated the immediate discharge of all officers and soldiers who were found to have used drugs. Some soldiers agreed with this approach. 'The rule should be clear – test positive, and unless you declared you'd been spiked as soon as you became aware and not on the day the drugs team arrived, you are out.' Doug K.'s last posting was in the same barracks as the CDT team. 'I know they were still getting many positive results when I left the Army in 2012.' This shows that the CDT's aim 'to provide an effective deterrent capability ... to prevent drug misuse within the services'[21] was not really working.

Figures released under the *Freedom of Information Act* show that between 2005 and 2015, each year the Army was losing the equivalent of a battalion of soldiers for taking drugs.[22] In October 2019, with the army facing a 9.2 per cent deficit in its numbers, Williamson's successor as Defence Secretary, Ben Wallace, scrapped the zero-tolerance approach. He said, 'I took the view that some people are young and irresponsible, and it should be up to Commanding Officers to decide ... whether they should be allowed to remain in the Armed Forces.'[23]

CHAPTER 9

The Changing Role of Women in the Army

Women have been involved with the British Army for hundreds of years. Whether it was as a nurse in the Crimean War, a member of the newly formed Queen Mary's Army Auxiliary Corps in World War I, or one of the 50,000 that served in the Women's Auxiliary Corps during World War II, women have always performed non-combatant roles. In 1949, as a successor to the Auxiliary Territorial Service, the Women's Royal Army Corps (WRAC) included all women serving in the Army except medical, veterinary, and nursing staff. During the 1980s, there were over 40 trades for women, but these were mainly in administration or support roles; no women were integrated into male units or allowed in combat roles. During the careers of women who joined the Army in the late 1980s, the status quo would be turned on its head.

There can be no doubt that Margaret Thatcher changed gender stereotypes. No one would again question whether a woman was capable of leading the country; young women grew up thinking there was no limit to their ambitions. But for those thinking about a military career, the Sex Discrimination Act 1975 and the Equality Act 2010 allowed the MOD to exclude women 'from those posts where the military judgement is that the employment of women would undermine and degrade combat effectiveness'.[1] So throughout this period, young female soldiers joining the Army were still limited to a small list of jobs that had been unchanged for years.

Despite the narrow field of job opportunities, women who joined the Army did so for very similar reasons to men. Catherine P. joined the WRAC in 1990. 'I grew up in a military family and joined the cadets until I signed up.' Pauline C. said, 'I wanted to have an adventure and see the world … The Army was a way for me to move away and widen my horizons.' Michelle W. was told by friends that she 'wouldn't stick it' after she signed up to join the Queen Alexandra's Royal Army Nursing Corps. She credits her 'stubborn nature' for the reason she had 'an amazing 22-year career'. As with male soldiers, a lack of employment opportunities encouraged many women to join up. Barbara G. had a job but was not content. 'Friends were into drugs … they were getting pregnant … I just knew I wanted more from life and knew that I wouldn't get it in my hometown.' Soldier F. grew up in Northern

Ireland. 'I wanted to do something for the British against the terrorists. I didn't like being told where to go, who to speak to ... I wanted to travel and I wanted a job.' Shelly L. came from a large family and was always active. 'Having four brothers helped as I learned from an early age to be assertive and confident, never showing that I was weak.'

Whether women's rights and opportunities actually improved during the Thatcher years is open to debate. But there was certainly no real improvement with regards to equality, especially in the workplace. The number of employed women went from 56 to 64 per cent, and although a woman resided in Downing Street, women doing the same job as men were still paid far less, and the sad irony is that during her premiership, the gender pay gap actually got wider.[2]

Surprisingly, many women joined the Army with very low expectations of pay equality. Some were just glad they were able to get a job, while others did not think it right they were paid the same while they didn't do the same job as men. 'At the time when pay was lower for women I didn't mind as we had different fitness standards and women were still classed as non-combatants.' For Pauline C., it wasn't equal pay that bothered her. 'Whilst we were WRAC and the limitations that were forced upon us at the time, I felt it was justified ... I was more frustrated by the lack of equal opportunities.' Some young women actually thought they were being paid the same as men, while others resented doing non-combatant jobs but being paid less than their non-combatant male counterparts.

> At the time, it wasn't explained to me that I was on a different rate of pay ... We did exactly the same job, and I would say I actually did mine better as the 'invisible' standards line was always higher for me than it was for them. I did everything exactly the same except for Basic and Combat fitness tests. My personal weapons test was the same, my NBC test the same, and I did guard duties, duty clerk, and went on exercises.

Apart from administrative jobs in Northern Ireland, women had not been deployed to a combat zone since World War II. This changed in the 1990s, when women were able to become members of a flight crew in the Royal Air Force, serve onboard surface vessels in the Royal Navy, and deploy to the Gulf War. Employed as drivers, medics, and other non-front-line roles, they carried out their duties as equals. But not all soldiers were impressed with the women being deployed. One soldier's first experience of women in a combat zone was during the Gulf War.

> The air campaign had just started and we were in Camp Blackadder waiting to be moved into the desert. While we were eating breakfast, between 30 and 40 women got off a bus having just arrived in country. At that same moment, the air-raid siren went off meaning that a Scud missile had been launched in our general direction. While I was shovelling eggs and bacon into my mouth before putting on my respirator, I witnessed the chaos of some of these women getting into their NBC gear. I know they were thrown in the deep end having just got off an overnight flight from the UK or Germany, but it wasn't a good advertisement for women being in a combat zone. Some of the younger girls just went to pieces in panic and seemed unable to

function and carry out this very basic task. I felt sorry for them, but from that day I held the view that there was no place for women in a combat zone.

Despite this negative first impression, women soldiers were employed throughout the Gulf War with the Army continuing to maintain the same high standards.

With the announcement of Options for Change, the basic structure of how women within the Army were employed was to change entirely. When the Women's Royal Army Corps was disbanded in April 1992, women were fully integrated into the Army's non-combat roles. All remaining WRAC soldiers were transferred to their appropriate corps, including many women joining the newly formed Adjutant General's Corps and the Royal Logistics Corps. Most younger female soldiers welcomed this change, but it was not greeted with enthusiasm by everyone. Some female officers and NCOs knew that female advancement might slow down, with men and women now competing on an equal basis. Many male soldiers throughout the Army complained that standards would drop in units where a woman was now doing a man's job.

For soldiers like Pauline C., it was what she had been waiting for. 'I found the lack of equal opportunities when I joined up very frustrating … I had many disagreements when we were WRAC asking why we couldn't go on exercise, instead of being left back in camp … I was really pleased when we changed from WRAC to Royal Signals.' Catherine P. also welcomed the change.

> In 1992, I was given the opportunity to take a posting to a Commando Logistics unit in Plymouth. It was a test to see how women could work alongside elite units. Three females were chosen to go … personally I loved it and was able to do the same fitness as my male counterparts. I was also the first female to pass an Arctic Warfare Commando course in Norway … at first there was a bit of grumbling from them, but they soon learned that I was fit and could dig in with the best of them.

But not all women integrated so well, and even for those who did, there seemed to be an intolerable level of animosity from male soldiers.

Many women were made to feel like they were invading a man's world and were not welcome. 'In the early '90s it really was a different time and I wasn't aware of how different I would be treated simply because I was female. When I joined the WRAC I was protected from the negativity.' This protection would end for Barbara G. when she was posted to a newly amalgamated cavalry regiment. 'None of them wanted a female in their ranks. It was awful. Teased, tormented and humiliated on a regular basis for the sin of being a woman. I, like many other women, tried to see the positives but it took many years (and it is still taking time) for women to be accepted fully.' Catherine P. had a unique way of combating discrimination. 'In phase two training, a male officer (second lieutenant), told me straight to my face that women had no role in the Army. Unfortunately for him my reaction resulted in him having a broken nose.' After two weeks' detention she was returned to training and the officer had been posted on. 'Twelve years later I came across the same officer who was now my commander; his nose was still bent but his opinion of women in the Army had definitely changed.' Shelly L. had a completely different experience when she joined the Royal Signals. 'I felt welcomed as a woman in all my postings. In fact, I had a problem with a female corporal who told me off for running too fast on PT runs. She said I should hold back so that the other ladies did not look bad.'

Before 1992, there was virtually no integration of women and men in the same units, meaning that some soldiers, especially those in combat units, had never worked with female soldiers. Many male soldiers had stereotypical views on the roles of women in the Army, and it is fair to say that this affected the way they treated women when they were integrated within regiments. Women were not treated as equals; many did not even regard them as soldiers at all. Most of the women I interviewed tell stories of how badly they were treated; some of their stories are shocking. Soldier K. joined the Royal Logistics Corps three years after women were integrated. 'The ripples were still there, and we were made to feel like it was our fault ... anything that went wrong with a female and they would hark on about a simpler time.' She said that female fitness standards had improved. 'It was physically demanding daily ... some women rose to the challenge and did fantastic but I felt like a fraud, not good enough to be there.' Things got so bad for Soldier K. that she left. In her final unit she said, 'They made me feel guilty about drawing a wage in the end.'

It was not only younger soldiers who felt unwanted in their new regiments. Now vying for promotion on a level playing field, women SNCOs struggled to be accepted. 'There were a few men who didn't believe in equality, and at times I was treated completely different to my male counterparts. This was more pronounced when I became a senior rank where some men often tried to undermine me. They acted as if they were jealous.'

One of the major issues when women were integrated into male units was fitness levels. When asking male soldiers how the Army had changed since women have been employed in many more roles, the responses were almost always about fitness. 'Women struggled to pass the most basic of fitness tests and when they did, they were often at an increased time to the men. Where is the equality here?' Owen C. said, 'The biggest bugbear I found was the double standards when it came to fitness tests. They had extra time to do less.' While Rich G. was an instructor at ATR (Army Training Regiment) Pirbright, he noticed that female recruits 'didn't have to meet the same physical standards as their male counterparts going into the same trade'.

While most women acknowledge that standards for physical tests were lower, this did not mean that they agreed with it. Shelly L. said, 'Women were allowed more time on the clock when doing fitness tests, and we carried less weight on our backs ... I did not agree with this. I worked extra hard at my fitness to ensure I could easily keep up with the men.' Pauline C. was the only female on her sergeant's course. 'I carried out exactly the same fitness tests and carried the same weight as the men.' And although she believes, 'We can't change a fact of nature; women in

The Iron Curtain separated east and west for 43 years. (Photo by Stefan Wagner from FreeImages)

Less than a year after the fall of the Berlin Wall, British Army soldiers swapped the green fields of north-west Europe for the Saudi Arabian desert. (Author's collection)

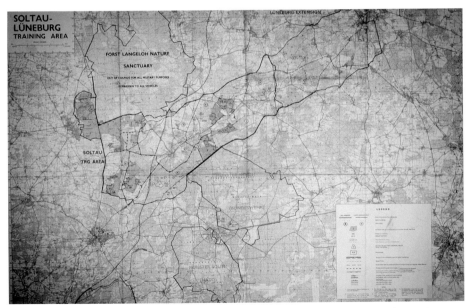

Since the end of World War II the British Army was prepared to defend large tracts of West Germany from any Soviet-led invasion. Training for this took place on the Soltau-Luneburg Training Area. (Author's collection)

The troop build-up was relentless, the Saudi Arabian desert, January 1991. (Author's collection)

Saddam Hussein had used chemical weapons before. All troops masked up every time a Scud missile was launched, even inside a Challenger tank. (Author's collection)

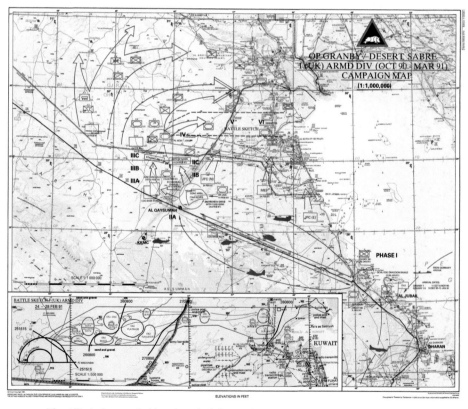

The Allied plan was bold and made full use of the open desert. (Author's collection)

Thousands of British Army vehicles entered Iraq once the initial breach was made. (Author's collection)

Midday in the Kuwaiti desert – day turned to night after fleeing Iraqi forces set hundreds of oil wells ablaze. (Author's collection)

The 'Highway of Death' – total devastation on the Kuwait to Basra road. (Author's collection)

On exercise at the British Army Training Unit Suffield in Canada. (By kind permission of David K.)

Large tracts of Bosnia were left in ruins, with atrocities carried out by all sides of the conflict. (By kind permission of Andrew T.)

The medical detachment at Konjic, Bosnia. (By kind permission of Andrew T.)

The UN checkpoint between Gornji Vakuf and Bugojno, Bosnia. (By kind permission of Jules H.)

Salvaging spares from a Scimitar destroyed by a mine. (By kind permission of unnamed soldier)

Task Force Alpha on Mount Igman. (By kind permission of unnamed soldier)

Spraying vehicles from UN white back to standard colours, Bosnia, 1995. (By kind permission of unnamed soldier)

Ready to deploy as part of NATO's Implementation Force, Bosnia, 1995. (By kind permission of unnamed soldier)

A Bosnian Serb radar station and listening post destroyed by a Tomahawk missile in 1995. (By kind permission of Jules H.)

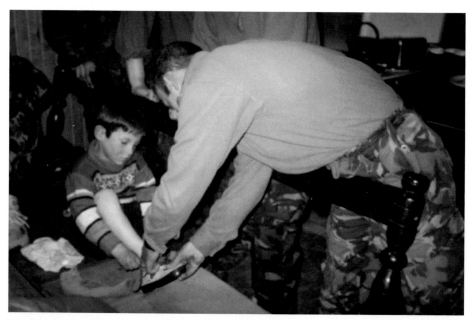

'My favourite memory of four Bosnia tours. Young Sayid (Sid) who was five years old and lived in a garage opposite our troop house. His dad had been murdered. He had nothing. I walked to a market and bought him these shoes. I've never seen delight like it … I hope he's still alive.' (By kind permission of Jules H.)

The Royal Engineers had an extremely difficult task keeping the roads open in Central Bosnia. (By kind permission of Jules H.)

Bosnia, 2002. The Household Cavalry patrolling in the mountains north-east of Prnjavor. (By kind permission of unnamed soldier)

Thessaloniki, Greece. Vehicles bound for Kosovo about to start the train journey north through Macedonia. (By kind permission of unnamed soldier)

German troops on patrol in southern Kosovo, 1999. (By kind permission of unnamed soldier)

Forkhill Police Station, South Armagh, 1997. (By kind permission of Conrad P.)

Snap vehicle checkpoint in West Belfast, 1998. (By kind permission of David K.)

Inside Springfield Road police station, 1998. (By kind permission of David K.)

Iraq, 2003. Patrolling Iraq/Iran border north-east of Amarah. (By kind permission of unnamed soldier)

Despite the warnings, British Army vehicles were still dangerously susceptible to being hit by American aircraft. (By kind permission of unnamed soldier)

The police station at Majar al-Kabir where six Royal Military policemen were murdered, June 2003. (By kind permission of Andrew T.)

The police station at Majar al-Kabir after order had been restored. (By kind permission of Andrew T.)

Conducting a raid on a village in Iraq. (By kind permission of Andrew T.)

Escorting special police to Musa Qalah. (By kind permission of Jules H.)

Signpost on ANP Hill, Now Zad. (By kind permission of Jules H.)

On patrol in Helmand Province, 2008. (By kind permission of unnamed soldier)

A close escape. Damage from an IED, Helmand Province, 2006. (By kind permission of Jules H.)

Casualty evacuation at Camp Nahidullah, Helmand Province, 2012. (By kind permission of Andrew T.)

Equipment improved but not before lives had been lost. (By kind permission of Andrew T.)

the norm are not as strong as men', she did not make excuses and went on to say, 'How can women expect to be accepted if they don't reach the required standard?' Another female soldier with 14 years' service told me, 'I agree with the men who felt standards were lowered to accommodate women's lower physical abilities ... I felt women lost respect from the men, and understandably so.'

In 1997, it was announced that a further 1,300 jobs would be available to women, increasing the roles open to women from 47 to 70 per cent.[3] This meant women could now serve in both combat support and combat service support roles. Soldier L. became a medic and served on four operational tours in the Balkans and Iraq. Throughout Bosnia, Kosovo, Iraq, and Afghanistan, hundreds of women were deployed where their roles took them into combat situations. Soldier H. completed a tour in Iraq attached to the Black Watch as a female searcher, plus two additional tours in Afghanistan. But even there she was treated differently.

> I was supposed to be top cover for a vehicle which had a female driver. It was a difficult mission and dangerous. I got pulled off just in case something happened. They said, 'It would look bad in the press if two females died.' I patted the guy taking my place on the back. 'Remember, your life isn't as important as mine, supposedly.' I did the same training, and had the same abilities; I wasn't too happy.

In 2006, the first female soldier was killed in action, and in the same year, Private Michelle Norris of the Royal Army Medical Corps became the first female British Army soldier to be awarded the Military Cross. After her unit came under attack at Al Amarah, and while under sustained sniper fire, she rescued the commander of her Warrior vehicle after he was shot in the mouth. Her commanding officer described her bravery, saying, 'Private Norris acted completely selflessly and, in the face of great danger, concentrated on her job and saved someone's life.'[4]

Regardless of the positive contribution made by female soldiers used in combat support and combat service roles in the Balkans, Iraq, and Afghanistan, women were still excluded from ground close combat roles. GCC was defined as 'roles that are primarily intended and designed with the purpose of requiring individuals on the ground, to close with and kill the enemy'.[5] The government said their decision was based on 'maintaining the combat effectiveness' of the Army and not on 'a stereotypical view of women's abilities'.[6] Although they didn't say as much, there were many people who were quietly voicing concerns that if women were to be allowed into GCC roles, then the quality of those units would go down because the standards required would have to be lowered. Some, like Colonel Tim Collins, were not so quiet. 'The infantry is no place for a woman, and to permit them to serve in close combat roles is a pure politically correct extravagance ... The physical bar for joining [close combat] units ... needs to be raised, never lowered.'[7]

Colonel Collins' view regarding standards was reflected by almost every soldier – female and male – that I spoke to. Female soldiers did not want any allowance, but they wanted a chance to try. Catherine P. never noticed standards being lowered but said, 'If they were I would not agree with it, especially if I wanted to do the same job as my male counterparts.' Shelly L. was a firm believer in equal rights. 'If a female is physically and mentally fit for the job then she should be allowed … in any role.' But she reiterated, 'I do not think that allowances should be made for any woman or man.'

Although many male soldiers were sceptical of females being able to do certain jobs, as long they were capable and standards did not fall, then most were in agreement that females should be able to try. Conrad P. never served with women but he did instruct them during training. He observed, 'Some, and by this I mean very few, are capable of front-line fighting on equal terms with men', but he went on to say that 'they should be welcome to try … but standards must remain the same.' Paul H. said he was 'a big fan of women serving … my view is that if they can do the job, then spot on!'

Before 1990, female soldiers were automatically discharged from the Army when they became pregnant. After that date women did not have to leave; the policy changed when the MOD realised that it had been in contravention of the Sex Discrimination Act of 1975. Supported by the Equal Opportunities Commission, two female nurses who had been discharged filed legal proceedings and were awarded compensation of £11,000. At the time, awards from industrial tribunals were limited. All this changed when the European Court of Justice set aside the limit of £11,000, allowing all 5,700 woman illegally dismissed between 1978 and 1990 to claim unlimited sums of money from the MOD.[8] It is an emotive subject. A retired nurse I spoke to said, 'Women were discriminated against by forcing them out of the Army for having a child' and that she knew several women who had sued the Army for compensation. She had herself been advised by her personnel officer that it was in her best interests to get out of the Army when she became pregnant.

Mismanagement by the MOD not only failed to implement individuals' rights, but also 'laid the public purse wide open'.[9] Ensuing lawsuits from some retired servicewomen resulted in pay-outs of up to £500,000, with the resulting total bill for MOD incompetence estimated to be as high as £200 million.[10] Even in 1994, these pay-outs were leaving a bitter taste in the mouths of many servicemen. One airman injured by an ejector seat said, 'I was paralysed and got nothing. She's getting half a million pounds for her normal function.'[11] And when casualties from Iraq and Afghanistan started receiving paltry sums by comparison, the bitter taste turned into outright anger. Andrew T. is in receipt of a war disability pension in line with the 2005 Armed Forces Compensation Scheme. He reflected the frustration felt by many soldiers returning from war affected by both physical and psychological wounds and who were getting poor levels of compensation, 'when they are paying out large amounts of money to non-combatant injuries'.

For soldiers who did have babies while serving, it was, and still is, a tough struggle. Michelle W. said she did not have a problem with women not being able to have children and serve when she joined up.

I still think it is difficult to juggle the two … they allow us to have children but put hurdles in the way … being a mum is hard enough constantly wrestling with, 'Am I doing it right?' But then there's the pressure of doing your best at work, best at home, deployments, postings, away from partners and spouses, odd shift patterns, and the CO's PT before the creche opens nightmare. The list is endless.

Soldier H. uses a couple of examples of how bringing up a family was extremely difficult for some military couples. One example was of a husband and wife who were sent on a tour at the same time then threatened by social services with losing their children if they did not make other arrangements. She told another story of a female soldier who had no choice but to allow her ex-partner parental rights so she could go on a deployment, only to lose custody of her child when she returned home.

Many female veterans worked extremely hard and struggled to integrate themselves into a male-dominated world that did not want them there, and the scars, both physical and mental, are still with them. Pauline C. had worked hard to be thought of as an equal. 'Towards the end of my career, the men in my troop treated me with such disrespect (including the Troop OC), that it led to depression … I never admitted it or did anything because I didn't think that I would be believed … I didn't want to be accused of being another woman trying to sue the Army for money.' Soldier O. said, 'The job I did was with a lot of extremely heavy equipment that even some of the men struggled to carry … Not every female that I worked with was capable of carrying the equipment. I even ended up in hospital with three slipped discs and sciatica down both legs due to lifting the equipment.' When I asked some women to describe their experiences with discrimination, some did not answer, and one was reluctant to respond, even with anonymity. She simply replied, 'Unfortunately, I can't.'

Like their male counterparts, the bonds and friendships women serving in the Army made have lasted over the years. Michelle W. describes a deep and lasting comradery. 'I have lifelong friends who I see once in a blue moon … when we do meet up there is nothing uncomfortable about that first meeting; we just pick up where we left off.' Soldier N. said, 'It was the best years of my life, and if the Army had not made it difficult for me and my husband … then I would have stayed in.' And despite how Soldier K. was treated, she said she would still join up. 'It's water under the bridge now … it made me who I am today and yes, I'd do it all again.' Soldier I. said, 'The Army gave me the perfect mental skills to deal with a couple of tricky situations in my life.'

The debate about a woman's role in the British Army is now over, whether male soldiers like the idea or not. In 2016, the ban on women serving in some parts of the Royal Armoured Corps was lifted, with the first officers joining regiments in the spring of the following year. In October 2018, Defence Secretary Gavin Williamson announced that all combat roles were open to women, including infantry and special forces units. Women are now free to apply to serve in all roles of employment within the Army. For the first time in the long and storied history of the British Army, its soldiers 'will be determined by ability alone and not gender'.[12] Of all the aspects of a soldier's life that have changed since the end of the Cold War, there is no doubt that the role of women is the one that has transformed the most.

CHAPTER 10

The Blair Doctrine and Humanitarian Interventions

On 24 March 1999, British Prime Minister Tony Blair made a statement to the House of Commons about Kosovar Albanians, who had been driven out of their province by the Serbian Army. He said, 'We have in our power, the means to help them secure justice and we have a duty to see that justice is done ... those nations that have the power, have the responsibility.'[1] With these words, the prime minister not only guaranteed British military involvement in any future intervention in Kosovo, but he also laid the foundation for future use of force wherever a 'humanitarian intervention' was deemed necessary. A month later, at the Chicago Economic Club, he gave a speech where he laid out what he called his Doctrine of the International Community, which later became known as the Blair Doctrine. In this speech can be seen the genesis of interventions not only in Kosovo, but also in Sierra Leone, Iraq, and Afghanistan.[2]

I believe that the strong international response to Kosovo was in part a collective guilty conscience regarding the failure to stop the massacre at Srebrenica, and a total indifference towards the Rwandan genocide. In 1994, when the full horrors of the slaughter in Rwanda became public knowledge, the world baulked; how could the international community have come to the aid of oil-rich Kuwait just three years before, yet do nothing to halt the slaughter of a million Tutsis in central Africa? After the 1993 withdrawal from Somalia, Washington was reluctant to be drawn into any more foreign conflicts. And even after a successful resolution in Bosnia, Washington initially signalled that it would not be involved in any ground war in Kosovo.[3] But Tony Blair was not going to let genocide happen again and made a promise to the people of Kosovo: 'We will not tolerate the brutal suppression of the civilian population.'[4]

Like other Balkan conflicts, the origins of the war in Kosovo date back to the middle ages, with hate and resentment between ethnic groups being passed down through the generations. After the battle of Kosovo in 1389, Serbia and Kosovo became part of the Ottoman Empire for over five centuries. Following defeat in the 1912 Balkan War, Kosovo was then ceded to Serbia. Throughout the 20th century there were simmering tensions between the ruling Serbs and ethnic Albanians. In the 1920s and 1930s there was an orchestrated effort to change the demography of Kosovo through colonisation by Serbs. After World War II Tito ended this policy, halting the return of many Chetniks to Kosovo. Tito understood that in order to keep nationalism under control, he had to make concessions to ethnic groups, so in 1974 the constitution of Yugoslavia was redrawn with Kosovo becoming an autonomous province within Serbia. After Tito died and Milošević took control of Serbia, despite demonstrations in support of independence, he seized Kosovo, stripping it of its autonomy.

After the Dayton Accords were signed, ethnic Albanians realised that 'an armed conflict might encourage the international community to intervene and resolve the situation sooner'.[5] Almost immediately, the Kosovo Liberation Army (KLA) was formed, releasing its name publicly in 1995.[6] The following year they began attacking Serbian police stations, which they saw as the chief source of repression. Funding to buy weapons and ammunition came from Albanian diaspora in many countries, including the United States and countries throughout Europe. It is estimated that $75–$100 million was raised from all over the world, allowing the KLA to become a potent force.[7]

Despite only making up about 10 per cent of the population, Serbia was determined to keep the province. In 1989, on the 600th anniversary of the battle of Kosovo, Slobodan Milošević spoke to a crowd of several million Serbians at the Gazimestan monument. Not only did the anniversary show how important Kosovo was to Serbian national identity, but it also showed what lengths Milošević would go to keep it. He spoke of so much 'Serb blood and Serb sanctity there that Kosovo will remain Serbian even if there is not a single Serb left there'. And with the crowd chanting 'Kosovo is Serb', Milošević stoked the fires, talking of future 'armed battles'.[8]

The Kosovo War began in March 1998, when Serbia launched an operation in Prekaz to apprehend known KLA members, including their leader, Adem Jashari. When they refused to surrender, the police stormed the Jashari compound, killing 58 ethnic Albanians, including 18 women and 10 children.[9] Later investigations revealed that the aim had not been to apprehend Jashari; the Serbian police and paramilitary forces were sent to wipe out the KLA fighters and their entire families.

Throughout 1998, the violence continued with numerous brutal massacres taking place. There were several attempts to broker some kind of agreement; Russian President Boris Yeltsin did convince Milošević to order a ceasefire, and then a diplomatic observer mission was deployed. After a withdrawal agreement had been made, and a date set, NATO deployed a verification mission. But even US President Bill Clinton declaring a 'national emergency' could not stop the violence. Milošević was put under pressure with sanctions, and an embargo on arms and oil. Regardless, human rights violations continued. A quarter of a million ethnic Albanians were forced from their homes, and the country descended into all-out civil war. Once again the west seemed powerless to stop it. In September, the UN Security Council issued Resolution 1199 demanding that all parties cease hostilities and maintain a ceasefire, but even as late as January 1999, there was still no firm plan in place to intervene in Kosovo. NATO had prepared airstrikes, but there was seemingly no will to intervene with ground troops.

All this changed on 15 January 1999, when '45 Kosovo Albanian farmers were rounded up, led up a hill and massacred'.[10] The murders were the turning point of the war, not because western countries and the U.N. condemned them, but because NATO realised the war was not going to end until a peacekeeping force was deployed in Kosovo. US Secretary of State Madeleine Albright reluctantly conceded 'that diplomacy with a credible threat of force would be the American strategy going forward'.[11]

Under the threat of a NATO bombing campaign, all sides met at the Château de Rombouillet in France on 6 February 1999. NATO Secretary General Javier Solana led the negotiations. The Rombouillet Accords were accepted by Albanian, US, and British delegations, but refused by the Yugoslavs and Russians. Although Milošević accepted some autonomy for Kosovo, he refused to allow armed NATO troops to replace Yugoslav security forces, instead offering to allow unarmed UN observers. After the collapse of the talks in France, NATO commanders were ordered to commence airstrikes.

NATO air operations began on 23 March 1999. NATO commanders and politicians alike thought it would take just a few days to bring Milošević to heel. Getting him to back down was not helped by weak signals coming out of Washington. Even as the bombing began, President Clinton said he did not 'intend to put our troops into Kosovo to fight a war'.[12] This statement did nothing but stiffen Serbian resolve. NATO airstrikes on their own had not worked in Bosnia, and Milošević knew it; if he could hold out, NATO countries might weaken and buckle when television images of collateral damage were broadcast worldwide and public opinion started to turn against them.

As the airstrikes continued into April and with no sign of Serbian capitulation, it became apparent to NATO countries that ground operations were going to be needed. Tony Blair, who had been an advocate of conducting ground operations all along, now had to convince others that it was the right thing to do. On 20 April, accompanied by Chief of the Defence Staff Sir Charles Guthrie, the prime minister flew to Washington. With falling approval ratings after his impeachment trial acquittal, and although he was in the last year of his presidency, Bill Clinton was 'nervous of the domestic political repercussions of committing US ground forces in a war'.[13] One American who was advocating for the use of ground forces was Supreme Allied Commander Europe General Wesley Clark. After he argued for an all-out ground offensive, then said as much to the press, he was told by Secretary of State for Defence William Cohen in no uncertain terms to keep his opinion to himself.[14]

One of the reasons Milošević was holding out was the hope of Russian support. Even in the eyes of a moderate like Boris Yeltsin, the west, and in particular NATO, was encroaching on Russia and seen as a direct threat. Since 1990, and the Bush–Baker 'not one inch eastward' promise that had been made when discussing German unification, three former Soviet countries had been coerced into joining NATO, and now it was bombing a Russian ally right on its doorstep. The Russian envoy to Serbia warned that nuclear war had not been closer since the end of the Cold War.[15] And even though Yeltsin would not support Serbia militarily, eventually forcing him to accept NATO troops, the crisis in Kosovo would have long-term lasting implications where US–Russian relations were concerned.

As the bombing continued, the British Army was busy preparing for all eventualities. Initially, figures of possibly 200,000 NATO troops were being suggested, but eventually a force of 50,000 was assembled in Macedonia. Tony Blair had considered calling up reserves and at one time talked of deploying 50,000 British soldiers if needed, so determined was he to see the conflict in Kosovo resolved.[16] British infantry battalions such as the Irish Guards and 1st Battalion, Parachute Regiment, arrived in late March, then spent the next month preparing on the Krivolak training area. The Kosovo Force (KFOR) had been preparing for combat operations, but in the end they were only needed for peace-enforcing duties after Milošević had agreed to withdraw.

Some 7,000 British soldiers were assembled into a 70-mile-long convoy that started snaking its way into Kosovo. Operation *Agricola* was now under way, and although the Yugoslav Army had agreed to leave, British troops entering Kosovo on 12 June 1999 were prepared to fight if they needed to. The main route into Kosovo wound its way north through the Sharr mountains. At Kaçanik, a small town that had been a Milošević stronghold, there was a natural defile. There were steep-sided mountains on both sides, with the Lepanac River squeezing through a deep ravine 12 miles long. The rail and road bridges that crossed had to be taken intact for the British, German, Italian, and American troops to move into Kosovo, so paratroopers and Gurkhas of 5 Airborne Brigade were tasked to secure it.

Stuart B. and members of 3 Para Support Coy had been sent from their base in Dover to join 1 Para for Operation *Agricola*. Just before entering Kosovo, he and other members of his platoon were to get their '15 minutes of fame'.

> While preparing to cross the border my .50cal gun team and I were snapped by a press photographer from the *Daily Mirror*. The next day it was on the front page of the *Mirror* with

the headline, 'Elite Paras march on Kosovo'. My wife was out walking our dog back home when a group of friends came running across the field towards her with a newspaper in hand. For some reason she said she feared the worst until they showed her the front page.

Once the armoured columns left the mountains, units moved into place to carry out specific tasks. Michael P. was in the KFOR column as it approached Pristina. 'The King's Royal Hussars BG with our No. 1 Company took off to the airport for a stand-off with the Russians, while the Irish Guards BG headed for Pristina.' A column of Russian soldiers with light armour had already secured Pristina airport, having entered Kosovo from Serbia. General Wesley Clark believed there was now a very real danger of Russia securing a partitioned sector of Kosovo that would remain in Serb hands, so he wanted to block the runway to stop the Russian troops being reinforced. KFOR Commander General Mike Jackson famously disobeyed the order and threatened to resign, saying, 'Sir, I am not going to start World War III for you.'[17] General Jackson diffused the situation and the Russian contingent eventually became part of KFOR but not under NATO command.[18]

While researching this book I have heard many different versions of the 'we-were-first-into-Pristina' story. Michael P. told me it was the Irish Guards. I heard from another source who said that it was members of the Parachute Regiment. The Household Cavalry also take credit, and even Norwegian Special Forces claim the prize. Soldier P. says the 'honour' probably went to the Royal Army Medical Corps.

> Two Land Rovers belonging to a medical unit lost touch with the vehicle in front, were not map reading, and at a junction went straight on instead of turning left to Pristina airport. As they entered the capital they were captured by Serb forces and went missing for a few hours. They were later released with the help of liaison officers.

Michael P. and No. 4 Company of the Irish Guards took over the Ministry of Interior Police's main station in Pristina. He says, 'It was an eye-opener when we discovered their torture chambers down in the cellars … it also had their Quartermaster's store, which made for some good souvenirs.' For the first two nights they stayed in a school ground after patrolling the deserted streets. Eventually the locals started to come out and 'made fresh bread which they gave us … we in turn gave them some of our rations. In time the kids came to sit with us; you could tell it was the first time that they had felt safe for a long time.'

After two weeks in Pristina, Michael P. and his company were moved into the countryside to a small village called Devet Jugovića from where they set up various patrol bases. As well as maintaining the peace in their AOR, they were tasked with collecting weapons from both sides. 'One weapon we collected was a Thompson machine gun that was dropped in by the OSS to the partisans during the Second World War – it now hangs in the Sergeants' Mess.' Michael's job when he arrived in the village was to look after the company's soldiers and the six interpreters who were working with them, but that was about to change.

> My task went from company medic to being the nearest thing to a doctor in the village … I had 39 casualties to deal with before we left Kosovo, ranging from gun-shot wounds, to rape victims, car crashes, three heart attacks, and one diabetic attack, and I'm glad to say they all survived … My other job wasn't so nice. I was tasked with the recovery of bodies (fresh or several months deceased) and to escort individuals (Serb and Albanian) to the city morgue to identify their loved ones. You could smell the morgue from a mile away as the refrigeration units weren't working so everything was decomposing … It is not a smell I will ever forget. It was that bad, the lads would complain about the smell on my uniform.

The brutality of the conflict shocked many soldiers. There is no doubt that the ruling Serbs had treated the ethnic Albanian population terribly. Upwards of 250,000 were displaced from their homes, seeking refuge in neighbouring Albania and Macedonia, and at least 2,000 ethnic Albanians were killed by Serb paramilitary and regular forces. But the KLA were every bit as brutal, and after 12 June, when KFOR entered the country, the KLA and many civilian ethnic Albanians were determined to have their revenge. During the first few days, it was clear what was happening. 'From the air you could see plumes of smoke curling up from burning buildings: the Albanian Kosovars were indulging in the typical Balkan behaviour of burning the houses of their enemy.'[19]

Many soldiers witnessed Serb civilians paying the price for what their soldiers had done. Soldier P. witnessed the hatred that overtook Kosovo in 1999. 'After the Serbs were talked into leaving, the remaining population were hell-bent on retribution, and to a large extent we were not able to protect them. I remember this pleasant old man we'd spoken to earlier in the day. He was taking food to a neighbour that was blind when he was shot dead by a sniper, because he was a Serb.'

After securing a helicopter landing site (HLS) for the battalion, Stuart B. and his company occupied a school in the city centre. From there they sent out patrols and were to witness what happened to Serbs.

> The only Serbs left were the old and weak … they would pay the price for the Serbian invasion … Homes were set on fire, killings and beatings against the old Serbs started taking place and the city turned into a lawless environment. We patrolled the streets day and night with Northern Ireland-style 12-man multiples … it was sad to see men and women in their 80s turning up at our school location with broken jaws and smashed faces. We caught quite a few of the scumbags who were carrying out the beatings … they were dealt with in a professional manner expected of the Parachute Regiment.

Many soldiers clashed with ethnic Albanians while trying to protect Serbs from the same brutality they themselves had experienced at the hands of the Serbian Army. Robert C. had deployed to Kosovo with The Queen's Dragoon Guards. His troop was sited close to an old Soviet-style apartment block where most Serbs had left after KFOR had entered the country and the Yugoslav Army had gone.

One old lady, 70, perhaps 80 years old, refused to leave as she had been living there most of her life. I was standing at the bottom by the entrance when a member of the KLA militia tried to gain access 'to talk to her'. It was obvious to me what would have happened if I wasn't there to tell him to 'Fuck off.' He left in a rage and reported me to the UN.

Michael P. was coming to the end of his tour in Devet Jugovića. They were due to hand over to the Norwegian Telemark Battalion. Before leaving, Michael would bear witness to how the barbarity in Kosovo knew no bounds and was obviously not going away anytime soon.

We had this one Serbian old lady in the village who had no family and was all alone, so we would look after her while we were there ... When it came for us to leave we were in our 432 [ambulance] when the CSM told me to head back to our old location and wait to be relieved (by the Norwegians). As we got back to the village we arrived just in time for a hanging fest ... The village had turned out to watch as they hanged this little four-foot-tall Serbian granny. I told my driver to head straight into them, make his rifle ready, and cover me ... I jumped down and entered the middle of the crowd – my rifle was made ready and safety catch off. I charged in, in a fit of rage pointing my rifle at the ringleaders ... There were only three of us and about 40 of them ... I got the old lady off the box they had her standing on – she was absolutely terrified ... We now had a standoff, us three against an angry mob of enraged Albanians. Just in the nick of time a company of the Telemark Battalion arrived and surrounded the mob. I pointed out the ringleaders ... They were arrested for attempted murder and off to prison they went. The new company in the village set up their HQ outside the old lady's house, and that was the last I saw of her.

Word of what had happened soon got back to the Irish Guards. When the 432 ambulance arrived back with his battalion, his company turned out to give him and the other two Irish Guardsmen a round of applause. Michael P. was later awarded a Joint Commanders' Commendation for his work in Devet Jugovića.

KFOR continues to keep the peace under UNSCR 1244. Thirty-eight different countries have contributed troops, which currently stands at just over 3,500.[20] There have been sporadic violent clashes over the two decades since the Yugoslav Army left the country, but NATO intervention has largely ensured that the peace has been kept. In 2008, Kosovo declared its independence and has since been recognised by 112 countries.

Kosovo would deeply affect many soldiers that served there – the terrible inhumanity shown by both sides would linger long in the memory. While negotiating with the Serbs, General Jackson heard for himself the Serbian attitude towards ethnic Albanians. 'One of their officers said to me while we were chatting during a break, "Of course, we in the Serb Army will treat you with honour. But Albania is not a proper country. The Albanians are not a proper people. There is no requirement to treat them with honour."'[21] Having seen the situation in Bosnia and Macedonia, Paul H. was shocked at 'just how violent Serbs were against the Albanians and the KLA. It was ethnic cleansing big time, people left with nothing, trying to escape ... Villages were left as ghost towns ... I found it was a step up from Bosnia in the levels of extreme violence and the speed that things escalated.' After several tours in Bosnia and now Kosovo, Soldier P. developed a very macabre skill set. He told me he had spent so much time dealing with death that he could distinguish the difference in smell between dead cattle and a human corpse.

The brutality of both sides scarred the young men who had witnessed it. One widely reported incident was of a soldier who had befriended a young boy while his unit was in Kosovo. 'This little boy, six or seven, would bring them bread and milk. They played football with him and would chat with him, and one day they found the little boy's body in pieces in their water supply.'[22]

Despite everything that had happened in the aftermath of the war in Kosovo, any clashes between ethnic Albanians and British soldiers who were protecting Serb civilians were soon forgotten. Kosovo would be forever grateful to the United Kingdom. Britain was one of the first countries to recognise Kosovo in its own right, and to set up an embassy in Pristina. In November 2019, Kosovo showed the depth of its appreciation when England played Kosovo in a Euro 2020 qualifying game. As well as warmly hosting visiting English football fans, banners and signs adorned buildings and walls all over Pristina. One read 'Welcome, brothers'.[23]

Most now agree that intervention and the threat of force in Kosovo was not only justified but necessary. Those same people would probably also agree that there was going to be a long-term price to pay as well. Former US Ambassador to the Russian Federation, Michael McFaul, saw first-hand the effect it had on Russia. Yeltsin and most of Russian society saw NATO's intervention as just another example of the United States using military force to expand its influence in Russia's backyard.[24] The irony is that the United States had always been reluctant to intervene.

In 2016, President Vladimir Putin was asked whether he thought that it was the annexation of Crimea or Russian involvement in Syria that had caused the overall decline in US–Russia relations. He replied, 'You are mistaken … think about Yugoslavia. This is when it started.'[25] If the Kosovo conflict had occurred 12 months later when Russia's new president would have been the one supporting Milošević's actions in Kosovo, instead of Boris Yeltsin, things could have turned out very differently.

***

Like Kosovo, Sierra Leone is another country where ex-prime minister Tony Blair is revered as a saviour. Blair would later write in his autobiography that the successful intervention in Sierra Leone was one of his proudest moments in office. It has been described as one of those rare moments in history when the motivation to intervene in another country was based on humanitarian interests alone.[26]

Sierra Leone was a former colony that had been under British influence since the late 18th century when freed slaves settled in an area that became known as Freetown. It was granted independence in 1961 and became a republic a decade later.

Wracked by corruption, abuse of power, interference from neighbouring Liberia, and influence of the 'blood diamond' trade, the country descended into a brutal civil war. In July 1999, the Lome Peace Agreement was signed. As well as an immediate ceasefire and disarmament of both sides, the United Nations sent in a mission consisting of unarmed observers to help with the implementation of the agreement. The Revolutionary United Front (RUF), a brutal organisation who regularly used murder and dismemberment as weapons of intimidation, was now legitimised as a political body. Heavily supported by Liberian President Charles Taylor, they were also given control of the diamond mines. Given their past history, this was akin to putting the fox in charge of the hen house.

The RUF's use of child soldiers was well known. Children as young as nine or ten would be abducted from villages, taken away into the bush, kept high on drugs, and trained to fight, murder, and mutilate. Their signature atrocity was to cut the hands off any enemy soldiers they captured. 'I wandered through villages that had been burned, trying to get testimonies from traumatized people. I saw so many hacked-off limbs that I began to think I was hallucinating ... Rebel soldiers asked adult villagers if they wanted "long sleeves" or "short sleeves", then hacked off their limbs with machetes.'[27]

Rich G.'s goal from very early on in his Army career was to pass selection and become a member of the Special Air Service. 'After I passed P Coy in '94 I became more focused and confident.' He first went on selection in 1996 when he was just 23 years old.

> I came off during test week after receiving two red cards (overtime on two test marches). I planned to go back in '97, but went on a crew commander's course and then to Bosnia ... I planned to go again in '98 but was enjoying being a commander ... and didn't get my arse in gear (completely my fault). I then planned to go in the summer of '99, but Kosovo happened, and I didn't want to miss out on an operational tour.

In 1998 he was told by his CO that he needed to go on selection the following year as it was starting to slow down his career. And towards the end of the Kosovo tour, his squadron leader said that he needed to go on selection in January 2000, or he would probably be posted to Knightsbridge on ceremonial duties.

> I think this was a threat to motivate me and put selection to bed, one way or another as you're only allowed two chances at selection. We didn't return from Kosovo until the end of October, so I decided that I didn't have enough time to get ready for selection and opted to go for Pathfinder selection instead, as this would give me a few extra weeks to prepare. The plan (in 1999) was to pass the cadre, do my time in the Pathfinder Platoon (three years for non-Parachute Regiment) and then go on to selection and Hereford.

The Pathfinder Platoon is the advance and reconnaissance force of 16 Air Assault Brigade. Stationed in Suffolk, the PF Platoon's main tasks are to mark and secure drop and landing zones before the brigade's main force arrive. It's the Pathfinders' role to arrive on the ground early and establish an intelligence picture.[29] Pathfinder selection, known as 'the cadre', is shorter in duration than other special forces selection courses but every bit as intense, and the six-week course has a very high attrition rate.

On 5 May 2000, the British government decided to send an Operational Reconnaissance and Liaison Team led by Brigadier David Richards to Sierra Leone. Arriving with a small staff and close protection force, the ORLT set itself up in the British High Commission in Freetown. At the same time, several other assets were being warned off for possible deployment. HMS *Illustrious*, HMS *Argyll*, and 42 Commando RM were ordered to sail to the area; four CH-47 Chinook helicopters flew directly to Lungi airport, and numerous RAF C-130 transport aircraft were put on standby. 1 Para, the UK's spearhead battalion, was also given a warning order and told to prepare for a possible operation in Sierra Leone. The CO of 1 Para requested that the Pathfinder Platoon be deployed with his battalion. In Windsor, Soldier P. and his troop were told to be ready to move as well. 'For three days our vehicles sat on the main square. In the end the troop was not deployed with the operation.'

Rich G. and other members of the Pathfinder platoon were on a square shoot jumps course at Brize Norton when they got the word that the platoon could be deploying. Just a few days later, as a member of the lead patrol, he took off in a VC-10 from Brize Norton. Landing at Dakar in Senegal, the paratroopers were loaded onto C-130s for the flight south along the west coast to Sierra Leone. Because the RUF had blocked the road from Freetown to Lungi airport, as soon the plane's wheels hit the tarmac, the paras ran down the ramps and took up fire positions. One of the reasons 1 Para had gotten the job of securing the airport over 42 Commando, who were the amphibious version of the spearhead battalion, was that they could be deployed to West Africa so quickly.

While the evacuation started to get under way, Rich G. and his patrol were picked up and taken to the High Commission in Freetown. As well as delivering a diplomatic bag, they helped secure the building for the next 24 hours until the remainder of the PF Platoon arrived. That afternoon, just around the corner from the High Commission, a group of locals protested outside the home of RUF leader Foday Sankoh. Journalist Janine di Giovanni witnessed what happened next. 'The people were marching for peace but Sankoh's men began firing into the crowd. People began falling around me, and I took cover in an alleyway, with a local teacher named Patrick. Crouched behind a bush, we watched soldiers continue to shoot civilians. Nineteen people died that day.'[30] Rich G. remembers the High Commission 'receiving a few rounds' from what he believed was the RUF leader being attacked. After Sankoh and his soldiers left the scene, the journalist took a huge risk and entered the house. Inside she found documents and notebooks containing information that would later be used in war crimes trials. It tied the RUF, Liberia, and the blood diamond trade to London's Hatton Garden and New York's diamond district. The notebooks also held the names of many African politicians, including Charles Taylor, and many UN officials.[31]

The Pathfinder Platoon were back at the airport the next day. Those eligible civilians in Freetown who knew what horrors were about to descend upon them made their way to Lungi, were packed on to C-130s and flown to Dakar. Just as most people were trying to get as far away from the country as they could, the Pathfinders were about to go deeper into it. Intelligence reports showed a huge force of RUF rebels massing about 70 kilometres to the north.[32] It was believed that the rebels' intentions were to attack the airport as the evacuation was under way, capturing British soldiers and civilians. What the Somalian rebels had done to America in Mogadishu, the RUF would do to the British at Freetown, or so they thought.

Lungi Lol is a tiny village 20 kilometres north of Freetown. It sits astride the main dirt road from the interior of the country; one road in, two roads out to the airport and Freetown. With no air support or artillery covering fire, the Pathfinders' orders were to insert by helicopter, then, acting as an early warning force, hold up any rebel advance for as long as possible.[33] Now fondly known by those who were there as 'Operation Certain Death', the Pathfinder Platoon inserted into the village and set about building defensive positions that would give the RUF a bloody nose if they were to attack.

> We were aware that if we were overrun and captured, that we were probably fucked. The plan was to conduct a fighting withdrawal, break contact, and then escape and evade back to the British lines or one of the small UN outposts along one of the routes. To be fair, we never had any doubt that we could defend the position and repel almost any attack.

The 24–36 hours they were told they would be there, soon turned into a week, then longer still.

While Rich G. and the Pathfinders were ensuring the RUF could not advance unnoticed on the evacuation at Lungi airport, in Freetown Brigadier David Richards was trying to even the odds by cutting the head off the snake. Having been in Sierra Leone twice before, he realised that 'with a little robustness' the forces at his command could make a huge difference. His mandate was to execute an evacuation of civilians and then leave, but 'he saw a chance, took a risk, and changed the fate of the country'.[34] Using tips from locals, British soldiers found and arrested Foday Sankoh.[35] This was a huge victory that boosted the morale of both government forces and the local population; at last someone was standing up to the RUF.

The same day that Sankoh was captured, RUF rebels finally arrived at the Pathfinders' position. 'The night before the contact, hundreds of people from a neighbouring village came into Lungi Lol. They said the rebels were just a few miles away and were intent on attacking the village.' Despite heightened tensions, the platoon carried out its well-tuned night routine.

We carried on as normal. I was one of the last stags with Bob. As it happens, Bob, who joined the platoon about a year before me, was my best friend; we joined up together … We had two codewords for getting the platoon into fire-positions. 'Stand-to' was the normal codeword for routine use at first and last light, whilst 'maximise' meant that something was actually happening. The moon had just gone down and it had gotten really dark when we heard 'maximise, maximise' over the radio. I was on the GPMG so Bob went to wake the guys up, telling them, 'maximise'. It was only an hour to go until morning stand-to and the guys were coming out of deep-sleep. 'Fuck off Bob, you're an hour early you dick,' they muttered. Literally 10 seconds later, it all went off with rounds coming into our positions and the village.

As the Pathfinders got into their positions, the RUF tried to advance but were cut down by accurate and sustained fire. With no night vision goggles they were helped spotting their targets by 51mm illumination mortar rounds. The firefight went on for several hours before the rebels seemed to melt away back into the jungle. The 1 Para QRF arrived at first light and took over their defensive positions, while the Pathfinders sent out two patrols to find and harass the rebels before they could regroup and attack again. The QRF had brought in extra guns and ammo, so Rich G. was given a GPMG for the patrol. 'I had 100 rounds on the gun, and another 1,400 in my backpack.' If the rebels were still looking for a fight, they would get one. 'There was blood, flip flops, and weapons discarded all the way to the neighbouring village.' But after going house to house, no enemy were seen; they had carried their dead and dying back from Lungi Lol, then left.

Four bodies were found in front of their positions, another 10 were later discovered in the jungle, and some have put the total number of RUF dead as high as 30.[36] Rich G. says, 'I saw a couple of the bodies; they weren't boy soldiers. They were young men in their late teens, early twenties. I didn't think anything of their deaths, as they had picked the fight and came off worse.' The next day 1 Para QRF went back to the airport. The Pathfinders were reinforced by a section of 81mm mortars and a small medical team, but the second attack never came; a few days later, they were withdrawn. 42 Commando RM replaced 1 Para who returned to the UK to resume their role as the UK's spearhead battalion.

There would be two further operations in Sierra Leone. Operation *Khukri* secured the release of Major Andy Harrison after he and other unarmed UN observers were trapped by rebels, and Operation *Barras* was authorised after a Royal Irish Regiment patrol were taken prisoner by a militia group called the West Side Boys. The Sierra Leone defence forces were now being trained by British servicemen, with increased help from the UN. The influence of Liberia came to an end with the prosecution of its president Charles Taylor. Sierra Leone was stabilised and has known relative peace ever since. Although Tony Blair deserves credit for the humanitarian intervention that secured a country destroyed in a brutal civil war, it was the actions of Brigadier Richards and the Pathfinders that deserve most of the plaudits. High Commissioner Tony Penfold later wrote, praising the leadership of David Richards.[37] The brigadier would go on to become General Sir David Richards GCB CBE DSO, Chief of the Defence Staff, retiring in 2013. Writing in 2014, he credited the Pathfinders for the success of Operation *Palliser*. 'Without a shadow of a doubt, their heroic actions that memorable night was the key tactical event in what has been held up as a model intervention operation.'[38]

CHAPTER 11

9/11

When I was growing up my father would often talk about the day President John F. Kennedy was assassinated. He remembered exactly what he had been doing, where he was, and often described in some detail the shock he felt. He also explained that it was not only him – his entire generation remembered where they were on 22 November 1963. For our generation of soldiers, the day they will never forget is 11 September 2001.

On that morning, 19 terrorists took control of four commercial airliners shortly after take-off. Three were deliberately flown into the World Trade Center buildings and Pentagon in New York and Washington and the fourth crashed into a Pennsylvania field. By the end of the day, 2,996 people had perished. It was the deadliest terror attack ever, and the world would never be the same again.

Most soldiers I interviewed vividly recall where they were that day. Paul H. was taking part in a Combat Fitness Test in Windsor Great Park in preparation for deployment to Northern Ireland. 'When we got back to Victoria Barracks the battalion held a Drumhead service ... I was really shocked.' Soldier B. had been visiting a school; the attacks took place while he was explaining to the kids what it was like to be a soldier. 'I heard it on the radio as we were driving out of the gates. I immediately knew this was a monumental historical occasion ... and knew it would have global ramifications which would include the UK.' Soldier E. watched the attack take place on television. 'I'd been up the North Tower of the World Trade Center (WTC) in the mid-'90s and had seen how many people worked in those two buildings. I stared in horror as the towers came down, knowing that I was watching thousands of people die.' Rich G. was in Macedonia on Task Force Harvest with the Pathfinder Platoon. 'My patrol had just come back from a five-day task. We were in the Special Forces compound getting ready to redeploy. I was in the TV tent watching Sky News when the first plane hit. I stayed to watch what was going on ... At first I thought it was a tragic accident until the second plane hit.'

Like most soldiers, Rich knew that there would be repercussions for whoever had done this. The scale and enormity of what had happened left most people with a feeling of dread and foreboding. Andrew T. recalls being a co-driver of an ambulance to Tidworth with his unit for pre-deployment training to Kosovo. Like most of the soldiers in the convoy, they got snippets of news headlines on their mobile phones and could not believe what they were reading or hearing.

> When we arrived in Tidworth, and once the vehicles had been parked up, everyone, and I mean everyone, pretty much ran to their respective messes or the Junior Ranks Club … The place was packed, all eyes were focused on the TV screens. There were gasps and grimaces, and then I saw it for the first time. Initially I thought I was watching a disaster movie; then the reality of what was unfolding across the pond hit me.

He recalls some excited banter among some of the younger soldiers.

> They said things like, 'Someone's in the shit for this,' and, 'This is going to lead to war.' I wonder if they shared the same enthusiasm a few years later? … Those of us with experience of the Gulf War, Bosnia, and Northern Ireland were a little bit more reserved and apprehensive of what may come … and we were correct, as many of us spent the next decade plus fighting in the Middle East.

Whether people heard about the attacks over lunch or watched in horror as the second passenger jet slammed into the south tower of the WTC, the effect was the same. It is sometimes easy to be hyperbolic when describing world-changing events. But on 9/11, words were inadequate; there was just utter disbelief that anyone would carry out such a terrible atrocity. Thousands of innocent civilians had been killed as they started their working day, and the most powerful country in the world had seemingly been brought to its knees.

What happened in the United States drew immediate condemnation from all over the world. Mixed with anger and revulsion, there was also unwavering support. Prime Minister Tony Blair pledged that Britain would 'stand full square alongside the US' and other European leaders such as German Chancellor Gerhard Schröder said the acts were 'a declaration of war on the civilized world'. Russian President Vladimir Putin said he would support a tough response to what he called 'barbaric acts'.[1] 11 September 2001 would mark a brief thaw in US–Russian relations, with both countries co-operating in the fight against a common foe.

Like the rest of society, most soldiers were shocked by what they had seen and felt genuine pathos towards the United States. Soldier B. said, 'I felt sorry for the US. No country deserved that… They are our allies.' Andrew T. said, 'I felt extremely sorry for the USA and the people involved… The horrific way in which some met their deaths was disturbing.' Her Majesty Queen Elizabeth II, who expressed 'growing disbelief and total shock',[2] broke royal protocol and allowed 'The Star Spangled Banner' to be played during the Changing of the Guard at Buckingham Palace. Journalist David Graves described the emotional reaction from tourists stranded far from home. 'Standing beyond the palace railings, many of the 5,000 Americans broke down in tears and held their right hands over their heart in salute.'[3]

Scarce by comparison, there were some who were not so sympathetic. Condemnation of the attacks had come from some of America's traditional adversaries: Iran, Libya, and Cuba all condemned the attacks. But Iraq said America had deserved the attack because of its 'crimes against humanity' in the Middle East. And although Palestinian leader Yasser Arafat expressed shock and offered condolences, with several Palestinian terrorist organisations denying responsibility, there were many Palestinians who celebrated 9/11 by firing weapons all over the West Bank.[4]

The legacy of Irish-American support for the Republican cause in Northern Ireland had left many soldiers with a bitter taste in their mouth. When asked if he felt sorry for the US at the time of the attack, Neil S. said, 'Nope, mainly due to their attitude and support of the IRA. But as you get older you realize they didn't deserve this.' Soldier G. held the same view because of the perception that the Irish-American community often turned a blind eye to the atrocities carried out in the name of Irish Republicanism. 'The USA needed to wake up to what was going on ... welcome to the real world.'

As the dust from the rubble of the fallen WTC towers started to settle, the fires at the Pentagon had been extinguished, and the bodies of the brave passengers on Flight 93 were recovered, what had happened on 11 September 2001 started to come to light. Almost immediately, the finger of suspicion was pointed at Osama bin Laden and his Islamic terrorist group, Al Qaeda.

The day after the attacks took place, a unique and unprecedented 'act of solidarity' left the United States with no doubt that it was not alone. After a meeting of NATO ambassadors, the 19 member nations voted to invoke Article 5 of its charter. For the first time since its formation in 1949, the organisation deemed that the 9/11 attacks on the United States 'shall be considered an attack against them all'.[5] Although NATO's Secretary General Lord Robertson said it did not mean that NATO forces would be committed to military action, it sent a clear signal to American military planners, one that would shape the future of any global war on terrorism.

On 14 September, two more events took place that would send the United States and its closest allies to war against the perpetrators of 9/11. Unscripted, standing on the rubble pile of the WTC buildings, now known as Ground Zero, President Bush, with a bullhorn in his right hand and his left arm around a New York firefighter, sent a clear message. 'I can hear you. The rest of the world hears you. And the people who knocked these buildings down will hear all of us soon.'[6] It was just what his country needed to hear. In the first few days following 9/11, there were those who wondered whether George W. Bush had what it takes to lead the country after such a debilitating attack. His words galvanised a nationalistic spirit not felt since Pearl Harbor. His appearance and words from the rubble silenced any doubters – his approval rating reached a record high of 90 per cent.[7]

The same day in Washington, D.C. a Joint Resolution that would have massive implications and far-reaching consequences for years to come passed both chambers of Congress. The Authorization for Use of Military Force (AUMF) would be signed into law on 18 September 2001 and gave President Bush sweeping powers. It authorised him to use all 'necessary and appropriate force against those nations, organizations, or persons he determines planned, authorized, committed, or aided the terrorist attacks that occurred on September 11, 2001'.[8] The authorisation passed 98-0 in the Senate, and 420-1 in the House of Representatives. The only dissenting voice against the AUMF was that of Congresswoman Barbara Lee (D-CA). She was not objecting to the use of force; rather, she opposed the language of the AUMF because it lacked specificity, had no expiration date, and looked very similar to the 1964 Gulf of Tonkin Resolution that had led to American involvement in Cambodia. She rather prophetically foresaw the authorisation being used far beyond what Congress had intended.[9]

Afghanistan was now in the centre of the US military's crosshairs. On 21 September 2001, speaking to a special session of Congress, President Bush gave the Taliban an ultimatum. He demanded that they must hand over all terrorists associated with Osama bin Laden's Al Qaeda terrorist network and close all terrorist training camps immediately. If they did not, he said that they would 'share in their fate'. Speaking to an expectant nation, interrupted by several standing ovations, the president warned of a 'lengthy battle'. He said, 'Tonight we are a country awakened to danger and called to freedom. Our grief has turned to anger, and anger to resolution. Whether we bring our enemies to justice, or bring justice to our enemies, justice will be done.'[10] In the audience, rising to his feet with the cheering members of Congress, was British Prime Minister Tony Blair. His presence left no one in any doubt that whatever was being planned with regards to Afghanistan, Britain and its armed forces would be involved, too.

***

After the Russian withdrawal in 1989, the Afghan people were euphoric. Despite a million dead and over 5.5 million displaced,[11] they had won the war, and most Afghans genuinely believed they would now be able to determine their own destiny. Despite the Soviet withdrawal, the Marxist government in Kabul led by Mohammed Najibullah was able to survive until 1992. Propped up with Russian aid which stopped after the cessation of the Soviet Union, it also survived for so long because of inter-factional fighting in a country awash with both Russian and American weapons. Having beaten the Soviet Union, the various Mujahideen groups could not work together to form a new government. Pashtuns, Hazaras, Tajiks, and Uzbeks all fought each other at one time or another. War with the Soviet Union had ended, but for the Afghan people, there would be no peace.

With both superpowers turning their backs on Afghanistan, the void was filled by outside forces who saw the instability as an opportunity to press their own political and regional ambitions. Iran, Saudi Arabia, and Uzbekistan backed and armed rival militias, but it was Pakistan that interfered in Afghanistan's affairs the most. With the withdrawal of Russian troops, Pakistan's Inter-Services Intelligence Agency looked to build a pan-Islamic coalition that could control the entire region and give Pakistan strategic depth against the threat of its long-term rival, India. They not only wanted the 'green Islamic flag' to fly over Pakistan and Afghanistan, but over the entire central Asian region.[12]

The Taliban rose out of the chaos of two years of civil war. When gunmen at a checkpoint in Kandahar began raping women, some locals sought out a former Mujahideen commander called Mullah Mohammed Omar. Together with 50 Pashtun students, Omar built an organisation that sought to end the suffering of the Afghan people, gain control of the government, and rid the country of its warlords.[13] At first both the Afghan population and some of the other Mujahideen factions welcomed the Taliban's stabilising influence, but under Pakistan's control, it soon showed its true colours. In Bamiyan and Mazar-i-Sharif they massacred thousands. And after taking Kabul, as well as brutally executing former leader Mohammed Najibullah, the Taliban turned Kabul's soccer stadium into a macabre symbol of its new power. 'The Taliban executed people publicly in this stadium. They cut off the hands of those accused of theft. They stoned to death women who were accused of adultery.'[14] By the start of the new millennium, the Taliban controlled 90 per cent of the country and governed under its own brutal interpretation of Sharia Law. Right up until 2001, Pakistan was the major influence on and financial backer of the Taliban. According to several sources, Pakistan provided 80,000–100,000 soldiers who were trained in Pakistan for the Taliban.[15]

General Tommy Franks, commander of Central Command, and his military planners had proposed invading Afghanistan with a conventional force of 60,000 soldiers that he said could be ready in six months. This proposal was immediately rejected by both President Bush and Defense Secretary Donald Rumsfeld. Not only were they worried about repeating past mistakes made by the Soviet Union in Afghanistan and getting bogged down in a protracted Vietnam-like war, but also they were not willing to wait six months for such a large force to be assembled. Rumsfeld snapped at the general when he heard the plan. 'I want men on the ground now.'[16] CIA Director George Tenet proposed the idea of using CIA and Special Forces operators working alongside Afghan fighters of the Northern Alliance.[17] Vice President Dick Cheney and Donald Rumsfeld were not happy that the CIA would be the lead agency. Cheney did not trust the CIA, and this decision started infighting between the CIA and the Department of Defense. Rumsfeld got his way later in the campaign when the president allowed him to direct the war effort.[18]

Operation *Enduring Freedom* began on Sunday, 7 October 2001, less than a month after the 9/11 attacks. American and British aircraft attacked known Taliban command centres and anti-aircraft defences. One of the first targets was the Taliban leader, Mullah Omar. One of his houses in Kandahar was destroyed just minutes after he had left the building. Among the victims of the laser-guided bomb was his 10-year-old son, his stepfather, and several of his bodyguards.[19]

While the airstrikes continued, over 400 CIA and special forces operators joined with the Northern Alliance fighters. Armed with laptop computers and laser target designators, riding on horseback, the Northern Alliance and special forces defeated the Taliban with the help of overwhelming air power, entering the stronghold of Kandahar on 7 December 2001. The quickly assembled force had achieved in two months what the Russians could not in 10 years. On 22 December 2001, Hamid Karzai became acting president of the Islamic Republic of Afghanistan. During the Soviet occupation, Karzai had been a major fundraiser for the Mujahideen. After the Taliban came to power, he initially accepted them as the legal authority. But after he witnessed the excesses being carried out in Afghanistan by Mullah Omar's men, he became a vocal opponent. After his father was killed by Taliban assassins in Pakistan, he then pledged to work with the warlords of the Northern Alliance.

When the 9/11 attacks took place, the United Kingdom was preparing for its largest single deployment since the Gulf War. Exercise *Saif Sareea* ('Swift sword') was a joint-service exercise involving 22,500 personnel in the desert of Oman. The purpose of the training exercise, four years in the planning, was to test the viability of the new Joint Rapid Reaction Force. The concept of the JRRF was to be able to rapidly deploy specialised units from all three branches of the armed forces anywhere around the world at short notice. Fortunately, the exercise would come at exactly the right moment. Some of the equipment needed in any future deployment in the Middle East was now placed by chance in a very strategic position. Ships, aircraft, and some ground vehicles would be left in Oman or deployed directly.

In a statement to the House of Commons on 26 October 2001, Armed Forces Minister Adam Ingram, MP, spoke about the exercise and laid out the government's immediate plans for deploying forces to be used in operations against the Taliban in Afghanistan. Operation *Veritas* would be initially based around the aircraft carrier HMS *Illustrious* and assault ship HMS *Fearless*, an unnamed submarine capable of firing Tomahawk missiles, along with a destroyer, a frigate, and other support vessels, all which would be diverted from Oman. The RAF were involved with support aircraft initially flying out of Diego Garcia, and 400 Marines from 40 Commando would sail on board HMS *Fearless*.[20] The Marines would support special forces operations out of Bagram Air Force Base (AFB) north of the capital, Kabul. On 19 December 2001, Secretary of State for Defence Geoff Hoon announced that the UK had formally offered to lead the International Security Assistance Force (ISAF) to help the new Afghan authorities with security in and around Kabul.[21]

2 Para and supporting elements from 16 Air Assault Brigade started to deploy over the Christmas holiday. Rich G., now a Pathfinder patrol commander, spent New Year's Eve at the Joint Air Mounting Centre at South Cerney before flying out of RAF Brize Norton on New Year's Day 2002. Rich and his fellow paratroopers first flew to Oman for a week before flying to Afghanistan. Because only a few of the RAF's C-130 Hercules transport aircraft were fitted with defensive counter-measures, it took some time to deploy the whole of 2 Para. The surface-to-air missile threat was very real; many of the American-made Stinger missiles that had been supplied to Mujahideen forces fighting the Soviets were still thought to be in circulation.

As well as a shortage of aircraft capable of getting them safely to Bagram AFB, there also appeared to be a shortage of ammunition. When Rich arrived, they made the journey south to Kabul virtually unprotected.

> We weren't issued with any ammo in Oman and were told we'd get it when we arrived. We didn't get it when we landed in Bagram, so they moved the lead company and PF contingent by road from Bagram to Kabul without ammunition. The Bedford driver I was with had one magazine, so I took it off him and rode shotgun in the cab.

After arriving in the diplomatic area of Kabul where the British and American embassies were situated, D Coy took over from the special forces support group (Royal Marines). 'Elements of the Pathfinder Platoon and D Coy did some local patrols to assess the atmospherics over the next few days.' Soon afterwards the remainder of his platoon arrived with their WMIK Land Rovers, and he was given responsibility for two districts of Kabul. He was told to go out and establish communications with the local security forces/police and local leaders.

> As always, we hit the ground running, out on patrols/ops within hours of arrival. Living on 24-hour ration packs and with only what we carried in our bergens. No showers, NAAFI [Navy Army Air Force Institutes] fresh food, or internet. The Coalition nations did nothing until they were fully set up and established with all the comforts of home. It seemed to take weeks before they started contributing to the effort. However, we did benefit from this, as we managed to blag the odd shower at the German base and one of the guys struck up a friendship with a German chef and got us some fresh scoff from time to time. The Finnish contingent even had a sauna in their compound.

It was decided that the rest of the Pathfinder Platoon was now not required and was stood down. After handing over their area of responsibility to another 2 Para platoon, the Pathfinder Platoon was tasked to work with brigade. As well as patrols and recces outside of Kabul, they were involved with 'brigade extraction planning'. Knowing how unstable Afghanistan had been for decades during and after the Soviet occupation, it was determined that there had to be contingency plans in place should the situation in and around Kabul became untenable and troops would need to be withdrawn. In 1842 a British force of 16,000 soldiers and civilians led by Lord Elphinstone was all but wiped out while retreating from Kabul. Plans would be put in place to ensure that history was not going to repeat itself.

In early March, Rich and his men were withdrawn to the UK. 'From my perspective, it was an interesting tour, as I was a patrol commander and our main roll was liaison. It was a little tedious for the rest of the guys as it was a lot of hanging around while I attended meetings.'

By early April 2002, when 2 Para handed over to the Royal Anglians, Kabul and most of Afghanistan was quiet. 2 Para had trained the first 600-strong battalion of the Afghan National Guard troops and had been involved in one of the most politically important football matches ever staged. Inside the national stadium, where public executions had taken place under the Taliban, in front of over 30,000 Afghan people, many of whom had clambered to get into the stadium, Kabul United played a match against a team made up of ISAF soldiers.[22]

***

The events of 11 September 2001 changed the world. Although it was the United States of America that was attacked, many countries felt the far-reaching consequences of that day and would be drawn into a 'war on terrorism' that their soldiers would have to fight. The 9/11 commission presented its findings in July 2004. The 20-month-long bi-partisan inquiry cited 'deep institutional failings' that had led to the tragic events. The report lay blame at virtually every federal agency, including the CIA, FBI, State Department, and Pentagon; a 'failure of imagination' that 'did not grasp the magnitude of a threat that had been gathering over a considerable period of time'.[23] In reality, inter-agency rivalry, a woefully bad security system on US internal flights, and a country distracted by a booming economy and preoccupied with the Monica Lewinsky scandal had allowed Al Qaeda terrorists to move freely and unnoticed into the United States.

Although Osama bin Laden had escaped capture by fleeing into Pakistan on horseback from the Tora Bora cave system in December 2001, the emphasis shifted throughout 2002 from combat to reconstruction and to helping the transitional government of Hamid Karzai. Despite several ground assaults, including Operation *Anaconda* in March 2002, against remaining Taliban and Al Qaeda fighters south of Gardez, the Pentagon actually started moving assets away from Afghanistan to another target in its war on terrorism.[24]

In May 2003, Secretary of Defense Donald Rumsfeld visited Kabul and announced an end to 'major combat'. He said that military commanders 'have concluded that we are at a point where we clearly have moved from major combat activity to a period of stability and reconstruction activities'.[25] The fatal flaw in Rumsfeld's announcement was that no one had told the Taliban or Al Qaeda that the fighting was over.

CHAPTER 12

The Invasion of Iraq

On the afternoon of 11 September 2001, Secretary of Defense Donald Rumsfeld issued orders for his staff to look for evidence of Iraqi involvement in the terrorist attacks that had taken place earlier that morning.[1] Notes taken by a senior policy official during the hours after the attacks clearly show that Rumsfeld's Pentagon had its sights set on Iraq from the start. Rumsfeld was not interested in firing cruise missiles at some abandoned training camp. 'The secretary said his instinct was to hit Saddam Hussein at the same time, not only bin Laden.'[2] With smoke still billowing from the Pentagon, it appears that Rumsfeld had already made his mind up. He is quoted as saying, 'Need to move swiftly ... near term target needs – go massive sweep it all up – things related and not.'[3]

The attacks on 9/11 had given the neoconservatives in the Bush administration the opportunity they had been seeking. President George W. Bush's words to a stunned world that evening gave them the platform they needed. Speaking from the White House, the president said, 'We will make no distinction between terrorists who committed these acts and those who harbour them.'[4] That same night the neocons[1] showed their hand during the first post-9/11 cabinet meeting when Rumsfeld suggested they should invade Iraq.[5] Although it was decided that Saddam would have to wait until the Taliban had been removed in Afghanistan, these comments show that the underlying justification for the 2003 invasion of Iraq was never about Weapons of Mass Destruction (WMDs) or terrorist acts; instead, it was about implementing a regime change.

In Britain, despite telling the public that he had made no decision about supporting any United States-led invasion of Iraq, Tony Blair had in fact promised to commit British troops as early as April 2002. At a meeting at President Bush's private ranch in

---

1 Neoconservatism (shortened to 'neocon') is a political movement that originated among disaffected liberals, in part a reaction to the 1960s counterculture, and resistance to the war in Vietnam. Although neocons started to reject liberal domestic policies as well, it is in foreign policy where they were more reactionary, advocating for the support of Israel, use of military strength abroad, and promoting American influence in the Middle East.

Crawford, Texas, Blair told President Bush, 'Britain will support an American attack on Iraq if Saddam Hussein refuses to accept resumed UN weapons inspections.'[6] Former First Sea Lord Admiral Sir Alan West told the Chilcott Inquiry that he knew months before the decision was announced. 'I was told ... that we would be invading Iraq with America in the beginning of the following year.'[7] The decision had been made in private, but both governments were now actively engaged in a public relations battle to justify military action to Congress, Parliament, and to the public of both countries.

In America, the media were being fed sanitised information from both inside and outside the government. So-called pillars of the media industry, such as the *New York Times*, were left embarrassed; they, and many other mainstream media organisations allowed themselves to be cynically manipulated by anti-Saddam Iraqis, pro-war lobbyists, and neocons within the government. The British media were convinced that Saddam had WMDs, too. Only a few papers, including the *Independent* and *Daily Mirror*, were vocal in their opposition. On 24 September 2002, just a few hours after the government had produced a dossier claiming Saddam Hussein had WMDs, the *Evening Standard* led with this apocryphal headline: '45 minutes from attack'.[8] 'Tony Blair was very convincing ... he had us all believing we were in imminent danger and action was required.' As well as scaremongering, Downing Street's Press Secretary Alistair Campbell and his well-oiled spin-machine ensured most of Britain's media 'meekly fell into line with government propagandists'.[9]

One of the reasons both the British and American public accepted their governments' claims is because there was confirmed evidence that Saddam had used chemical weapons in the past. During 1987–88, Saddam launched chemical attacks against 40 Kurdish villages using deadly mustard, sarin, tabun, and VX gases.[10] The worst of these attacks was against the Kurdish city of Halabja on 16 March 1988, when mustard and nerve gases killed up to 5,000 people, injuring another 10,000.[11] At the time there was a muted response from the international community, with some even claiming that Iran was responsible.[12]

From the moment the Gulf War ended in 1991, Saddam Hussein seemed to be more secure in Baghdad after his troops were forcibly ejected from Kuwait. Because America and its allies had not attempted a regime change then, he erroneously assumed they would not do so now. Consequently, he became more belligerent, not afraid to ignore the rules the world now wanted him to follow. As an insurance against any attempt to topple him in the future, he distributed a large amount of weapons to be secretly stock-piled in the south so loyal followers could conduct a Ba'ath Party led insurgency.[13]

After the implementation of UN-mandated weapons inspections, Saddam deliberately misled inspectors. In 1998, he pushed his luck too far when he refused them entry altogether. The UN responded in usual fashion with immediate condemnation, followed by security council resolutions; however, Saddam's refusal to accept weapons inspectors would have far-reaching consequences. The United States Congress took the unusual decision to vote for the removal of Saddam Hussein as leader of Iraq. The Iraq Liberation Act, which became law on 31 October 1998, declared it should be US policy to 'remove the regime headed by Saddam Hussein from power', replacing it with a democratically elected government.[14] It was this law that President George W. Bush would later use to justify the 2003 invasion.

In October 2002, 13 months after the 9/11 attacks, the United States Congress passed the 'Authorisation for Use of Military Force against Iraq Resolution of 2002'.[15] With the Republican Party in control of the White House and both the Senate and House of Representatives, there was little chance of it being rejected. All but seven Republican lawmakers voted in favour; even 81 congressmen and 29 senators from the Democratic Party voted for the resolution. It passed 296-133 in the House, and 77-23 in the Senate, then was signed into law by President Bush on 16 October 2002. In January 2020, this law was still being used as justification to take action in Iraq.[16]

Unlike the United States, when the House of Commons voted to grant parliamentary approval of the use of British troops in an invasion led by the United States, those same troops were already poised and ready on the Iraqi border. Opposition to British involvement became more vocal as the months went by. Even though Prime Minister Tony Blair did not need Parliament's blessing because of Royal Prerogative, Britain's involvement had become such a political hot potato that he and some members of his cabinet felt they needed parliamentary approval. There was talk of a full-blown Labour rebellion, with party whips reporting that as many as 200 Labour MPs could vote against the government.[17] But in the end, resignation threats by the prime minister and some of his cabinet should he lose persuaded most rebels to vote yes. The gamble paid off; the prime minister had his parliamentary approval to go to war, and the next day, 19 March 2003, the invasion of Iraq began.

Throughout 2002, it was obvious to anyone watching the political manoeuvring and media coverage that British soldiers were going to be involved in any invasion of Iraq. Most retired soldiers I interviewed thought it was the right thing to do. There is no doubt that Saddam had defied UN weapons inspectors and persecuted his own people. Rich G. said, 'I thought Saddam needed to be removed and should have been in 1991.' Andrew T. reflected the mood of most soldiers. 'At the time I think we all believed the government and the media hype. The threat was made to feel very real, and for that reason I was behind the war.' David K. said, 'Saddam Hussein did little to deny these allegations, especially having openly used them against the Kurds in the north.' Simon J. was directly involved in the invasion and one of the first soldiers to cross into Iraq. He echoes the attitude of most soldiers who had deployed. 'We all thought it was the right decision due to WMD and other factors … We all firmly believed in what we were doing.' There were some who thought otherwise. 'I knew from the start that this was a bad idea … there is a huge difference between removing someone who had invaded another country and invading a country in order to change the regime.' Michael P. did not think that either America or Britain was justified in its actions. 'To me it felt that we were just finishing off what Bush senior had left unfinished ... There was just not enough proof and not enough time given by Bush or Blair; they had their own agendas.' Shaun G. thought Saddam should be removed. 'We were convinced he had the nasty stuff and was willing to use it.'

By March 2003, the world was now aware that a powerful coalition force was assembling in the Kuwaiti desert preparing to enter Iraq. Away from public scrutiny, some military commanders voiced disquiet about the preparations for war. The Pentagon's plan, which was now several years old, had originally called for an invasion force of 500,000.[18] This figure was quickly dismissed by Donald Rumsfeld. Both he and the Deputy Defense Secretary, Paul Wolfowitz, 'suggested the war could be done on the cheap',[19] with 'a light, manoeuvrable force that could handily defeat Iraqi President Saddam Hussein'.[20] They are reported as having said, 'Surely 125,000 would suffice ... with a little imagination, you could probably get away with far fewer than that.'[21] Before the 1991 Gulf War, General Schwarzkopf had threatened to resign if he was not given the time or resources he needed to get the job done. For some generals who were close to the planning of the 2003 invasion, there is now deep regret that they had not spoken up when Rumsfeld had put forward such 'dangerously low' troop numbers. One three-star general said, 'I should have had the gumption to confront him ... the right thing to do was to confront, and I didn't. It's something I'll have to live with for a long time.'[22]

The plan that was finally approved would involve around 150,000 troops. The United States, United Kingdom, Australia, and Poland would provide the troops for the invasion, with troops from 37 other countries that formed the 'coalition of the willing' being involved in its aftermath after the fight was over. Rumsfeld and Wolfowitz had gotten their way, but it was not long before both serving and retired military officers started to criticise 'civilian micromanaging' of the invasion plans. More than a dozen officers interviewed by *The Washington Post* less than two weeks after the start of the invasion blamed Rumsfeld for an 'invasion force that is too small, strung out, under protected, undersupplied and awaiting tens of thousands of reinforcements who will not get there for weeks'.[23]

In Britain, getting a substantial fighting force ready for the invasion was also not without issues. The initial plan for any British troop involvement had been based on the assumption that the main British force would enter Iraq from Turkey. However, it soon became apparent that the Turkish government, who were under huge domestic pressure, were not going to allow that to happen. 'The plan had to be rejigged at short notice ... increasing the pressure on time.'[24] This shift to the south not only caused issues with moving everything they would need from Turkey to Kuwait, but it also made it necessary to increase the size of the British force to a three-brigade division.

This dramatic increase in size added to an already enormous logistic task. A much smaller Army and the MOD's Defence Planning Assumptions, based on the future use of smaller, more mobile forces such as the new Joint Rapid Reaction Force, would make the task of equipping a division at short notice almost impossible. British military planners were now under extreme pressure to make sure that the 1st (UK) Division's military assets involved in the invasion were ready to go when the date was set. Some of the problems the planners were to face came directly from the same political masters that were telling them to prepare to go to war. Downing Street feared a leak to the press, so it prevented the MOD from making vital preparations like ordering essential equipment from contractors.[25] This deliberate delay would prove to be fatal.

Most of the soldiers I spoke to talk of 'huge supply issues' leading up to the invasion. Because many Army supply depots and stores were now being run by civilians who were employed nine-to-five, some soldiers found it difficult to prepare their units for deployment outside those hours. Another issue was that because no official decision had been made by the government regarding military action in Iraq, 'the Army was not on a war footing, so civilian-run stores that issued war equipment would not issue it'. Simon J. was a troop corporal with The Queen's Dragoon Guards, who would be one of the lead reconnaissance units of the invasion. He describes the haphazard way his regiment were equipped for such an important task. 'We had to drive in mini-buses to various Territorial Army centres around London to collect Scout Land Rovers. We got them back to Catterick, then proceeded to paint them in desert colours and kit them out.' Units like The Queen's Dragoon Guards would arrive in Kuwait without essential pieces of equipment like desert combats and body armour. 'We literally sent a Land Rover with a trailer back down to a logistics hub somewhere near Kuwait City. Ironically, when driving into the Royal Logistics Corps camp the gate sentries were all wearing brand-new desert combats and the latest body armour.' Michael P. deployed to Kuwait with the Irish Guards as a company medic. He says, 'Equipment wise it was a joke.' Any uniform he took with him he had 'acquired', and for the whole time he was in Iraq, he had no body armour plates. Even special forces high-readiness units like the Pathfinders who were 'deployed with almost everything we needed' had some problems. After they had been issued with 'a new night sight for the snipers' rifles' it was discovered that 'no one in theatre had any batteries for them.'

After the invasion, some of the issues were quickly rectified, but the logistics supply system was often found to be wanting throughout Operation *Telic*. 'Post-invasion logistics was a joke. There was not enough body armour and what we had was sub-standard. We were still wearing desert combats that were issued during the first Gulf War.' Although the clothing shortage was an issue, it was communications that concerned Soldier G. the most. The Clansman radio system had been an ongoing problem in Kosovo and on Exercise *Saif Sareea II*. The issue in Kosovo had been negated by soldiers' use of personal mobile phones, but in the Omani desert there was no mobile phone coverage. 'Unable to communicate by radio, tank crews frequently had to pull up in the middle of manoeuvres and check their orders with each other.'[26]

On one patrol in southern Iraq, Soldier G. was tasked with delivering new HF radios to the Australian detachment and the Iraqi border police. 'This was the same system as the Aussies used for their ranches and with the Flying Doctors ... Each border station was issued a base station and they had a smaller version in their patrol cars ... They could talk from North Maysan all the way down to the southern Iraqi coast', a distance of 200km. After delivering these 'state-of-the-art' radios to the Iraqi border police, Soldier G. had to hit his Clansman radio's tuning unit on the outside of the vehicle with a plastic mallet to make it work; the sad irony was not lost on him.

Another problem for British commanders was the issue of what should happen after the invasion and Saddam Hussein had been removed. Known as 'Phase Four',[27] being able to manage and maintain peace in a devastated country the size of Iraq had many planners concerned that they would not have the numbers or resources. During the planning of the invasion, British generals raised the issue of what would happen. General Mike Jackson, Commander-in-Chief (Land Forces), and his colleagues frequently aired their views. 'Within meetings of the Chiefs of Staff, I voiced my concern that management of the post-conflict period was essential to the success of the operation ... In our discussion it became clear that the American State Department had done plenty of planning for Phase Four, and we placed our confidence in this.'[28]

In October 2002, Michael P. was with other soldiers of his battalion at Hannover airport about to return to the United Kingdom to help cover the impending fireman's strike. 'We were seated on the plane when one of the crew said, "Can the Irish Guards put up their hands?" ... We were told to get off the plane and pick up our stuff.' They were soon informed that they would heading to the Middle East instead of the UK.

Stuart B. was a sergeant, mortar section commander, with 3 Para, based in Colchester, when the battalion was told it would be involved.

> The battalion deployed on exercise to a cold, wintery Brecon to prepare for the inevitable. I remember the main topic of conversation being about the anthrax injection we were all supposed to have ... Initially our OC said if we didn't want it, we weren't required to have it. After a visit from the CO to our company location the OC changed his mind and told us we must all have it. Many of us were none too pleased ... One of the lads in my platoon had a father who was a naval surgeon. We asked him to ask his old man what he should do, on the basis that a father would not want his son taking anything unsafe. He advised his son to have the jab, so the whole platoon followed this advice.

Anthrax and preparing to go to war were not the only things on his mind. On 7 March 2003, in the Kuwaiti desert, he was told that he was now a father.

> I was called to the RSM's tent … he informed me my wife had given birth and I was given a mobile phone to call her. He was 6lb 2oz, healthy, and all was good with wife and son … I remember telling my wife before I deployed that I was sorry but I had to go to Iraq and had no chance of staying on the rear party back in the UK. In all honesty If I had pushed for it I could have probably got out of it due to the impending birth, but there was no way I was going to miss something that I'd waited my whole career for. My wife was very good as always and understood my feelings. She knew the Reg came first.

In January 2003, Rich G. was trying to fulfil a lifelong dream of passing selection for the Special Air Service. 'I was on winter selection when the OC of the Pathfinder platoon called me and asked me to come off selection and return to the platoon to deploy.' This was mid-January; he was in Kuwait by the end of the month.

As expected, the invasion of Iraq started with an air assault. The initial plan had been to start by taking out the top 55 men in the Iraqi leadership with a massive 'decapitation' strike. But at the last minute this plan was changed when the CIA received information of Saddam Hussein's whereabouts. On 19 March 2003, stealth bombs and cruise missiles hit the house of Saddam Hussein's daughter, but the information had been inaccurate. Not only was Saddam still alive, but because the original attack had been cancelled, the Iraqi leadership was still completely intact.[29] This would be the first of many similar intelligence blunders.

The allied invasion plan differed from that of the Gulf War in 1991 in so much as there would be no prolonged gap between the air campaign and the ground invasion. The use of ground forces would begin almost immediately as the Iraqi defence infrastructure was being systematically dismantled from the air. The ground plan was for the US Army's V Corps to enter Iraq and head north towards Baghdad through the desert to the west of the Euphrates River. The US Marine Corps would move through the more inhabited areas east of the river towards Nasiriya and head north to Baghdad parallel to the V Corps line of advance. The 1st (UK) Division, under the command of Major-General Robin Brimms and with support from US Marine Corps troops, would secure Iraq's second city, Basra. General Brimms had three fighting brigades under his command: 7th Armoured Brigade, 16 Air Assault Brigade, and 3 Commando Brigade.

The morning after the attempted strike on Saddam Hussein, the forward elements of the 1st (UK) Division crossed the Kuwaiti border into Iraq. 'I was a Troop Corporal in 2nd Troop, B Squadron, Queen's Dragoon Guards … There was a big berm made of earth that separated Kuwait and Iraq on its border. They blew holes in it and cleared the minefields which I then led the squadron through.' 16 Air Assault and 7th Armoured Brigades were tasked with securing the strategically important Rumaila oil field. There were fears that retreating Iraqi troops would ignite the well heads as had happened during the 1991 Gulf War in Kuwait. Of the 500 oil wells rigged with explosives, only nine were set alight by retreating Iraqi soldiers.[30] Expecting a prolonged air campaign, it was the quick movement of ground forces that caught the Iraqi Army by surprise and prevented another ecological disaster. Along with US Marine Corps troops, Stuart B. and 3 Para moved quickly.

> From miles away we could see the oil fields burning, large plumes of smoke raising high into the sky. The USMC were to take us as far as the Rumaila Bridge where we would conduct a relief in place, then we would push on and secure the oil fields while the USMC were re-tasked elsewhere. A Coy were lead Company and we got to the bridge with little fuss. There were mine fields either side of the roads in various locations but no sign of enemy troops … The USMC had Abrams tanks and all sorts of amphibious vehicles, we had our normal Land Rovers, Pinzgauer, and 4 Tonners. Quite comical really.

It had been predicted that most Iraqi soldiers would offer very little resistance. Donald Rumsfeld was forecasting as much; his planning and strategy had depended upon that assumption. 'There will be Iraqis who offer not only to help us but to help liberate the country and to free the Iraqi people.'[31] As British soldiers moved into southern Iraq, there were the first signs that Rumsfeld might be right. 'It was around this time we started to see young fighting-aged males in groups of four to five walk close by. Dressed in civis they had clearly removed all uniforms and weapons and had no intention of fighting. Nothing came of it and we left them to go on their way.' Both British and American troops would soon find out that not all Iraqis were willing to meekly surrender.

Rich G., who had swapped a freezing winter for the Iraqi desert with his Pathfinder Platoon, was involved from the start.

> The PF plan/mission changed several times before the invasion and as we crossed the border into Iraq a couple of patrols were sent on the 'famous' task to Qalat Sikar airfield. I was tasked with leading half the platoon (3 patrols) to push north towards the Euphrates and get eyes on the road between Nasiriyah and Basra then interdict any significant enemy movement between the two cities. The area that we tried to cross into was extremely difficult with the vehicles and we were prevented moving north by the canals and railway. Most of the bridges had been dropped and the ramps onto the railway line had been dug out on the northern side; we could get onto the rail line, but couldn't find a place to get the vehicles off and go north towards the river. We canned this task and set up an OP screen to cover this area and report on enemy movement.

At the Rumaila Bridge, Stuart B.'s mortar section was soon in action as 3 Para carried out an operation to cross the river on a damaged bridge.

> We supported the operation with deception fire missions firing illumination rounds in depth. The bridge was taken safely and A Coy pushed over and secured the other bank … the lead Platoon from A Coy identified possible enemy positions further up the road into the oil fields. A Coy were given permission to carry out a quick attack. I deployed my mortar line over the other side of the bridge to give us greater range into the oil fields. We set up on a quick action

and waited. Fire missions were sent by our MFCs [mortar fire controllers] and we engaged … It was the first time 3 Para mortars had fired in anger since the Falklands war and I felt quite privileged. We fired in the region of 180 rounds … A Coy carried out the quick attack and I believe the enemy withdrew. We then moved to another mortar line as we slowly pushed into the oil fields.

Although many Iraqi conscripts were either surrendering or just laying down their arms and heading home, many were not, and decided to fight.

It was not long before tragic news reached soldiers' ears; once again British soldiers had died and been injured because of friendly fire. D Squadron, Household Cavalry Regiment, were deployed on Operation *Telic* as reconnaissance troops for 16 Air Assault Brigade. The squadron – whose job was to scout ahead of the brigade, identify enemy positions, and call in artillery, air power and ground forces – was making their way north towards Basra when they came into contact with Iraqi armour. Mick Flynn, who was later awarded the Conspicuous Gallantry Cross for his actions, described what happened.

> I could hear the A-10s above so I scanned between the berms waiting to see a fireball when the tanks were hit. But there was nothing. What were the pilots firing at? Suddenly I felt the pit of my stomach drop away. I looked to my right where I could see a pair of 2 Troop Scimitars about two clicks away. Smoke was rising from that location then frantic calls on the net. 'This is Whisky two two; we're being engaged by A-10s! Check Fire! Check Fire! Check Fire!' I could see men scrambling out of the vehicles, others trying to help. It was total devastation.[32]

Two Idaho Air National Guard A-10 aircraft had mistakenly fired at a group of Household Cavalry Scimitar and Spartan CVR(T) vehicles. Lance Corporal of Horse Matty Hull, the commander of one of the vehicles, was killed with four others injured.[33] Trooper Chris Finney was awarded the George Cross for his brave action in rescuing a fellow crew member from the burning vehicle while being fired upon and injured by the A-10s when they came around for a second run. The pilots were not on the same radio frequency as D Squadron or the US Forward Air Controllers attached to the squadron and were oblivious to the frantic calls of 'Check Fire!'

Reactions from soldiers after the incident were mixed. There was initially no time to grieve or for recriminations; they still had a battle to win. Most soldiers I spoke to about the incident said their first emotion was profound sadness and there was very little anger towards the Americans. Mick Flynn said, 'The Americans were just as devastated when they heard of Matty Hull's death. Even in the age of advancing technology, war is chaos at times. In combat, fratricide still happens. The thing is to learn from the mistakes and make sure they never happen again.'[34]

The problem was that it appeared that lessons were not being learnt. As happened in the 1991 Gulf War, yet again it was British soldiers being killed by American A-10 pilots. Soldier E. said he did not blame the Americans either, but he was not shy in saying whom he did blame.

> Blue on blue happens in war, we all know that risk, but you would have thought by 2003 the MOD would have been able to issue front-line troops a better Friend or Foe indicator than a large dayglo orange panel. American troops all had an IFF tracker, a transponder that clearly signals to an aircraft when you are a friendly callsign. It's disgusting that recce soldiers who were in close contact with the enemy were not given IFF equipment. How many times does this need to happen?

In 1992, the MOD was warned that front-line vehicles needed IFF, but it took 10 years just for a policy paper on combat identification to be published.[35] And just weeks before the Iraq invasion, Lieutenant Colonel Andrew Larpent, former commanding officer of the 3rd Battalion, Royal Regiment of Fusiliers, who lost nine soldiers to friendly fire in 1991, tragically predicted that it would happen again.[36] He went as far as to suggest 'that British forces should not be sent unless a system was introduced to prevent accidental attacks by American aircraft'.[37]

3 Para were making steady progress into the oil fields. Every time the vehicles stopped, Stuart B.'s mortar section got out and dug shell scrapes to ensure there was cover if they came under direct fire from enemy artillery.

> Rumours of an Iraqi D30 gun line came down the chain of command and were soon to prove correct. C Company were targeted as was our mortar line. The fire wasn't accurate and the nearest rounds landed around 300m away. This enemy fire continued over the next 24 hours. The LEWT [Light Electronics Warfare Team] team identified a possible location so we deployed to a new mortar line with all three sections coming together, providing nine barrels in total. We bedded in, then carried out a harassing, searching fire mission which enables the mortars to engage a complete grid square, firing on different firing information until the grid square has been covered. It was during this mission that the rain came.

On 25 March 2003, most of the Tigris and Euphrates valleys in Iraq were hit by a severe weather system that would last several days. A debilitating sandstorm was to hinder US forces closing in on Baghdad, and in the south the same weather system produced huge amounts of rain.

> The now famous storm came hard and fast and the mortar line was soon flooded. The water was so high it sat just below the mortar sight. We ceased fire and tried to make our way back to our three original section mortar lines. We managed to get about three of the Pinzgauer vehicles off the mortar line and on to the canal bank but the rest were stuck in the thick mud. We worked for hours recovering the vehicles and finally help came from the Household Cavalry Regiment attached to the battalion. They pulled us out with their CVR(T) and we went on our way, tired, wet, and cold.

Despite the thick mud and bad weather, the threat from Iraqi artillery was still very real.

> The next day we were engaged again by the D30s. At the same time a pair of enemy forward observers were identified on a motorcycle; as soon as they extracted the firing stopped. One of the platoons from A Company planned to set up an ambush on the enemy forward observers. My mortar line moved forward to ensure we could cover the ambush site and beyond. We were placed way too far forward and had to provide our own security. Feeling like we were

well into enemy-held ground we spent a sleepless night waiting for the ambush. Right on time the two enemy observers rode straight into the ambush and were swiftly dealt with. Maps were recovered from the enemy dead and the grid of the enemy artillery gun line was passed up the chain of command. A-10s were then tasked to destroy it. It's great when all goes to plan. No mortar support was required. We then extracted back and reoccupied our original mortar line.

Once 16 Air Assault Brigade had captured the Rumaila oil fields and the bridge over the Al Hamra canal was open, Rich G.'s Pathfinder Platoon passed through 3 Para's positions and headed north up to the Euphrates towards Chibayish about 25km in front of their own troops.

We spent about six days in the area. Moving up to the river at night to observe and set up ambushes, pulling back to a lay-up position during the day. We were then re-tasked back to the oil fields to resupply and mission plan for the next task. This task (two patrols) was to watch and interdict the road between Amarah and Nasiriyah. The Americans were worried about Chemical Ali's Division moving down the road, re-enforcing Nasiriyah and cutting off the US move towards Baghdad.

Two patrols with four WMIK Land Rovers in four Chinook helicopters were inserted at last light 80km behind enemy lines.

We flew in two pairs conducting several dummy drops before finally off-loading both patrols 35km from the target area. We had to insert this far back due to enemy positions in the area. We inserted through the night and had eyes on the road by first light. We spent six days on target watching the road and reporting on activity (or lack of), moving position before first light and after last light each day. During this time the US entered the outskirts of Baghdad. After a couple of days I decided to patrol the area (maintaining eyes on the road) to meet the locals and gauge the atmospherics for future ops … We were also tasked to find a possible command and control post. EW had located a strong electronic signal in the area and we went to find and destroy it. We got close to the area, but found nothing and snapped the half shaft on one of the vehicles, losing four wheel drive. We were eventually picked up off the task and flown back to 16AAB HQ for a debrief and resupply.

On 21 March 2003, just two days after the start of the invasion, British troops had arrived at the outskirts of Basra. It is widely reported that lead elements of the 1st (UK) Division met immediate resistance from the Iraqi Army's 51st Division and units of the *Fedayeen Saddam*, a paramilitary group loyal to Saddam Hussein and the Ba'ath Party.[38] Robert C. was in one of those lead elements with The Queen's Dragoon Guards.

After the initial invasion and advance into southern Iraq, we moved quickly to the outskirts of Basra. We found it completely undefended and it's my opinion that it could have been taken much earlier if we had been given permission to press on. Elements of the QDG had advanced into the city where it was relatively peaceful, but they were soon ordered to withdraw back across the river. It then took two weeks of fighting to take the city.

BBC correspondent David Willis was confidently reporting the fall of Basra from inside the city on 22 March. 'Coming into Basra as part of a massive military convoy,

I encountered a stream of young men, dressed in what appeared to be Iraqi army uniforms, applauding the US marines as they swept past in tanks ... US and British marines seem confident that they have secured Iraq's second largest city.'[39]

At first British commanders tried to negotiate with Iraqi troops in Basra. They offered for them to join the Coalition to provide security for the city if they surrendered. But when units started to probe the outskirts of the city, they came under heavy fire. Iraqi forces in Basra were commanded by General Ali Hassan al-Majid. 'Chemical Ali', as he was known, one of Saddam Hussein's most brutal henchmen, was determined to ensure there would be no easy victory for the British. Captured soldiers taken during the early stages of the fighting in Basra said that regular Iraqi soldiers wanted to surrender but were being forced to fight by the *Fedayeen* and Chemical Ali's secret police. Some soldiers whose families were still inside the city were being threatened with violence to their families if they did not fight.

General Brimms and 7th Armoured Brigade commander, Brigadier Graham Binns, both came to the conclusion that any forced entry into Basra would destroy the city, cause countless civilian deaths, and in all probability lead to mass casualties of their own troops. So the decision was taken to encircle Basra and allow civilians to leave while MI6 agents tried to incite a rebellion against Chemical Ali and the *Fedayeen*.[40]

There was now pressure coming from inside the United States military 'to encourage the British to actually take Basra at an earlier date than they wanted to do so'.[41] The Pentagon claimed that British caution made Saddam and his army look strong, while in reality they had targeted Basra to 'yield immediate photogenic results or demonstrations of the liberation of the country from its current regime'.[42] But General Brimms was not interested in appeasing US military officials' desire for a photo opportunity, at the expense of the strategically important city, Iraqi civilians, or his own soldiers. He would not be swayed from his cautious approach. Instead, he would bide his time and tighten his grip on the city by conducting raids designed to gauge the enemy's strength.

Chemical Ali and the *Fedayeen* were desperate to lure the British Army into Basra; they wanted to fight a guerrilla war, making British soldiers go from street to street inside Basra's old city where they believed they could inflict a huge blow upon the invaders. Frustration grew as the British refused to take the bait. On 26 March, a convoy of about 120 T-55 Iraqi tanks heading south out of Basra was spotted by troops encircling the city. Dispersed during the night by Coalition artillery and air support, the next day 14 of the tanks reformed and were destroyed by Challenger 2 tanks of the Royal Scots Dragoon Guards. One officer described the engagement as like 'the bicycle against the motor car'. Trying to understand the logic behind this futile attack, the commander of the UK's forces in Iraq, Air Marshal Brian Burridge, had his own theory. 'Iraqi soldiers in Basra were being forced by Saddam Hussein's security forces to get into their tanks and attack the encircling British forces ... Iraqi troops appeared to have been coerced by Ba'ath Party militias in the city to fight.' He went on to say that there was evidence of 'exemplar executions' to terrify the conscripts.[43]

Although British tactics appeared to be working, as the stranglehold on Basra became tighter every day, there were British casualties. There had already been a large loss of life in two separate helicopter crashes that claimed the lives of 14 British servicemen, and both crew members of a British Tornado were killed when their aircraft was shot down by an American Patriot missile while returning from a bombing raid over Baghdad.[44] Two Royal Engineers, Staff Sergeant Simon Cullingworth and Sapper Luke Allsopp, were brutally murdered after their convoy was ambushed,[45] and Lance Corporal Barry Stephen, Black Watch, died after 'a rocket-propelled grenade exploded near his armoured vehicle'.[46]

There was another tragic case of fratricide, but this time it was between two British Challenger 2 tanks. Corporal Stephen Allbutt and Trooper David Clarke, Queen's Royal Lancers, were killed when their Challenger 2 tank was hit by a high explosive (HESH) round fired from a Challenger 2 of the Royal Tank Regiment. Although the Board of Inquiry, held over a year later,[47] listed a catalogue of reasons why the tragedy happened, not one individual was blamed. But in 2007, the Oxfordshire Assistant Deputy Coroner accused an officer in the Black Watch of 'failing to pass on vital information to his men' – that there were friendly tanks near their position – then 'lying to cover up his blunder'.[48] Although the family of Corporal Allbutt called for the officer to resign, like many families of soldiers killed in Iraq, their focus of anger was the Ministry of Defence. Whether anyone was to blame in the fog of war is irrelevant. If the MOD had heeded warnings after the Gulf War in 1991, all British vehicles would have had some form of friend-or-foe identification system that would have avoided this tragedy and taken human error, fatigue, and communications failures out of the equation.

General Brimms used pinpoint airstrikes against the Ba'ath Party HQ, the *Fedayeen*, radio transmitters, and other strategic targets to pile the pressure on the city's desperate defenders. On 5 April, one such attack took place in the Al-Tuwaisi district, a residential area in downtown Basra. The target was Chemical Ali. The United States-run operation dropped a guided bomb onto the targeted building, destroying the two neighbouring houses as well. This resulted in the deaths of 17 civilians while they slept. General Al-Majid was not in the building – another example of poorly gathered intelligence, resulting in one of the worse cases of collateral damage of the war. But both in Basra and around the world, it was being reported that Chemical Ali had been killed.[49] Realising the effect this news may have on the city's beleaguered defenders, the Coalition forces were not in a hurry to correct the media's mistake.

Throughout the next day, around the city it was being reported that Iraqi troops were now melting away, losing their weapons, taking off their uniforms, and disappearing into Basra's civilian population. That afternoon, Brigadier Binns briefed his battle group commanders on two raids that were being planned for the following day. He instructed them to 'Knock on the door, if the door opens, keep going.'[50] The next morning, the doors did indeed open. Once the lead elements of the battle groups had breached the outer defences, they were able to race to the centre of the city unopposed. When Brigadier Binns heard that the Royal Scots Dragoon Guards were in the centre of Basra, he ordered in the entire brigade.[51]

British tactics had been vindicated. British soldiers now controlled most of Basra, and it had not turned into a complete bloodbath. Lieutenant-General James Conway, Commander of the 1st Marine Expeditionary Force, was one American general who was not critical of British tactics, impressed with what General Brimms had achieved. 'We had a great level of satisfaction because, I think he played it just about right.'[52] The only thing left to do before security in Basra could be guaranteed was to ensure that die-hard *Fedayeen* soldiers would not be a threat, and for that General Brimms turned to 3 Para.

After the oil fields had been secured, Stuart B. and 3 Para were moved to a gas and oil separation plant. They spent several days there where they rested and were resupplied. The battalion were then suddenly tasked to move 50km to Basra, where the previous day armoured infantry and tanks had taken most of the town.

> The armour had set up defensive locations around the city. Intel reports said many of the enemy had retreated into the old town whose streets were too narrow for the armour to operate in. 3 Para's task was to clear the old town, house by house. Around 400 *Fedayeen* were reported to be in control of the old town so a tough fight was to be expected. As the battalion planned through the night to take the old town, British Intelligence agencies dropped thousands of leaflets by air stating that a battalion of British paratroopers were going to enter and clear the old town so the enemy were advised to give up their weapons. The following day at first light we started the operation. The tankies looked on in surprise as the battalion drove into Basra in our soft skin vehicles, straight up the same road they had to fight up the night before. I set up my mortar line in the grounds of the deserted Basra University. We had the range to cover the whole of the old town. The battalion were up for a fight and carried as much ammo as possible. Slowly street by street was cleared with no *Fedayeen* encountered. They had taken the advice given by the leaflets, upped sticks, and buggered off. Looking back it was probably a good job as we would have lost many men had we been required to fight. The lads moved back to their company vehicles disappointed, tired, and dehydrated, but alive.

On 9 April 2003, a large statue of Saddam Hussein was pulled down by American soldiers and hundreds of jubilant Iraqis in Firdos Square, Baghdad. As the statue fell, civilians jumped on the fallen effigy hitting it with their shoes, sticks, and anything they could lay their hands on. It was a moment the Coalition forces wanted to show the world: Iraqis celebrating their newfound freedom. But with Saddam Hussein still on the run, and no sign of WMDs, the war in Iraq was far from over. Regardless, the United States declared victory over Iraq on 14 April, and on 1 May, President Bush gave his infamous and controversial 'Mission Accomplished' speech. Although he never said the words, a huge banner stretched across the bridge of the aircraft carrier USS *Abraham Lincoln* acted as a backdrop. Announcing an end to major combat operations, in hindsight, was a huge mistake. His victory speech was premature and did not reflect what was happening in Iraq. Critics of Bush would use this moment as an example of how unprepared his administration was for a war it should have never gotten into in the first place.

Secretary of State Colin Powell had warned President Bush of the dangers of going into Iraq. He'd said to the president, while trying to convince him to go back to the United Nations for a resolution, 'Iraq is like a piece of crystal. You're going to shatter it, it's going to be in pieces all over the place and you're going to have to put it back together. And you're going to need help to do that.'[53] Just how shattered and broken Iraq really was would soon become apparent.

In both Baghdad and Basra, scenes of joy were followed by mass looting. Iraqis who had been used to obeying the authority of Saddam's regime now went wild. They stole anything they could get their hands on; nothing was left unbroken. Both British and American soldiers stood by and allowed it to continue, unsure what they should do. But it soon became apparent that the looting was so widespread that the infrastructure of the country was breaking down. In Basra, the looting was so bad, trying to convince essential government workers to return to their jobs was impossible because they could not be paid. Ministry offices had been ransacked with most employment records destroyed.[54]

President Bush appointed Paul Bremer as special envoy (de facto president) of Iraq. On arrival he had foolishly suggested to the media that looters be shot, and his first formal decision was just as controversial. Coalition Provisional Authority Directive No. 1 called for de-Ba'athification. As had happened in Germany to the Nazis after World War II, all Ba'ath Party members would be investigated. He was advised that by nightfall 50,000 people would be driven underground. The Sunnis, who had occupied positions of responsibility in both local and national government, suddenly had no voice, and there was no one to replace them, creating a power vacuum. Bremer's next move would also have long-lasting ramifications.

The security situation in Basra was aided by Iraqi police and soldiers maintaining law and order. The newly formed 'Basra River Patrol' was a start but had to be disbanded when Directive No. 2 was published on 23 May 2003. Bremer took it upon himself, without White House approval, to order the disbandment of the Iraqi Army. Now hundreds of thousands of disgruntled Sunni and Shia soldiers were going home with their weapons. Attacks on Coalition forces started within 72 hours.[55]

Donald Rumsfeld had convinced President Bush to hand over 'Phase Four' to the Pentagon. All the work done by the State Department in preparation for a post-war Iraq was put to one side. The internal feud and power struggle between the State Department and the Pentagon began to have real-time implications. The Rumsfeld plan was simple: after hostilities, hand over leadership to Iraqi dissident Ahmed Chalabi, then start bringing US soldiers home. The problem was that the

Iraqi people did not accept Chalabi. Suddenly there was now no plan, a massive power vacuum, and soldiers expecting to go home soon.

By May 2003, British soldiers involved in the invasion did start to go home, and were being replaced. After Basra had fallen, Michael P. and the Irish Guards moved back to Kuwait. They had lost two men during the final operation to take Basra; Lance Corporal Ian Malone and Piper Christopher Muzvuru were killed in action by enemy fire. The fact that only three soldiers were killed during the operation to take Basra was of no consequence to the Irish Guards; they felt their loss deeply as they headed back to Germany.

> They moved us over the border into Kuwait for a week to deflate which was frustrating ... then we moved on to Doha for our flight out ... Our return journey to Munster was uneventful, but we all felt that we were being sneaked back in under the cover of darkness. As we passed by the married quarters we could see that they had all strung out messages of welcome. But since it was 2.30 a.m. we figured they would all be in bed. As our transport pulled into Oxford barracks they were all waiting for us which was quite emotional to say the least.

After 3 Para cleared Basra's old town, they were moved to an abandoned Iraqi airfield. After a few days' rest each company was allocated an area of responsibility. Stuart B.'s support company was deployed to the Iran/Iraq border to conduct patrols.

> We soon realised we were patrolling old battle grounds of the Iran/Iraq war. There were old defensive positions everywhere with empty shells and live mines scattered around. It was quite interesting looking around these old positions but we didn't venture far from the road ... After a few weeks around the border I was called in to see the Coy OC. He informed me that my wife's mother was not well and my wife had been travelling from Colchester to Cornwall with our young son on a regular basis and maybe I should return home to help out. The war was over and I returned home to find out my wife's mother was dying of cancer. On one hand it was great to see my wife and my son for the first time but unfortunately I was too late to say my goodbyes to my mother-in-law.

After being extracted from his operation behind enemy lines, Rich G. and his Pathfinder patrol were resupplied and back on the road within 24 hours.

> The platoon was tasked to drive north to Amarah Airfield to prove the route and report back on what we found. We were the first British troops into Amarah, secured the airfield, and conducted local patrols to gauge atmospherics. The locals were very friendly and pleased to see us. There was widespread looting and revenge killings across the city. A number of local groups set up road blocks to secure their neighbourhoods, utility buildings and the hospital. The brigade moved up in the next 48 hours and PF identified an old barracks (close to the airport) for Brigade HQ.

Richard flew back to the United Kingdom in mid-May. The 'atmospherics' he found in Amarah with 'friendly locals' were about to change.

Andrew T., a Royal Army Medical Corps combat medic, had volunteered for deployment on the initial invasion but was sent on Operation *Telic 2* instead. He was attached to C Company, 1st Battalion, The King's Regiment. 'By the time I arrived in Kuwait at the end of May 2003, the war in Iraq was declared over and combat operations had ceased.' But if Andrew and his colleagues thought he was going to have a quiet tour of duty, then, like every other British soldier deployed to southern Iraq on Operation *Telic 2*, they were in for a shock.

> We spent two weeks in a tented camp in the Kuwaiti desert, acclimatising, training, and zeroing our weapon systems. Heat casualties were commonplace, and I made plenty of trips to the UK field medical unit with casualties. Eventually the time came to move forward to our new base in Basra. We boarded coaches and headed to Camp Cherokee, an Iraqi naval base on the edge of the Shat Al Arab river. We spent a few days here, the infrastructure was non-existent, no toilets, showers, etc. There was one working ceiling fan which we all sought solace under from the oppressive heat. We made the best of it. Eventually our armoured vehicles arrived. Warriors mainly; I had an AFV432 ambulance variant, but it was already broken before it arrived. In fact, it was never repaired during the entire tour, and I spent the whole time following the AFVs in a normal battlefield ambulance. This was full of bullet holes and had smashed windows. But the engine started, and the wheels turned around, so it was classed as road worthy.

In the marshland of southern Iraq where Shia Arab tribes had lived among fertile lands since biblical times, there was hatred and a deep resentment. They hated Saddam's Ba'athist regime that had destroyed their ancient homeland with a series of dams, turning their Garden of Eden into a stagnant wasteland in the early 1990s. But there was also a deep resentment for the British. Long before Saddam came to power, British colonialists had looked to turn the southern marshes into a profitable food source for the empire.[56] As late as the 1950s the United Kingdom had worked with the pro-British Iraqi government with plans to dam off the marshes, plunder its natural resources, and bring the Marsh Arabs to heel. In 1992, after British and American Coalition forces did not support or come to the aid of the Shia uprising, that resentment was complete. Politicians or military leaders who thought the people of towns and cities in southern Iraq, such as Majar al-Kabir, were going to greet British soldiers as liberators showed no understanding of the country's history.

The tragic events that took place in Majar al-Kabir on 24 June 2003 mark the start of the insurgency in southern Iraq. Keen to remove as many weapons from the town as possible, British paratroopers had angered the 80,000 inhabitants with aggressive house-to-house searches using dogs. The town's tribal chiefs and officers of 1 Para came to an agreement to halt the house searches. But a misunderstanding about what they had actually agreed to would have fatal consequences. The Iraqi leaders thought the agreement meant an end to British soldiers on the streets, but 1 Para had agreed to stop house searches; it was not about to stop patrolling altogether.

What happened on 24 June has been covered by many writers and journalists, so repeating details of that day would be a redundant exercise. Some writers have rightly laid blame at the feet of those who put soldiers into harm's way without adequate ammunition and reliable communications. But some have criticised individual soldiers on the ground, one in particular accusing a paratrooper (who was later decorated for his bravery) of 'recklessness'.[57] Non-combatants and civilians who choose to write about such tragic events need to remember that soldiers who have to make life-and-death split-second decisions do not have the luxury of hindsight and have to live with the consequences of their actions for the rest of their lives.

About 120 miles south, in Basra, news that something terrible had happened in Majar al-Kabir was starting to filter down the chain of command. Andrew T. and men of The King's Regiment were about to be thrown into combat.

> Around mid-morning the OC came and called us all together. 1 Para was in heavy contact up north and needed armoured support. As the theatre ops company, we were to prepare to move immediately. Pack for 24 hours and load up … however, we had no ammunition, not a bullet. I still had no filler for my body armour nor any medical equipment. We loaded our vehicles, a mixture of armoured and soft skinned vehicles and headed to Camp Breadbasket. The Fusiliers were there, winding down before their return to the UK. Orders were to beg, borrow, or steal something to fight with. We were given containers of loose rounds and other bits. I begged a few field dressings and crepe bandages. We then acquired water and rations and headed north. There was still no ammunition for the 30mm main armament on the Warriors.

The company was ordered to travel to a base occupied by Danish forces and wait for an emergency resupply convoy to catch up. While they waited for the resupply, the company formed up for a briefing.

> The OC informed us that there had been a major contact in a town called Majar al-Kabir involving 1 Para, and that sadly, six British Royal Military Police had been killed … Also, the Quick Reaction Force Chinook helicopter had been badly shot up, having to return to base with a number of severely wounded on board. You could have heard a pin drop, stunned silence. *The war's over for Christ's sake.* The OC reiterated we were not here to play games, this was serious, and we were to be at the forefront of future combat operations.

As the briefing was being concluded, the resupply convoy arrived.

> I had never seen so much ammunition in one place: Javelin anti-tank missiles, grenades, 30mm for the warriors, 7.62 link for the GMPG and chain guns, 5.56 rounds in the tens of thousands, smoke grenades, flares, more than we could carry. The vehicles were filled to bursting. 'Any medical kit, mate?' I asked. 'Just this.' I was thrown a box; inside was hundreds of morphine auto jets. *At least we can bleed to death painlessly,* I thought to myself. I was now concerned as the med situation was pretty dire.

At first light the company travelled to Camp Abu Naji, an old Iraqi Army base, being used as the main British base in the area, just a few miles southwest of the city of Amarah.

> On arrival we were met with stares. These were men of the Parachute Regiment; they didn't fight with armour … Over the next few days, we trained and planned to go back into the town … The paras were taught how to de-bus from a Warrior, we trained hard, attended briefings and understood the plans. The anticipation was high; this was going to be a major show of military force to the townspeople. We also heard the full details of the battle in Majar al-Kabir,

of how the RMPs had been cut off with no radio communications in the town's police station, surrounded by a baying mob, overrun, and then brutally executed.

The British Army went back into Majar al-Kabir just a few days later. The locals were about to see what forces the British Army could bring to bear if they were foolish enough to resist. Challenger 2 tanks from 2nd Royal Tank Regiment provided a cordon around the town, while USMC Cobra helicopter gunships circled above, with ground attack aircraft making regular shows of force. The townspeople had been told in air leaflet drops that the British Army would be coming back.

> We left just before dawn. I was in the OC's command warrior, the third vehicle in the convoy. Crammed in with me were Iraqi interpreters, Para Regiment officers, and radio operators. I was by the back door but couldn't move. Hatches were battened down, it was hot as hell and there was no air … We rolled into town, not knowing what to expect, but we were prepared for anything. I constantly went over casualty procedures in my head. Gunshot wounds, blast injuries etc. I had to get it right. I looked out the small window in the door; instead of being met by a barrage of RPGs and small arms, the streets were filled with locals and the world's press. Journalists jostled to get pictures and footage of us rolling in. Regardless of this anti-climax, we stuck to the plan and took up our defensive positions around the police station. Once in place, the Household Cavalry Regiment and 1 Para Regiment officers arrived and started patrols. REME recovery arrived to clear the British vehicles destroyed in the battle.

One of the main reasons for the show of force was to get scenes of crime officers into the police station to collect evidence of the murders. The next time C Company would go back into Majar al-Kabir would be on their own, tasked to turn the police station into a patrol base.

Back at Camp Abu Naji, while the company prepared to return to Majar al-Kabir, they now had a roof over their heads.

> We now had an old barrack block to sleep in. Too hot to sleep inside though, so at night cots were carried to the roof where it was cooler, and the sand flies couldn't reach us … I had also built up a rapport with some of the RAF nurses from the dressing station … Now that plans were afoot to put us back in the police station, the urge for revenge was strong. The day before we left, one of the nurses came to find me … She took a crucifix from around her neck and gave it to me to wear, telling me it would keep me safe and give me the strength to go on no matter what was to happen in the coming days.

The days before establishing the new patrol base in Majar al-Kabir had been spent gathering equipment, filling sandbags, and working out how to deal with the radio communications blackspot that had been a major factor in the deaths of the six RMPs. They were also given new satellite phone equipment as a back-up.

> We drove into Majar al-Kebir, hatches open this time. It was eerily quiet. We approached the front of the police station and reversed the Warrior so we faced outwards. Guys debussed their wagons and took up all-round defence. I climbed out the back and looked up at the front of the station. It was covered in bullet strikes and burn marks. Shell casings still littered the ground. The front door was a huge metal gate. The OC called out, 'Cpl T*****, open the fucking door.' 'Yes, Sir,' I replied. Weapon at the ready and adrenaline pumping, I ran at the door and gave

it a hefty boot. To my surprise the entire frame tore away from the wall. Shoulder barging it further, I entered the building and was followed by another soldier. We went room to room, ensuring they were clear. Going left through the front hall, we entered a small courtyard, where there was a distinct smell of burning. We came to a short dark passageway. There were two rooms, one left and one right. I looked left and it appeared to be an office; burnt papers and ID cards littered the floor. I swung right and stopped. *Jesus Christ, this is it. This is the room.* It was fairly dark apart from a small window on the outside wall. It gave enough light to show me all I needed to know. I lowered my weapon and took in the horror … I felt physically sick; those guys had surrendered and were huddled in this room. The mob had them cornered and then executed them … One of their comrades was already dead in the corridor outside, so they must have known what was coming. *Can you imagine the fear?* We moved on, up the stairs, checking the roof, and then back out the front door. 'Building clear,' I shouted. Then it dawned on me, what the hell was I doing, I'm the bloody medic!

Almost immediately the new patrol base became a hive of activity as the British Army re-established itself back in the town and set up operations.

We had brought in a huge mast which was attached to the side of the police station in the hope we could get comms with Abu Naji. An RMP arrived and we set up an office for him by the front door. He was there to recruit a new police force. Engineers arrived, and a detachment from my old medical unit, 12 Medical Squadron. We built bunkers on the roof, established a small Regimental Aid Post, toilets and showers were built. The engineers started to build protective walls. This was a huge team effort. We were back to stay, and the locals weren't going to like it. Things seemed okay at first, but then we'd have occasional small-arms fire. I recall watching an engineer jump off a wall as he came under fire. As he ran for cover, I watched the dirt being kicked up behind him as rounds struck the ground.

A routine was established that involved patrolling, guard shifts, and the constant fortifying of the new patrol base. After the area was classed as safe due to C Company's presence, Andrew T. experienced something macabre that still disgusts him to this day.

I can only describe it as gore tourism. The patrol base was getting a constant flow of visitors from Abu Naji. Most had legitimate business there, though a large number seemed to have come for one reason in mind – the room. We saw numerous people going to the room to pose and take pictures; myself and another soldier found this totally abhorrent. To that end we took it upon ourselves to seal up the room. Using some engineer supplies we created some doors with which to close it up. Before we did this, I walked to the small courtyard; in the centre of it was a lone flower. I picked this and placed it in the room. I then removed the crucifix the nurse had given from around my neck and hung it from a nail in the wall, and said a prayer for the six. One last look around, then we fitted the boards. Job done. I'm happy to say I never took a picture of the room; it felt wrong and disrespectful to the memory of those guys.

The King's Regiment continued operations in and around Majar al-Kabir before they eventually moved back to the south. For an operation that soldiers were told would last 24 hours, they returned to Basra three months later.

By the summer of 2004, the deteriorating situation in southern Iraq had reached crisis point. Politicians and senior Army officers were sugar-coating what was happening, describing the insurgency there as 'a few difficulties'. In reality, 'Britain was facing strategic defeat.'[58] It had not delivered since the invasion; inadequacies had stoked a resentment that grew into the insurgency. Forty-five thousand British troops took part in the invasion; by May 2003, that number in southeast Iraq was down to 26,000. In July, as the insurgency was in full swing, there were only 9,000 left[59] – soldiers on the ground really had no chance of succeeding.

Fuelled by long-held grievances towards both Britain and America, the insurgency was now led by Shia militants such as Muqtada al-Sadr's Mahdi Army who were being helped and funded by Iran.[60] The British government was either naively ignoring Iranian involvement or deliberately trying to hide it altogether. Rather than reinforce beleaguered troops in southern Iraq, or admit defeat and withdraw from the country entirely, the government bumbled along for another five years. To make matters worse, as the war became increasingly unpopular in the UK, politicians were turning towards Afghanistan. Within a year, on the recommendation of senior military officers, in part looking to rebuild the reputation of the Army, thousands of British Army soldiers would be deployed to Helmand Province. Suddenly, Britain was fighting a major war on two fronts.

For the next five years soldiers continued to arrive in southern Iraq on Operation *Telic*. Some soldiers did multiple tours with short breaks in between. As the British Army's commitment in Afghanistan escalated, the turnaround for many troops became tighter. Between 2003 and the final withdrawal in 2009, Robert C. found himself on three tours to Iraq. Another member of the QDG who had been in the initial invasion of 2003, Simon J. would return to Iraq in 2005 and 2008.

David K., who had transferred to the Royal Military Police in 2000, narrowly missed out on deployment to Iraq. He was posted out of his Provost Company three weeks before they were deployed. Involved in helping train fellow policemen before deployment on Operation *Telic 3* and *4*, he did not deploy himself until *Telic 6*.

> I was employed, primarily, as a Court Liaison Officer, providing support to the Iraqi Judicial System, ensuring that they were carrying out business as usual and were safe from external, nefarious influences. We would carry out weekly visits to the main courts in Basra and meet with the judges, discuss cases they had ongoing, and review evidence. Apart from the usual mortar attacks, roadside IEDs and the new threat of passive infra-red IEDs that arose during this tour, I was involved in two incidents of note.

One of the incidents was an argument between two rival police stations that occurred at Al Maqal Court Room and resulted in an armed stand-off between policemen from the two different stations.

> My interpreter had disappeared, along with my escort team (Coldstream Guards) and I was left in the middle of the group. Fearful of cocking my rifle in case it enflamed the situation, I shouted '*Kiff* ['stop' in Arabic]. This shocked the police into pausing and I grabbed hold of who I thought was the main protagonist and started shouting and gesticulating to him. After my interpreter reappeared I told him to get them lined up. I then told them that they should be setting an example to the civilian population and not arguing in public. I noticed that a

number of rifles had appeared and went about doing a full unload drill, using the interpreter to translate. I used this as a tactic to diffuse the situation; looking back in hindsight, it does appear quite silly.

Silly or not, his actions prevented what could have been a bloodbath, and for this he was awarded a commendation from the General Officer Commanding.

Michael P. had been involved in the initial invasion in March 2003, with the Irish Guards. His battalion had tragically lost two men during the invasion, and in 2007, when his battalion returned to Iraq for a second tour, tragedy would strike again.

> The worst incident I had was our two lads that were killed, one of them being a good friend … along with other medics we had to look after their bodies, searching them for private items like rings, wallets and that sort of stuff – it was harrowing, they were friends. We didn't even have body bags issued, so we put them in their ponchos … as it was all we had. We brought them to the bombed-out building where we were staying and laid them on top of tables so that they were off the ground and in the morning the Duke of Wellington's Regiment were tasked with collecting them. There was quite a turn out to see them off.

Soldier G. was attached to the Prince of Wales's Royal Regiment (PWRR). He spent most of his tour patrolling the Iran–Iraq border and manning Observation Posts at night, trying to catch insurgent mortar teams who routinely attacked Camp Abu Naji. On 14 May 2004, during a routine journey back to camp from Basra, Soldier G. and his men would become unwitting witnesses to one of the most well-known incidents of the war.

> On the return journey we had to pass through a village called Qual Al Salih. It had a truck stop cafe just before you entered the town. This was the first combat indicator on the way back as there were no trucks to be seen. As we drove past the cafe and entered the village all hell broke loose. An IED went off behind my vehicle and we had small arms engage us from the right. We returned fire and sped through the ambush. I saw a man who appeared to be wearing a police uniform … he was carrying an AK-47 … An RPG was fired straight over my head. I looked in my mirror and saw that the policeman had dropped to the ground.

Having escaped an ambush relatively unscathed, about 1.5 miles up the road, Soldier G.'s vehicles were stopped by a soldier who was guarding some Land Rovers.

> On the right the QRF from PWRR was assaulting a position with a platoon of Argyll and Sutherland Highlanders … we stopped, gave them some ammunition, and helped with one of their wounded … by this time a company commander from the Highlanders was running the show. He made us pick all the Iraqi dead up and load them into the Land Rovers. We then set off back through Checkpoint Danny Boy. When we arrived it looked like a scene from World War II. There were Warriors engaging into a field on the left, and half the battle group was ready to assault. We were now all dismounted; they placed us on the left flank on a sand dune. The five troop lads did fire support while the rest of us guarded the rear. I was running around dishing ammo out. It was like a film set: burning fields, infantry with fixed bayonets, Iraqi dead all over the shop. After the battle we mounted up, drove back to camp, and dropped the dead off at the Medical Centre. Then we all stood in a hollow square. I remember looking around and there were PWRR lads covered in blood. The medics checked us all, then we were interviewed by the RMPs.

The battle of Danny Boy was one of the most widely known engagements of the war. At first it was associated with bravery and courage, against overwhelming odds. Twenty-eight Mahdi Army insurgents were killed with the loss of no British lives, and Sergeant Brian Wood of the PWRR was awarded a Military Cross. In later years it was synonymous with accusations of murder, lies, deceit, professional misconduct, and finally, vindication for soldiers wrongly accused.

Rich G. had returned home in May 2003. Two months later he was posted back to the Household Cavalry Regiment in Windsor. He went from being a patrol leader in an elite Special Forces unit back to his regiment. 'It was a bit of an anti-climax really.' The one consolation was that it was not a desk job, and just 11 months after returning from the desert, he was back in southern Iraq. His squadron's task was to mentor the Iraq border police so that they could operate independently. Most of the tour involved spending their days visiting border police installations and teaching them their jobs. Rich G. said it was 'Very frustrating at times. We were responsible for 70–80km of border. We were totally aware that that not all crossings could be controlled.'

The invasion of Iraq was the most controversial military deployment of British troops since the Suez Crisis of 1956, has been continuously debated, and the effects are still felt today. For years after the invasion there were calls for an independent inquiry or other punitive action to be taken by Parliament,[61] although it was not until 2009, after Tony Blair had left office, that Prime Minister Gordon Brown authorised the Chilcott Inquiry. The findings were finally published in 2016.

During an October 2015 interview with Fareed Zakaria on CNN, just before the release of the Chilcott report, Tony Blair unreservedly apologised for going to war on the basis of 'flawed Iraq intelligence'. During the interview, which many criticised as nothing more than a well-managed public relations opportunity ahead of the report's release, he accepted blame 'for some of the mistakes in planning and … in our understanding of what would happen once you removed the regime.'[62] But he stopped short of apologising for going to war to remove Saddam Hussein. 'I find it hard to apologise for removing Saddam. I think, even from today in 2015, it is better that he's not there than he is there.'[63] The ex-prime minister's words were met with harsh criticism by most British media outlets. The *Daily Mail* said, 'Blair's weasel words insult Iraq war dead',[64] and the *Daily Mirror* called it 'too little too late and so cynical'.[65]

I am not in a position or qualified to apportion blame, but if I neglected to highlight some of the major shortcomings of the conduct of the Iraq War, then I would be doing a disservice to those soldiers of our generation who served in Iraq and to the families of the 179 soldiers who lost their lives. Many of the political leaders involved have been highly criticised, and there are still calls for those responsible, for initiating what many consider to be an illegal war, to be held accountable. General

Sir Michael Rose had called Blair to be held to account in 2006, saying 'The only way Parliament can regain the trust of disaffected voters is to admit that it was wrong to support the war.' General Mike Jackson has no doubt who should shoulder blame for the way the war was prosecuted and the aftermath. 'In my view, Rumsfeld is one of those most responsible for the current situation in Iraq.'[66]

It is not only political leaders that soldiers now look to blame. The decision to send soldiers into battle without everything they needed was a calculated risk taken in Whitehall but one that would be paid for with the blood of its soldiers. The National Audit Office report after Exercise *Saif Sareea II*, published in July 2002, highlighted the problems with equipment that failed in the Omani desert in 2001.[67] One of those failures was the ageing Clansman radio system. The report clearly stated that while the radios could be used in 'environmentally controlled conditions' such as headquarters units, 'they proved completely inadequate for field units in the heat and dust of the desert'.[68] The report explicitly and clearly warned the Ministry of Defence that 'Clansman is now incapable of providing availability for war-fighting operations. This capability gap will persist until Bowman is introduced from 2004.'[69] The findings of the report appeared in the media. Writing for *The Telegraph,* Philip Johnston says, 'Problems with the Army's ageing Clansman radio system had become so severe that it was now judged to be "incapable" of operating in combat conditions.'[70] Yet, the MOD still sent its soldiers into harm's way without radios or communications equipment that had been tested and proven to work. As Soldier G. attested, there was communications equipment available that could have been used. Although the Board of Inquiry into the deaths of the six RMPs in Majar al-Kabir in June 2003 did not apportion blame, it is clear that poor communications directly contributed to their deaths. The inquiry said that the RMPs 'had not taken a satellite phone with them because a "culture" had grown up in which they did not bother with an unreliable technology'.[71]

The shortage of personal body armour was another supply and logistics issue that would directly contribute to a soldier's death. One of the first British fatalities in Iraq was Sergeant Steven Roberts of the 2nd Royal Tank Regiment, who died after being struck by a bullet. The new enhanced body armour was in such short supply that some non-infantry soldiers, including tank crews, were ordered to give it up. Sergeant Roberts was one such soldier, handing over his body armour just before the invasion. The coroner's report into his death recorded, 'Sergeant Roberts lost his life because he did not have that basic piece of equipment.'[72] The coroner clearly pointed to who he thought was to blame. 'To send soldiers into a combat zone without the appropriate basic equipment is, in my view, unforgiveable and inexcusable and represents a breach of trust the soldiers have in their government.'[73]

After the drawdown of military units in Northern Ireland, the MOD was left with a surplus of certain equipment that because of budget restraints they were keen to re-use. One of these items was the Land Rover Snatch variant. Based on the Land Rover Defender 110 design, it was fast, manoeuvrable, and perfect for use in Northern Ireland. But, as had been proven in Ulster, the lightly protected vehicle could not withstand much in the way of incoming fire, mines, or Improvised Explosive Devices. 'You drive over a landmine in a very lightly armoured Land Rover Snatch – it's not much different from driving over it in a Ford Escort.' There were lots of them left over from Northern Ireland,[74] and those controlling the purse strings obviously wanted them used. To troops that used them in both Iraq and Afghanistan, they would soon become known as 'Mobile Coffins'.[75] The decision to use vehicles that 'were not suitable or safe for the operations they were used on' led to the deaths of 37 British servicemen and women.[76]

Soldiers who had been sent to fight the war were even more scathing when asked if it was it all worth it. Former Chief of the General Staff General Sir Lord Dannatt told the Chilcott Inquiry that he thought 'going to Iraq was an error of near biblical proportions'.[77] Although he thought removing Saddam Hussein was the right thing to do initially, Rich G. believed 'no thought or planning was done to deal with the aftermath of his removal'. And as for culpability, he has no doubt about who is to blame.

> Bush and Blair are a couple of crooks who should be held to account. The current state of the region can be directly attributed to them and their lack of thought for the consequences and inability to listen to sound advice … I'm sure Haliburton, the defence industry, and all those that have financially prospered from the invasion think it was worth it.

From the outset, the legality of the invasion has always been questioned. The United Nations' founding charter, signed by both the United States and United Kingdom after World War II, is clear: no country has the right to invade another unless acting in self-defence or with the authorisation of the UN Security Council.[78] Even Foreign Secretary Jack Straw, a lawyer by trade, knew that 'regime change' was based on 'thin' evidence and was not legal.

Novelist, poet, academic scholar, and native Iraqi Sinan Antoon wrote an article for the *New York Times* in March 2018, 15 years after Operation *Iraqi Freedom* was launched. He wrote, 'The invasion of Iraq is often spoken of in the United States as a "blunder," or even a "colossal mistake." It was a crime. Those who perpetrated it are still at large.'[79]

CHAPTER 13

Helmand

While the eyes of the world were focused on Iraq, the Taliban, who had been defeated and removed from power in Afghanistan in December 2001, had quietly reorganised and regrouped. Taliban fighters had started to cross the porous border back into southern Afghanistan. Small, well-hidden training camps were set up along the mountainous border area, where new fighters who had been recruited from Pashtun areas were taught to fight.

General Mike Jackson was critical of the US global war on terror and its focus on the single military means. He went on to say that, 'Any use of military force must, by definition, be in pursuit of a political objective.'[1] Maybe the Americans already had one eye on Iraq. General Jackson added, 'The Americans did not seem much interested in what would happen within Afghanistan after the Taliban had gone.'[2] Some cynics might point to Afghanistan's lack of a natural resource or commodity such as oil, to explain America's disinterest. But Bush's staunchest ally had a different view. Tony Blair had made a promise to the Afghan people in October 2001, when he said, 'We will not walk away from Afghanistan, as the world has done many times before.'[3] These comments would have been welcomed by the Afghan people looking to shake off the tyranny of the Taliban, but they came at a time when Britain's military was not heavily committed. Just a few years later when the British Army was needed to help stem the tide of a resurgent Taliban insurgency, it was stretched dangerously thin.

In May 2003, after combat operations had concluded in Iraq, the House of Commons Select Committee on Defence opened an inquiry into Operation *Telic*; the report was published in March 2004. While its scope and recommendations were far-reaching, the Select Committee applauded Britain's servicemen affording them 'the highest praise for their conduct and performance in Iraq'.[4] But for both policy makers and the MOD, there were significant warnings. Even before the start of the insurgency in Iraq, the Select Committee gave a dire warning that should have set alarm bells ringing all through government. 'The UK Armed Forces have become a one operation force – one operation which must be followed by a lengthy period of recovery before they can be in position to mount another operation, even within a coalition.'[5] If Britain had withdrawn from Iraq completely in 2004, then the argument could have been made for involvement in Afghanistan in 2006. But as we now know, this did not happen.

In January 2006, Defence Secretary John Reid announced that Britain would be sending a Provincial Reconstruction Team (PRT) to Helmand Province. He said it would be backed up with several thousand troops and the deployment would last for at least three years. Helmand Task Force Commander Brigadier Ed Butler would later say, 'I think there was a naivety on a corporate level that people felt we were going into Afghanistan to hand out bread and milk and deliver development and reconstruction.'[6] During a visit to Afghanistan in April 2006, the Defence Secretary made a statement that would come back to haunt him. 'We are in the South to help protect the Afghan people construct their own democracy ... we would be perfectly happy to leave in three years and without firing one shot because our job is to protect the construction.'[7]

Many of Britain's top military commanders have since faced criticism for not speaking out in 2004 and 2005, when the Helmand operation was first proposed. Professor Hew Strachan not only lambasted Bush and Blair for committing troops 'without any coherent vision of what they can achieve', but he also criticised Britain's military leaders, saying they were wrong 'to put up and shut up', and that 'the services had been silenced', having 'undergone a massive loss of status and authority.'[8]

After returning from Iraq in 2003, Stuart B. was promoted to colour sergeant and posted to the Support Weapons School, Infantry Training Centre at Warminster. For two years he taught the SNCO Advanced Mortar and Platoon Commander courses. He returned to 3 Para in January 2006, as the 2IC Mortar Platoon and to the news that the battalion would be deploying to Afghanistan with 16 Air Assault Brigade in April. After an exercise at Thetford, then live firing at Otterburn, the battalion stepped up its training by deploying to the desert.

> After a brief period back in Colchester, the battalion flew out to Oman. We spent three weeks conducting platoon and directed training (normal tick in the box stuff) ... then one week intensive live firing exercises culminating in full battalion attacks supported by Oman Air Force Jaguar aircraft and for the first time from the Army Air Corps Apache attack helicopters. It was all singing and dancing live day and night attacks – our final tick in the box before deployment.

For troops deploying on Operation *Herrick IV*, the centre of operations would be based in the newly constructed Camp Bastion. The largest British military installation since the end of World War II was sited in the desert northwest of Lashkar Gar. After the experience of nightly insurgent attacks in Iraq, the British Army would be safe in their isolated encampment, or so they thought. With the official handover from US forces taking place on 1 May 2006, most troops were not expecting to be in combat. One Gurkha officer was told his company should prepare for nothing more arduous than guarding Camp Bastion. Little did he know that within a few weeks he and his men would experience fierce fighting.[9]

The British forces in Helmand were tasked with establishing a secure triangle of territory between Camp Bastion, Lashkar Gar, and Gereshk, so that within this area the PRT could start their work.[10] But this plan would change very quickly. Just a few weeks later, the decision was made to occupy the district centres of Now Zad, Musa Qala, and Sangin to the north.[11] The expansion of the area of responsibility would have huge implications for every soldier deployed to Afghanistan, but it was a decision that was not made in a vacuum. Not only was the increased Taliban activity a direct challenge to British authority, but also pressure was immediately placed upon British commanders by the governor of Helmand Province, Mohammed Daoud. He later said, 'Their mission was to maintain security in Helmand, if they were not deploying to those districts to the north, then we may lose those districts.'[12] Daoud, whose nephew had been shot in the stomach in Sangin, said the situation was so bad that Now Zad, Musa Qala, and Sangin were about to fall to the Taliban.[13] Brigadier Butler confirmed this when he said, 'Both he and President Karzai said if you are not prepared to fight to protect our flag and our people, then what are you doing here?'[14]

Brigadier Butler and the CO of 3 Para, LtCol Stuart Tootal, were left with a tough choice while trying to balance conflicting priorities. Of the 3,500 British soldiers in Helmand, only 600 were infantry.[15] From the start they lacked the resources, but with no real alternative, they agreed to go in. Tootal would later say, 'Yes, it was a stretch; yes, it was a risk, but hey, we're paratroopers; we're British soldiers, that's what we do.'[16]

Stuart B. joined the CO's planning team and Tac HQ when the mortar platoon commander was tasked to lead a small team from support company to the Kajaki Dam. This strategically important site had come under attack and the Afghan security force there needed strengthening. After LtCol Tootal agreed to intervene, 3 Para Tac HQ and A Company deployed to Sangin. 'The district centre was occupied and the nephew of the governor was found and extracted. I left with the CO and A Company stayed in the district centre. Things were very quiet for the first few days but little did we know what lay ahead.' Soldiers deploying to Sangin were told they would only be there for 96 hours – they ended up staying for 95 days.[17]

After his second tour in Bosnia, Jules H. went on ceremonial duties for a year. In 2001, he was promoted to corporal of horse and posted to ATR Harrogate as an instructor. When he returned to his regiment, he spent the next two years as the designated troop CoH of the 'Airborne Troop' to deploy with 16 Air Assault Brigade. During this time his troop was constantly on 48 hours' notice to move. In January 2006, D Squadron, HCR, were warned off for deployment on Operation *Herrick IV*. After training had taken place Jules H. and his squadron received their vehicles from the CVR(T) fleet, they were prepared, loaded onto containers, and shipped by sea to Karachi.

One day into pre-deployment leave, Jules H. was informed that he would be flying out to Afghanistan within 36 hours, a full six weeks before the squadron. As a qualified Joint Terminal Attack Controller (JTAC), he needed to obtain USAF accreditation before being able to work with American aircraft engaged in close air support. Once he got accreditation he was supposed to fly home and finish his leave. But the situation in Afghanistan had quickly changed; JTACs were in such short supply he could not be released, so he was attached to the Guards Para Platoon who were apart of B Company, 3 Para, until his squadron arrived.

On return from Sangin, Stuart B. was asked to command a patrol with soldiers from the machine gun and anti-tank platoons.

> B Coy had been tasked to take control of Now Zad and were to fly forward in Chinooks. Our convoy was to move cross-country and secure a Helicopter Landing Site just outside the town and bring the company in. The Pathfinder Platoon had already been up to Now Zad and had a fire fight with the Afghan Police. Luckily no one had been killed but it showed how trigger happy the Afghan police were ... It took around four hours to move up to the HLS and secure it just before B Company arrived. I had time to meet with a group of police on the old Russian defensive position they were manning before the Chinooks arrived. The last thing we needed was the police shooting at the choppers as they came in. The insertion went well and B Coy occupied the district centre along with a platoon of Afghan National Army soldiers, and the police.

By this time, 3 Para were fully committed to manning 'Platoon Houses' throughout Helmand Province, but this would leave them stretched very thinly on the ground.

> The battle group was now manning five locations: Camp Bastion (HQ), FOB Price (C Coy), Sangin (A Coy), Now Zad (B Coy) and Kajaki (SP Coy minus attachments). Each company group had attachments consisting of mortars, anti-tanks, machine guns from support company, patrols, snipers, assault engineers and sigs from D Coy. MFCs, JTACs, and Forward Observation Officers formed the new Fire Support Team concept. Each company also had a section of combat engineers from 9 Squadron RE. It was a formidable fighting force with the fire power to over match anything we might encounter.

Stuart B.'s optimism that they could match anything the Taliban could throw at them was about to be thoroughly tested. After a few weeks, he left Now Zad and was back in the JOC at Camp Bastion.

> It was then the shit started to hit the fan. Sangin became a hotbed of Taliban activity. Contact after contact ... A Coy were getting hit numerous times a day while both out on patrol or in the District Centre ... C Coy at FOB Price had a big contact with the Taliban, and B Coy carried out an operation to take ground in Now Zad that ended with huge fire fights. The lines were so close, B Coy were throwing grenades at them. The lads in Kajaki were in contact most days with the place lit up like a firework. There were far too many incidents to mention and many more acts of bravery from the lads.

Stuart B. was not a stranger to losing members of his own platoon, but it was something that never got any easier. 'I had six MFCs deployed and three mortar sections who were bolstered by a section from the Royal Irish and a section of two barrels from the Fusiliers. By the end of the tour 50 per cent of my MFCs were either dead or injured.' Corporal Mark Wright was killed in Kajaki while trying to rescue a member of a patrol who had inadvertently walked into a minefield.

Another was shot in the shoulder during a patrol outside Sangin, the same patrol when Corporal Bryan Budd VC was killed, and a third MFC from Stuart's platoon was injured at Sangin during a rocket attack that killed three paratroopers and an Afghan interpreter. 'Mark was posthumously awarded the George Cross. Fortunately Robbo and Hoss recovered from their injuries. Any death is hard to deal with, but when it's from your own platoon, it cuts deep.'

Brigadier Butler, who was widely criticised for the approach he took in Helmand,[18] was constantly asking for reinforcements. 'I asked on a daily, weekly basis for more troops, more capability, more helicopters. I remember saying to the Chief of the Defence Staff in 2006, on one of his visits, that we probably needed a division – 10,000 troops – to achieve what we set out to do.'[19] The gap between the policy laid down by politicians and top military commanders and what could be implemented with resources available on the ground was too wide, even for paratroopers. Limited reinforcements were sent. A Company of the Royal Regiment Fusiliers stationed in Cyprus from the 'Theatre Reserve Battalion', along with two platoons (Barossa and Somme) and a mortar platoon from the Royal Irish Regiment, were flown in. Once reinforcements for the hard-pushed paras arrived in Afghanistan, they were quickly sent where they were needed. The Fusiliers took over in Now Zad, while the Royal Irish, along with an ad hoc 3 Para HQ element, moved to Musa Qala and took over from a Danish contingent when they pulled out.

With two of the 'Platoon Houses' manned by non-3 Para soldiers, this meant the battalion could now launch operations aimed at attacking the Taliban away from the district centres.

> The battalion was asked to plan an operation in the north to attack a Taliban training camp. We planned a two company operation, with one company carrying out a parachute insertion and the other company a heliborne insertion. We had the parachutes, the Parachute Jump Instructors, and aircraft. It was looking good for the battalion to carry out the first Airborne operation since Suez in 1956. It was given the green light by all parties until it got to Northwood back in the UK and some general turned it off saying it was too risky. We were all gutted, from the youngest Tom up to the CO. I am sure some craphat general had it in for the regiment and couldn't bear the thought of the Parachute Regiment actually jumping in to battle even though it was the best option due to a lack of helicopters and any ground move being way more dangerous.

Despite the disappointment of not being able to jump into combat, Stuart B. was involved in a number of operations. One, called Operation *Augustus*, in the Sangin Valley, he would remember very well.

> We deployed by Chinook to capture a high-value target that was known to be operating in the area. I was the chalk commander of the support weapons helicopter and we were packed in. Many lads standing so we could load more men on. On approaching the landing site the Chinooks came under fire from small arms and RPG. The pilots did a great job of getting us in with some evasive flying. Our Chinook came in hard and fast, and on landing, the cable the standing lads were holding on to snapped. Lads fell all over the place as the door gunners were letting rip with their M60s. After a little delay we debussed. I was the last man off, and on my

way down the aircraft I noticed that four jerry cans full of water to be used for our resupply throughout the operation had been left in the confusion. I went back, picked two up, and threw them off the tail gate. I then went back for the last two, but as I did this the Chinook took off. I dropped the remaining jerry cans and ran off the tail gate into the pitch black night. I was unsure how high the helicopter had got in the few seconds it had left the ground but I couldn't remain on board … It felt like I was in the air for ages before I hit the ground with a thud. On return to Bastion I spoke to the loadmaster and he said we were between 20 and 30 feet up when I jumped. I waited for the Chinook to clear the area before I stood up to look for the lads. I fell over immediately and realised then that my leg and ankle were fucked. I flipped down my night vision goggles, then, using my rifle as a makeshift walking stick, I hobbled off towards the lads. I could already hear them entering the compounds with explosives. In the background I could hear both our Apaches and a US C-130 Spectre gunship engaging targets close by. It was a surreal experience. I was patched up by the battalion doctor and cracked on until the end of the operation. We didn't catch the HVT but we did capture a number of Taliban who were extracted for interrogation.

Stuart B. spent three days in Bastion Hospital. X-rays showed that he had broken his right fibula and ruptured the ligaments in his ankle.

In the bed next to me was a young NCO from 216 Parachute Signal Squadron. I knew him quite well from my time in Now Zad. He had been on the roof sorting out a comms problem when he was shot. The bullet entered his back behind his armpit under the body armour and exited the same place on the other side. He had one hell of an injury all the way across his back from one side to the other. He was in good spirits and glad to be alive. I could have gone back to the UK but I decided to stay and work in the JOC, crutches and all.

A few weeks later, it was decided there would be a battle group-sized assault on Now Zad to clear out the Taliban who had been attacking the main compound and ANP Hill (an old Russian defensive position), then replace the Gurkhas and paratroopers with A Company, Royal Fusiliers. The Fusilier mortar section, which had gone in as a fire support group just two days after arriving in Bastion,[20] were having a few problems with their mortar computer.

The CO asked if I was able to deploy and sort the problem out … the med centre gave me strong pain killers and strapped up my leg nice and tight. I deployed on the operation and landed on the HLS I had secured at the start of the tour when we first occupied Now Zad. I made my way up the hill and met the lads from the Fusiliers' mortars. Some of our anti-tank platoon were also positioned up there which was nice to know. After investigation I found the problem … For the next few days we carried out the relief in place and cleared much of Now Zad. We were constantly targeted by Taliban small arms and RPG fire up on the hill which was a bit of a pain in the arse with my leg strapped up. However, we got the job done and extracted back to Bastion.

D Squadron HCR were also involved in the operation. Jules H. was the lead callsign, providing mutual support for 400 paratroopers that cleared the town, going from house to house, compound to compound. Despite coming under sustained small-arms and RPG fire, the mission was a success, with no losses and about a dozen Taliban killed.[21] 'D Squadron got split up after the assault … It was decided that Now

Zad didn't have enough protection so my troop was left behind while the remainder headed for Musa Qala … I kept my own Scimitar in the police station and my other three vehicles were on the hill in overwatch.' The operation in Now Zad had been a success; armour and infantry working together, providing mutual support. However, D Squadron was now tasked with moving towards the beleaguered garrison in Musa Qala to secure a landing site so that the defenders could be resupplied. The problem was that they would be doing this without infantry. When the news arrived at Now Zad that the squadron had lost four men (three killed, one seriously injured) in an ambush at Musa Qala, Jules H. said he was absolutely devastated. 'Losing four men out of 88 in the squadron was a big hit.' Despite not being the same regiment, the deaths had affected the Fusiliers too. Out of respect for their fallen comrades a memorial service was held in the compound.[22]

Jules H. and his troop were relieved and other troops took over during the tour, but his troop spent most of the tour on top of the ANP Hill defending Now Zad, in contact every one of those days. As a JTAC he was responsible for bringing in air-assets to support the defenders of the police station compound and ANP Hill. During his time at Now Zad, he developed a great respect for the officers and men of the Royal Fusiliers. He said, 'For me, the most important unit was 2RRF … Absolutely outstanding soldiers. Their company commander, Major Jonathan S., was the finest officer I ever served with.' The Fusiliers left Now Zad after 104 days; for those who had been on ANP Hill, it is unofficially regarded as the longest defence of a static trench system in British military history.[23]

During Operation *Herrick IV*, reports regarding a lack of supplies, reinforcements, and failing equipment started to leak out to the media. Jules H. said, 'There was a leaked report from Now Zad about being ill-equipped, out on a limb. It was true, I was there. We were the poor cousins.' Journalist and author, James Ferguson, had heard the stories too. He interviewed several Fusiliers who complained about being left on their own without adequate support and equipment. He was sceptical at first, because soldiers have a reputation for moaning about everything, and he could not believe that a modern Army would be sent to war so poorly equipped.[24] However, like in Iraq three years earlier, British soldiers had been sent into a war zone to do a job without the tools to complete it.

Stuart B. did everything he could to support all troops in his platoon – paratroopers, Fusiliers or the Royal Irish.

> The Danish who had manned the DC in Musa Qala were extracted. 3 Para decided to replace them with an ad hoc company of individuals from across the battalion and from the Royal Irish. The new company became known as Easy Company. They went through hell … I supported the Royal Irish mortar section when possible and tried to resupply them with mortar ammo as they were running very low. I spoke to their section commander (whom I had taught at Warminster) when possible and sent him up a cigar for when it was all over. They were stuck on their own with very little resupply. Only when they had a casualty was it possible to send ammo and stores to them.

When Jules H. finally left Now Zad, no one would have blamed him for not holding a very high opinion of a country or its people that had cost his squadron so much. But an incident towards the end of his tour left him with a different opinion.

> After the squadron met up with us in Now Zad, we handed over to 3 Commando Brigade. On the way back to Camp Bastion, I was leading the convoy, when an Afghan local ran towards my wagon. You never take any chances so I shouted for him to halt a safe distance away and gestured for him to lift his clothing so I could see he was unarmed. He wasn't threatening, so I called for the interpreter. He had a 12-year-old son who was crying in pain – he had an earache. Our medic treated him with syringes and medicine, then we went on our way. A few weeks later, I was back patrolling the area, about to cross the same dry wadi, when the man came running across to me waving his hands. I immediately called the medic and interpreter assuming his boy was still in pain. The interpreter told me the man had watched the Taliban planting bombs. So I asked him, 'How do I know they're not holding your family hostage and you're going to direct us over the IEDs?' He smiled at me, climbed on the front decks of my Scimitar and said, 'What happens to you will happen to me, my friend.' And we crossed the wadi safely together.

3 Para would hand over responsibility to the Royal Marines, who in turn handed over to the Grenadier Guards six months later. As new units and commanders came and went, new tactics and ideas were tried, but between 2006 and 2010, nothing much changed. The British Army was still stretched to breaking point. They were reinforced in 2007, with an extra 1,400 soldiers, bringing the total number of British troops in Afghanistan to 7,700.[25] But trying to cover an area half the size of England, while unwanted by most of the population, was a huge task. The warlords competing for regional domination, those involved in the narcotics trade, and the Taliban all worked together with the sole aim of killing as many foreigners as possible. This was reflected in the casualty figures: 37 were killed in 2006 (including 14 in an RAF Nimrod crash); 42 in 2007; 51 in 2008; 108 in 2009, and another 104 in 2010.[26]

The situation became so bad that the Chief of the General Staff, General Richard Dannatt, made the unusual decision to speak out publicly about the deplorable stress and conditions his troops were now facing. Dannatt, who believed 'it was an error not to reconsider the deployment (to Helmand) when the situation in southern Iraq deteriorated during 2005 and 2006',[27] said in September 2006, 'We are running hot, certainly running hot. Can we cope? I Pause. I say "Just." We are meeting challenges on the hoof.'[28] Dannatt, who left two years later after being snubbed by politicians he had criticised, also would openly call for better pay, better support from the general public, and an earlier exit from Iraq.

Brigadier Ed Butler, who had commanded 16 Air Assault Brigade in Helmand, resigned in 2008. Lieutenant Colonel Stuart Tootal revealed to *The Sunday Times* why he had decided to leave the Army, despite being promoted and, like Brigadier Butler, having been told he had a bright future ahead of him. The article details a list of failings during the Helmand deployment, particularly expressing anger at the government's 'wishful thinking' about the mission. But most of all, he felt he could no longer serve while soldiers were being treated so badly – whether it was pay, accommodation for the soldiers and their families, or the way injured soldiers were being treated in civilian hospitals when they returned to the UK. 'Being a good soldier was not about rank, but about how you treat people and look after them.'[29]

Stuart B., who had been heavily involved in the decision-making process during *Herrick IV*, said, 'There is so much to tell about Afghanistan.' On return to the UK he was promoted to WO2 and became the company sergeant major of Support Company for the battalion's second tour of Afghanistan in 2008. He describes the tour as the height of his military career and proudly boasts that the battalion were the first to return from a six-month tour to Helmand without loss of life.

Shaun G. was involved with the retaking of Musa Qala in December 2007. 'We were tasked with securing the high ground around the villages to stop the enemy leaving or reinforcing.' He describes the six months he was in Helmand Province as 'his best tour'. He goes on to say, 'The boys in my troop became men. I was tough on them and used discipline to ensure all of my troop returned home alive.' He also had some close calls too. In a position near FOB Edinburgh he was giving formal orders (O Group) to his troop when he was hit by small-arms fire that penetrated his body armour. On a patrol back to Camp Bastion he was lead vehicle and saw a suspicious dip in the ground. 'My sixth sense told me that something was not right so I told my driver to stop.' His right-hand track was just 6 inches from a 500lb IED. He said, 'I learnt that day to always trust my instincts.'

Jules H. returned to Afghanistan in 2008, on *Herrick VIII*. He, too, had been promoted. But unlike Stuart B. and 3 Para, tragedy would once again befall D Squadron, HCR, who would lose two more soldiers during the tour. One would die on the very first patrol, and in a terrible twist of fate, another on one of the last patrols of the tour. As the SQMC of the squadron, Jules H. spent most of his time in Camp Bastion with his Admin Troop, working hard to make sure that troops on the ground had everything they needed to carry out their mission. On 2 May 2008, Jules H. was tasked with carrying out one of the worst things any soldier could ever be asked to do. During the squadron's very first patrol of their deployment, a Spartan CVR(T) suffered a mine strike that took the life of Trooper Ratu Babakobau and injured three others. 'Babu and his family lived next door to me in Windsor … His kids used to come round my house because I gave them sweets.' As the senior Household Cavalryman in Camp Bastion at the time, it was his responsibility to formally identify the body.

> The Warrant Officer in charge of the hospital was really helpful and considerate; I could tell he knew what I was going through … it was a really harrowing experience, one I will never forget … After I had positively identified my friend, I had to make a statement to a captain in the Royal Military Police. The final thing he said to me was, 'We will treat this as murder, and it will be vigorously investigated.' I knew this was a lie.

In October 2008, Jules H. left Afghanistan for the last time. He told me in a conversation, 'Afghanistan was fucking awful, but I wouldn't have missed it for the world.'

By 2010, strategy had changed. The clear-hold-build strategy that had been used in Iraq was now in vogue in Afghanistan. No clearing of the enemy from a populated area would now take place unless assets were in place to hold it and prevent insurgents from returning. ISAF also made it public knowledge that they were intent on moving into an area in hope that it encouraged insurgents to leave. This way, there would be no major destruction or collateral damage. Then, within these key population centres, ISAF troops would maintain law and order, while Afghans got on with rebuilding their lives. This worked to an extent; the Taliban realised they could not match ISAF firepower and continue to take unacceptable losses. But the Taliban switched up their strategy, too, with devastating effect. The use of IEDs and mines had already been effective; however, it soon became the Taliban's weapon of choice in a newly focused insurgency. Anywhere that troops patrolled on foot or in vehicles, the Taliban would target them.

Also in 2010, as part of the 'Obama Surge', US troops took over the northern district centres of Musa Qala, Sangin, and Now Zad. In an ironic twist, the original territory troops of *Herrick IV* had been sent to secure in May 2006 would now become Britain's sole responsibility in Helmand. This was reflected in the casualty figures. In 2011, the number of those wounded in action had gone down to 274. In 2009 and 2010, 508 and 510 respectively were wounded. This figure went down further to 222 in 2012, then to 95 in 2013, and 17 in 2014.[30]

Soldiers deployed in Afghanistan, whether they were in Camp Bastion, at a forward operating base, or patrolling a town, knew the situation on the ground. Despite talk of improved security, a six-month tour to Helmand Province was still an experience few would ever forget. Added to the mix was the fact that a majority of soldiers who had five to six years' service under their belts had probably already seen combat or at least been on an operational tour. In 2006, General Dannatt had warned that the Army was being pushed to breaking point, and this was starting to have a terrible effect upon individual soldiers, too.

Andrew T. was one such soldier. In 2006, he was a staff sergeant working as an intake medic at the Royal Military Academy, Sandhurst. Despite having had some mental health issues after Bosnia, Kosovo, and Iraq, he was enjoying life. He got married in 2006, and by the time he deployed to Afghanistan in 2012, he had three children.

> At this point Helmand was making the news. I followed events in both Iraq and Afghanistan closely. When I was due a posting again, against my better judgement I asked to go to a medical unit due to deploy to Afghanistan … Really I was far too gone to deploy again, but I kept quiet about my issues and deployed with 4 Medical Regiment in March 2012 on Op *Herrick XVI*. I was assigned as a medic to C Squadron, The King's Royal Hussars.

During his deployment, he spent most of his time at Camp Nahidullah, a patrol base in the Lashkar Gar district constructed in 2010, which closed just a few months after he left in 2012. Andrew kindly sent me a transcript of the diary he kept while he was there. He told me, 'I haven't changed anything, names, places, or thoughts at the time.' As well as being a moving insight into what life was like in Afghanistan – the harsh conditions they faced, the incessant patrolling in the ever-increasing heat of an Afghan summer – it also shows the mental strain and pressure that everyone was under.

One thing that immediately stood out was the number of ISAF casualties still happening in 2012. Every soldier who has ever served in Afghanistan would have heard the message 'Op Minimise' called over a radio or broadcast on the tannoy system at Camp Bastion or one of the patrol bases. Whenever there was an incident with soldiers killed or seriously wounded, 'Op Minimise' would be called. This informed soldiers that there would be a complete ban on external communications, a total blackout of phone calls and internet use, until the next of kin of those involved had been informed, eliminating the risk of rumours being spread back home. It was absolutely the right thing to do; no soldier would wish another's family hearing a rumour that a loved one had been killed or seriously injured. But 'Op Minimise' had a debilitating effect on morale. Every time it was called, soldiers knew that somewhere a soldier's family was having the worst day of their lives.

From late March to mid-August when Andrew made daily entries, 'Op Minimise' is recorded almost every day. On 26 March, his first day at Bastion, he wrote, 'Just after 10 a.m. "Standby for broadcast, Op Minimise, Op Minimise, Op Minimise". Already? Fuck me we only just got here – the colour drains from some of the younger faces – this shit is real.' In other entries he wrote, 'Can't call Tracey due to Op Minimise. Hope she doesn't worry', and 'gutted I can't call Tracey due to Op Minimise, will try tomorrow morning.'

Like most soldiers' experiences of an operational tour in Afghanistan, there is enough material in his diary to fill a book on its own. Between 26 March and 23 August 2012, Andrew carried out his duties as a combat medic and med team leader. It is full of incidents while on patrol or designated operations. It describes friends and comrades being injured and of having to deal with grief and loss on a daily basis. If you read his final entry (after a six-week lapse), just a week before he was due to return home, you get a full picture of what he had been through and the struggles that lay ahead.

> Well, ashamedly, it has been almost six weeks since I last wrote. I'm not sure why I stopped writing, laziness, lack of interest, or maybe a continuing disbelief in the cause we are supposed to be fighting for. An enormous amount has happened in the last six weeks, and as I sit here and reflect, I have mixed emotions. I feel pride, sadness, bitterness and contempt. Pride in the fact I helped in some small way when Camp Bastion … was attacked. Sadness that I am still suffering the psychological effects of past conflicts. Bitterness that this war has continued unabated for over 10 years, the lies and deceit told to our troops. And I now have nothing but contempt for a religion and the people who worship it … and casualties have been steady over the past six weeks.

I spent just over two weeks in Bastion as a guest of the Field Mental Health Team. I went there in late August after some bizarre nights of sleeplessness. I was feeling vulnerable and scared for my life, believing people were trying to kill me. I woke one night after a terrible nightmare to find I was clutching a loaded pistol. I was jumping at every bang, and tearful at anything that reminded me of the Bosnian War. During two weeks of rest in Camp Bastion, I had regular meetings with Mel, my assigned CPN. I still never felt safe in Bastion, but went day to day.

On the night of 14 September, Bastion came under attack from a highly trained group of Taliban in American uniforms. The evening was total chaos, and everyone was on lockdown in their workplace.

I watched and listened to the battle unfold across the airfield. Explosions, tracer, and fire lit the sky. Casualties started to arrive. Our ambulances also came under attack. The Taliban had got onto the airfield and were causing total destruction and chaos. I watched gunships doing strafing runs of the airfield, and the clatter of gunfire was incessant. As most people were in nightclothes, and I was in uniform, I volunteered to man the armoured ambulance with a few others. It had taken some time to get it from the REME some 500 metres away as rounds had been coming through the compound. Once loaded we headed to the main gate of the airfield and waited. We had heard reports of five casualties. The gate was held by two US Marines, two RAF Policemen, and some civilian security contractors. Now on the edge of the airfield, I watched the battle only a few hundred metres away. Fuel dumps were ablaze, gunfire crackled away, and RPGs thumped into targets. Reports came in that the runway was littered with the dead. I stayed there all night, helping where I could. The RAF Regiment fought gallantly, suffering numerous casualties. We resupplied them with ammo and water throughout the night … As dawn broke, the first of the dead arrived. I helped carry LtCol Chris Raible (USMC) from the back of a truck. He was draped in the Stars and Stripes and we loaded him into an ambulance for the trip to the hospital … Later on another body arrived. Sgt Bradley Atwell (USMC). We loaded him onto an ambulance and along with his best friend I accompanied him to the mortuary. That was the most unpleasant drive I have ever had. We were relieved later that morning. The Taliban dead had to wait as they were, in most cases, badly burned and covered in ammo and grenades, and had to be cleared before removal … The whole of Bastion was numb to what had happened, everyone was on lockdown. Gun positions had been set up everywhere. Damage is estimated at £200 million. Three fuel dumps, six Harrier jets, buildings and vehicles all destroyed. 15 enemy dead, one captured, two ISAF dead and nine wounded. A Taliban victory if ever there was one.

It was the 15 September, Tracey's birthday. I didn't even remember. Minimise came off for about 20 mins later that day, then back on because two guys had been shot dead in a green on blue … That night in the cookhouse, Bastion came under mortar fire, the first time ever. I lay on the floor in the dining area and laughed. Looking around, people looked terrified. KBR private contractor guys were crying with fear. It wasn't until the morning of the 16th and looking at Facebook that I even knew the previous day was Tracey's birthday. I felt awful.

Well it is now 3 October and my time is nearly done. Replacements are arriving every day. Mine arrives on 10 October and I leave for Bastion on the 12th, Cyprus on the 15th and home on the 17th.

Home to my family, my wife, my children. Ryan was a baby when I left, now he is a toddler. Talking, climbing, and nearly walking.

We have not been on patrol in nearly three weeks. The Taliban are free to return. The areas that had been fought for so hard for over the years, British blood spilt and lives lost, have been retaken by the enemy. The Taliban sit 600 metres from our west wall, about 30 strong. But it's technically over the battle group boundary, so we do nothing. A high-level commander lives 300 metres from our north wall, but it's over our boundary.

Patrol Base Nahidullah will close eight weeks after we leave. The Afghan Uniformed Police, in whose hands we leave this area, are corrupt to the core and not fit for the task. This area will flood with Taliban within weeks. We know they are here already, waiting. And when we are gone, they will reappear. The war is lost. We have built a few roads, some schools, and maybe a health centre, and the population feels safe because we are here. When we go it's all over. Back to square one. But the generals and politicians will tell us it was worth it, and a great success. They will praise the sacrifice of the dead and the wounded. Tell that to a generation of young men and women, who have fought in Iraq and Afghanistan, seen friends die, had limbs blown off, and lives crushed.

In the spring of 2014, Task Force Helmand came to an end, and Camp Bastion was handed over to Afghan security forces. The last British combat troops left the country in October 2014, with about 450 remaining to train and advise local Afghan security forces. Between 2002 and 2014, Britain suffered 456 casualties, 405 killed as a result of hostile action.[31] The British Army fired 46 million bullets,[32] and the conflict cost the United Kingdom £40 billion.

CHAPTER 14

The Aftermath

Soldiers who joined the British Army in the late 1980s, then served a full 22-year career, would have left around 2009–10. Some left earlier, deciding that it was, for varying reasons, the right time to leave. A few actually served longer than their 22-year point because of manning short-falls, and there are some who are still serving today as Late-Entry Commissioned Officers.

Like many generations of soldiers, this group has the distinction of having served through an unprecedented and tumultuous period of history. They belong collectively to a remarkable generation, but also each one has an individual story, and their stories reveal that some have adapted well to life after the Army, while others have not.

In October 1992, after returning from Knightsbridge with his regiment about to move back to the UK, Martin M. decided that it was the right time for him to leave the Army

> I left because I thought I'd missed my chance of a war when I didn't go to the Gulf. After all, that was the first real action since 1982. How wrong was I? The regiment promptly went out to Bosnia, and later deployed to Kosovo, Iraq, and Afghanistan … gutted doesn't even begin to describe it. If I'm honest, it still bugs me that I made such a rash decision and left when I did. But you can't put an old head on young shoulders.

Martin M. exchanged one uniform for another and went on to serve 25 years in the Hampshire Fire Service, retiring as a watch manager in 2018. He credits the leadership style he learned in the Army for helping him in his second career. 'I've since applied the same method of leadership and management in the fire service, and have been thanked more than once by firefighters on the watches that I have managed for treating them with respect.' Although he left the Army after just eight years and 54 days, he noted, 'Strangely, despite the 25 years I served, the fire service means considerably less to me than the Army.'

After serving in the Gulf War and Bosnia, Soldier M. decided to leave the Army, also after eight years. 'It was the best job in the world, despite the stress, heartache, and suffering from the effects of serving in the Gulf War and with Bosnia constantly on my mind.' He admits now that he struggled with mental health issues. 'It wasn't on anyone's radar back in those days.' He moved to London, landing a great job and a steady girlfriend. He was doing really well for himself, but he knew things were not right. 'I was aware that my head was very much off centre, and I struggled to comprehend and cope with a civilian work ethic. I remember being very angry at times, and had the odd bar scuffle or two, one of which landed me in deep shit.'

As well as losing his job and girlfriend, Soldier M. ended up in court on charges of assault.

> It was my first offence, I was ex-Army, had a decent brief, and good references, but the judge threw the book at me … he said he was making an example of me as I should have known better as a trained soldier … I got six months and served three. My girlfriend dumped me and had an abortion while I was there … Pentonville Prison is a scary place and three months seemed like years. I got out safe but totally traumatised.

Soldier P. saw service in the Gulf, Northern Ireland, Bosnia, Kosovo, and Iraq. In 2003, after returning to the UK, he was getting ready for his annual parachute jumps.

> Every year to maintain para-pay you have to complete a certain amount of jumps, and before you carry out these jumps you have to be cleared by a doctor. During my medical I was diagnosed with leishmaniasis caused by sand flies in Iraq. The doctor prescribed me with antibiotics but I was cleared to jump. I was never comfortable with heights, so I normally didn't sleep the night before a jump and certainly not on the plane on the way to the drop-zone, but this time I did both. As I came to the door, I felt very relaxed which also had never happened before. On the way down I didn't check my canopy or steer away – it was if I was just going through the motions. When I hit the ground I must have had my legs apart because I broke my leg and couldn't move. Once I was found I could tell by the look on their faces that it was really bad – my foot was facing the wrong way.

When he was taken to hospital, it was discovered that instead of taking antibiotics he'd been given antidepressants for the leishmaniasis by mistake. After several weeks in hospital he was then moved to RHQ as the Intelligence Warrant Officer where he spent two years before finishing his service with the Royal Yeomanry.

Having served in the Gulf, Bosnia, and Kosovo with his regiment, then in Macedonia, Sierra Leone, Afghanistan, and Iraq with the Pathfinder Platoon, Rich G. was at a crossroads in his career. After returning from Iraq with his regiment he expressed a wish to return to the Pathfinder Platoon.

> The regiment wasn't happy with that and wanted me back at regimental duty to follow a more traditional career path … I was picked up on the 2004 promotions board … but the Pathfinder Platoon offered me the CQMS slot early so they wouldn't lose me. I said if I didn't go back to the Pathfinder platoon I would leave, so off to the Pathfinders I went. The CO wasn't happy and barred me from staying in the platoon past my CQMS posting.

After six months in the post there was a change in leadership at the Pathfinder Platoon. 'The new OC confirmed that I would have to go back to the regiment and that I could try and get back to the platoon at a later date as Ops WO. At that point I signed off.' After serving 17 years, just five years short of a full pension, Rich G.

left the Army, taking his considerable skillset into the private sector. 'I'm not bitter about my time in the Army and loved both my regiment and the Pathfinders. It was just time to move on and find a new challenge.'

Owen C. left the Army as a WO1 after 22 years and found the transition to civilian life 'rather difficult'. He finished his career at the Royal Armoured Corps Centre in Dorset, 'away from the regimental family'. He found that even as a warrant officer there was little help. 'Nobody wanted to go out of their way and just left me to it. As you get to the end of your career less time was invested in the older guys … Added to that I was diagnosed with cancer so that put any career transition on hold.'

Angus T. also finished as a WO1 posted away from the regiment where he had spent most of his Army career. But he was better prepared than most when he left because he had bought a house in the mid-1990s, and that meant there was less disruption for his family. 'My last posting in Manchester was perfect because my house was less than an hour away. The children were in good schools, never had to worry about moving whenever I was posted, and being in the property market at a young age was a huge benefit later on.'

Paul H. was medically discharged as a staff sergeant because of injuries he had sustained in a climbing accident in Alaska several years prior. Having served 24 years and in almost every operational deployment conducted by the British Army since he joined in 1985, he found the sudden change hard at first. 'I received no support at all, nothing. In one day, civilian the next. Nobody goes out of their way to help, and there was no respect given for being a veteran.'

Conrad P. left the Army as a WO2 after 24 years, then served as a policeman for another six. Scarred by his service, carrying serious anger issues, and still not fully aware of what he had become, he says it took him nearly 30 years to realise that he was a bully. He had several wake-up calls that eventually helped him. He came across a Facebook page written by former Sandhurst officer cadets entitled, 'Cadets scarred by Conrad P.', and while coaching his son during a rugby match, he was approached by a teacher who told him his coaching was verging on child abuse. 'I keep my anger in check now, but I know it's there just simmering away at the surface.'

Soldier B. left the Army as a WO2 after 22 years. 'Whilst I had the opportunity to commission in my own regiment, I opted to leave regular service so that my wife could pursue her dream of becoming a midwife, and my kids could have some stability in school.' Having previously served as a permanent staff instructor with the TA, he always intended to get back into uniform one day. 'When I left I had no issue getting a good civilian job but I missed the lifestyle, camaraderie, and pride of being in uniform, so when the opportunity came along, I jumped at the chance.' He has since been commissioned with the TA and served as a troop commander in Afghanistan.

Soldier G. left as a WO1 and is another soldier who seemed to adapt well to life out of the Army. 'For me it's been easy as I joined late at 21 and owned my own house during my service. I always had a civilian outlet; either football, rugby or cricket clubs around where we lived.'

After his close escapes in Afghanistan, Shaun G. was happy to take a couple of desk jobs in Windsor. Because of the manpower shortages created by Options for Change many soldiers were asked if they wanted to serve an extra five years. 'They realised there was a massive gap ... so they asked certain people if they would like to go back for five years, giving them a 27-year career. It was sold as a good thing, as they said you could still be promoted as normal. But it soon became clear that we were being passed over as the younger guys were coming through.' His family have now settled in the Windsor area, thankful for being stationed in one place for the majority of his Army career. It meant his family could put down roots. 'Apart from a little stress regarding purchasing a house and me getting a job once I left the Army, there was very little disruption for the family, making the transition easier on all of us.'

Jules H. also agreed to serve longer. 'I had already finished my 22-year engagement, but in 2006, whilst in Afghanistan, I was offered a five-year extension which would have taken me to my 45th birthday. However, I was in my second year of continuance when the redundancy package came out.' He left the Army in 2012, with a bad taste in his mouth, after he and his family were put into financial difficulties over his married quarters. Because he had volunteered for redundancy, unbeknownst to him, he was charged at a much higher rate after he left. By the time he moved into the new house that he had just bought using all the money from his redundancy package, he was suddenly faced with a massive bill. Despite being deeply affected by his service experiences, he still has a sharp sense of humour. 'When I came out of the Army I was employed as a driver and personal assistant to a wealthy landowner. I went from having the ability to order life or death over an entire grid square on a map to deciding which piece of peacock shit to pick up.'

Stuart B. returned from a second tour of Afghanistan in 2008 as the support company CSM. The following year he was posted back to the mortar division at the Support Weapons School, ITC Warminster, as the division sergeant major. He stayed in this post until he left the Army as a WO2 in 2012.

> I have been lucky since I left the Army ... I worked in the maritime security industry alongside ex-forces, like-minded people in a military environment. I worked at sea for two years before being offered a job in the UAE as a military advisor/instructor ... My current job is also similar to serving in the Army so I haven't had to deal with issues most ex-military are required to deal with in a civilian workplace. I'm happy in an environment that I feel comfortable with.

Doug K. left the Army as a WO1 and became a doctor's practice manager but found the transition out of uniform very difficult. Despite a rough baptism into a new working environment that he called 'something of a shock', he has been able to bring his colleagues around to his way of thinking. But for him, the struggles of life after the Army have taken their toll.

Integration into the civilian world is an area I feel I have failed at. I have tried to make new friends but struggle … I guess the connection you have with Army friends cannot be replicated. I chat online with guys I've not seen for years and it just flows. With civilians it is just hard work and I don't feel they are worth it. Since none of the people I served with live near me it creates a certain amount of loneliness.

Andrew T. returned to the UK from Afghanistan in October 2012. 'I was never the same. I showed all the signs of chronic PTSD but my superiors never clicked. I picked it up in a half-dozen of my younger soldiers and got them help, but I didn't help myself. I was the Sergeant Major now, I'm not allowed to be weak … eventually it got too much and I gave in.' After seeing his unit medical officer, he was referred to a mental health specialist. He was again diagnosed with severe and complex PTSD. In 2014, after 23 years in the Army, Andrew was a WO2, but he felt like he was being treated like he had committed a crime.

I was downgraded and put on permanent sick leave to await medical discharge. I was sat at home for nearly a year with next to no support from my parent unit … I felt ostracised and forgotten … There was no dine-out or final CO's interview. When I went to hand in my ID card I was ignored and ended up giving it to a junior AGC private. I walked out the gate and that was it. I was not offered any mental health care or a referral to the NHS. I was totally alone and had never felt more disappointed. I didn't know how to be a civilian as I had lived in a military environment since the day I was born.

Andrew now lives with his family in the New Forest and runs his own business.

***

Although it is soldiers that go on operations and have to deal with the Army and all that it has to throw at them, when they leave their family and spend lengthy periods of time away, the strain it places upon those they leave behind is immense and sometimes overwhelming. Many relationships have failed because of the pressure placed upon them. However, others have thrived, with soldiers crediting the strength of their partners and family helping them through some very difficult times.

Conrad P. credits his family – his wife 'for keeping him sane', and his son for being brutally honest when it was needed.

My wife and I have been together since she was my girlfriend at school. Our relationship is stronger now than it's ever been … My son was offered a commission in a Welsh infantry regiment. He told me, 'I'll end up like you if I join … there is 10 per cent of you that is nuts, and I don't want to end up like that.' So he turned it down.

Soldier D. recalls the strain one operational tour placed upon his wife and family. 'It wasn't until I got home that I realised what my wife and parents had been through. It had been really easy for me – I just did my job. But she was alone in a married quarter in Germany with very few friends, and my parents were beside themselves worrying about me. They were all glad when it was over and I was on my way home.'

Stuart B. says his wife always knew before they got married that his regiment would come first; 23 years later they are still happily married. 'She has supported me through thick and thin, and I couldn't have asked for a better partner.' His son has had to watch him leave home many times so he is empathetic to others in the same situation. 'I feel for families in general who never get any recognition for the sacrifice they make being married to service personnel.'

Paul H. said his service has had a massive effect upon him and his family. Whenever he returned home, he 'had huge problems settling back into the family routine'. He remembers hearing one of his children saying to his wife, 'When is Dad returning to camp?' Although he and his family have remained intact, he said, 'You can never make this time back.' He also spoke of many of his close friends who have since separated or divorced.

Doug K. says three decades in the Army was hard on his family. 'By the time I came to hand in my ID card the damage to family life had already been done ... I was single again so I was walking out of mess accommodation into the big wide world on my own.'

Andrew T. was not married until 2006, with his first child being born that November. But by the time his son was seven, he had spent four years of his life on operations or training exercises. 'That level of separation is very hard on families, especially the children.'

Some soldiers attempted to shield their families from the dangers they faced. Jules H. sometimes told his wife 'white lies' in letters and on the phone that he was not in harm's way and was miles away from danger. 'During one call she suddenly said, "You're such a liar." A few days earlier she'd been in camp for a family's lunch when she heard from a senior officer that my vehicle had been hit by an IED.'

The thought of being reunited with their loved ones is what got many soldiers through gruelling operational tours. Soldier A. said, 'It was my family, thinking of them in the worst of times that stopped me descending into some very dark places.' For Andrew T. it was the ability to be able to talk to his wife and children from Afghanistan. And for Jules H. it was the thought of walking in the English countryside with his family and dog. Next to a photograph he posted on social media he wrote, 'Fabulous day this. Got back from Afghanistan the day before. Took my dog and the girls for a walk around the Great Park. Felt the fresh air, and was with the people I love the most.'

***

Where social issues are concerned, the Army that this generation of soldiers left is a very different place from the one they joined. With regards to diversity, Shaun G. thinks 'the changes the Army has made are amazing'. He goes on to say, 'I served through the time when it was deemed okay to throw bananas at Black soldiers and gays were deemed to be evil.' Where diversity is concerned, all soldiers I interviewed are in agreement that the changes have been positive. Paul H. says, 'People need to be treated equally, even if they are different in some way.' And Andrew T. said differences should not matter, 'so long as they can do their job'.

There is no doubt that the changes made by the British Army have not only been necessary and the right thing to do, but we're all better for it – the Army, soldiers, and society. Soldiers are now more empathetic and better equipped to deal with situations they might face on future operations. I've seen a video of a young rifleman giving a lesson on assault pioneering to Afghan soldiers in both Punjabi and Hindi. I've felt huge amounts of pride as a young female medic was awarded the Military Cross for bravery on an operation in Iraq, and watched numerous ethnic minority and female soldiers riding on the Trooping of the Colour in both the Household Cavalry and King's Troop, Royal Horse Artillery.

Even though some of the answers I received during my interviews might not be what the Army of today is looking for from its soldiers, not once did I think that someone was being racist, homophobic, or misogynistic. They sometimes had views that that differed from official policy, but never did they demean someone because of their race, sex, or gender.

Even though attitudes have changed and the Army is actively taking action, it does not mean that prejudice does not still exist. An army is a mirror image of society, and so in a world that has become more polarised and divided, both Army and society still have a long way to go.

Regarding women serving on the front line in combat, some soldiers I interviewed have retained deep misgivings, but their opinions centre around a woman's physicality to do a particular job that few men can do rather than prejudice against women. Stuart B. has seen war and death and is adamant in his view that 'There is no place for women on the battlefield.' Both he and Dave M. also believe they are distractions. 'I have seen first-hand what happens when loads of male soldiers are posturing around a pretty girl', but he is quick to point out that this is not the fault of the female soldier. Shaun G. thinks the new ruling regarding women in combat could be a good thing. 'We will have to wait a few years to see what effects if any it has on the Army.' Angus T. agrees and says, 'We have been one of the last armed forces to let females into combat arms. Israel has had them for years.'

Despite the seismic social changes that took place during their careers, most soldiers appear to have coped well. Although they embraced the upheavals, with many changing long-held opinions, some have become extremely bitter towards an Army that appears to want all its soldiers to now be 'politically correct'.

Soldier E. says there is blame enough for all. 'The generations before ours started this – the racism and bigotry that ran through the Army had to change, no question. It changed all right, but now we have a generation of self-entitled barrack room lawyers who are easily offended and seem to have no respect for authority.' One soldier has such strong views on the subject that he says he 'came to loathe' what the Army had become. Another was equally scathing when he said, 'I have no time for the snowflake generation at all.' Like many he admits that he has struggled with demands to be more politically correct. 'I have to hold my tongue and engage brain before mouth in order to not upset people.' A third soldier said, 'Luckily I was coming up to the end of my service when the real snowflake invasion started. There were times when I would look around camp in disbelief.' Soldier G. says that living in the PC world is something he has had to adapt to. 'It's taken the fun out of everything. You have to watch what you say all the time and it can be very uncomfortable when you can't relax.'

But there are soldiers who see things very differently. Soldier B. believes, 'The so-called snowflake generation are no different to others that came before them ... They are a product of our society and I have no doubt they will perform just as well on operations if called to do so.'

Jules H. told me a story that shows soldiers of any age can cope on operations. During his 2006 deployment in Afghanistan, his vehicle was hit by an IED while out on patrol. After the blast the Scimitar came to a sudden halt. His driver was closed down at the time, so he was closest to the origin point of the explosion and therefore most exposed. 'I climbed out to open his hatch, terrified at what I might find in there. When I ripped the hatch open, I was met with two thumbs in the air, a big grin, and the words, "That was fucking brill, can we do it again?" Not bad for an 18-year-old on his first deployment.'

***

One subject that unites everyone is the continued prosecution of retired soldiers. This first started after the Good Friday Agreement and the PSNI's Historical Enquiries Team. Several soldiers, one of them in his seventies, was charged with offences even though years earlier he had been found not culpable. Then, after the 2003 invasion of Iraq, came the Iraq Historical Allegations Team. Two soldiers who have helped me with this book gave witness statements before it was shut down.

Soldiers' opinions are strong, heartfelt, and show a depth of anger that successive British governments have not fully understood. Paul H. and Soldier G. called the harassment of former soldiers 'a disgrace'. Soldier G. went on to say, 'The hypocrisy of the GFA winds me up.' Both Soldier A. and Dave M. agreed that 'soldiers should be held accountable if they have done wrong, but if they've already been cleared, then they should not be dragged through the courts years later because of newly discovered hearsay evidence.'

Angus T. said the situation made his blood boil, asking why retired soldiers were being harassed. 'Tony Blair should be in the dock with all his cronies ... Giving a get out of jail free letter to a terrorist has to be the most despicable things our government has ever done.' Stuart B. also attacks those who have allowed the prosecutions. 'Northern Ireland was a war zone and every time you went on patrol your life was on the line … these people have never been in such situations.'

Future governments, including the new Office for Veteran Affairs, established in October 2019, have to understand that how these soldiers have been treated by their country will have massive implications for the future of the British Army. In recent years, recruiting and retention has suffered. In 2019, it reached crisis level when numbers plummeted to the lowest level in modern history.[1] These highly publicised cases and the resulting outcry from the veteran community are seen by both potential recruits and serving soldiers alike who are asking themselves if they want to be in an Army that might turn its back on them in years to come.

The Army is based on discipline; these prosecutions erode that away. Will serving soldiers start to call into question orders given to them on a battlefield? Owen C. thinks so. 'I like to think that we follow orders given to us in the knowledge of being given a certain amount of protection.' Shaun G. actually thinks this issue 'will affect future deployments'.

Soldier B. not only calls the prosecutions despicable, but also he fears for the future. Writing to me on 24 February 2020, he said, 'Unless the persecution of Northern Ireland and Iraq veterans is addressed with the government taking a robust stance … then we are simply storing up problems for the future. How long is it before we see historical crime allegations from Afghanistan?' Just 10 days later, a BBC News article appeared on its website: 'Afghan Conflict: Top court backs war crimes probe'.[2]

***

In 2007, a report appeared in the *British Medical Journal* publishing the results of a three-year study looking at the mental health of 5,547 members of the UK armed forces.[3] The results show a direct correlation between the frequency with which soldiers go on operational tours and the chance of them suffering from PTSD. The report also concluded that soldiers who deployed for 13 months or more over a three-year period were consistently associated with problems at home both before and after deployment, and displayed psychological symptoms.[4]

Thirteen years since the report was published, the results are obvious to society – a marked increase in soldiers who are suffering from PTSD, who have been convicted in civilian courts, are homeless, or who have taken their own lives. Many who are suffering from untreated PTSD turn to drink and drugs and even become homeless. In January 2018, it was reported that as many as 13,000 ex-servicemen are now living on the streets.[5] Others end up in prison. In 2010, it was reported that almost 3,000 ex-servicemen, or 3.5 per cent of the entire prison population, were serving jail sentences within the British judicial system.[6] This sustained high rate of incarceration has led to calls for action to be taken. Since retiring as Chief of the General Staff in 2013, General Lord Sir Richard Dannatt has been a vocal advocate for better conditions for veterans, especially regarding the treatment of PTSD. In 2018, he called for mental health assessments for all servicemen upon discharge and for it to become part of the resettlement process.[7]

Almost every soldier I interviewed knows someone who has taken their own life after leaving the Army. The alarm bells have been ringing for decades; 400 ex-servicemen and women have committed suicide since 1995.[8] But the full scale of what is happening now, with an alarming rise in the number of suicides by Afghanistan veterans, has only just started to sink in.[9]

Stuart B. agrees that suicides are on the increase. 'I have had a few lads who I know committed suicide for reasons only known to themselves. You need to be in one hell of a dark place to even contemplate such actions. More support needs to be given when required but you can only help if the person asks for it. Many a time these lads do not show any key signs that enable others to step in and help.'

The rise in suicides has affected Andrew T. badly.

> I have lost four friends to suicide in the last few years. I have been that low, but the love of a good wife and family have pulled me through. It's a total lack of understanding from the civilian health service to veterans' needs that is the fundamental problem. If the help isn't there and the guys are at their lowest there can seem to be no way out but suicide.

Shaun G. has also been affected by the increasing number of veteran suicides. 'Losing a number of mates to suicide has really hit me hard. Luckily, I have a number of friends I can talk/drink with, and we deal with it in our own way.'

Soldier G. believes it is a much broader issue. 'I believe it's not just a forces thing … men between the age of 24 and 45 are more likely to commit suicide regardless of their background.' His experience in the ambulance service gives weight to his assertion. 'No matter where in society they were, rich, poor, civilian, or ex-forces, it was always men.'

Owen C. agrees and thinks the solution could be to talk. 'There certainly is a problem with people committing suicide. Men can be very stubborn and will not talk about problems and are very reluctant to go to the doctor if they are unwell, until it is too late.'

Soldier B. thinks more study is needed. 'It's not affected me personally, but it has made me question whether all these suicides are as a direct result of army service (PTSD) or does it just happen that the victims served at some time in the Army? It's difficult to get a clear, unbiased picture.'

Data analysis from the Office of National Statistics seem to support these opinions. In 2018 there was a 'significant increase in the rate of deaths registered as suicide … largely driven by an increase among men who have continued to be most at risk'.[10] Whether the increase is driven solely by veteran suicides or a general trend among men (civilian and ex-military) is not clear.

Some think that there are those that are taking advantage. Stuart B. openly admits that he finds the issue of mental health 'a very difficult subject to quantify'. He acknowledges that PTSD exists and many serving and ex-service personnel suffer with it. But he also believes many have jumped on the 'PTSD bandwagon ... Half of these people have never seen war or death and everything that goes with it but still cry PTSD at the earliest opportunity.' Although Soldier B.'s opinions on mental health are not as clear cut, he does think there are some that are being dishonest, playing the system. 'Invisible injuries are just that and in my opinion they are being exploited by a small number who are using this for their own financial gain.'

Andrew T. was not looking for an excuse or financial gain. He had just been promoted, but his military career was brought to an abrupt end when he asked for help.

> I referred myself, and as a result lost my career. As a warrant officer I was made to feel that I had no right to suffer from PTSD. I tried for nearly 28 years to deal with it, but it got worse, and I couldn't hide it anymore. I had the audacity to seek help and be downgraded which was all an inconvenience for the unit.

One of the many incidents that was to cause Andrew T. to have recurring nightmares and flashbacks took place in Basra, which led to him having to give evidence during the IHAT investigations. The company of infantry he was attached to conducted a house search operation when an Iraqi civilian was shot. Andrew went into the house and tried to save him. 'I had a part of his stomach in one hand and his liver in the other. His last words before he died were, "Why Mr. Bush, why?"'

***

Marcus Tullius Cicero supposedly said, 'Where there's life, there's hope.' For soldiers who have left the Army after an unprecedented period of history, have experienced the hardships and heartbreak of multiple operations over two decades, and who have learned to live with its effects, there are signs of hope.

There are also signs that the British Army are now taking mental health seriously and have learned from mistakes of the past. Soldier B. certainly thinks so. 'The Army attitude to mental health has changed immeasurably and recognisably over the last five years. The long-held stigma around it being perceived as a weakness is starting to recede and this has been helped massively with the two princes publicly talking of their own experiences. Access to trained individuals is easy and soldiers are signposted to them if necessary.'

Over recent years there has been an emergence of 'Breakfast Clubs', where veterans of all ages and regiments can get together and talk over a cup of tea and a bacon sandwich. Founded in 2007 by ex-soldier Dereck Hardman, the Armed Forces and Veterans Breakfast Clubs now have over 300 clubs in 14 countries with over 100,000 members. The club exists to simply help veterans 'return to the tribe'.[11]

After getting his life back on track after his short prison sentence, Soldier M. has become a successful businessman and advocate for veterans, working with several charitable organisations that assist retired soldiers suffering from PTSD. Paul H. had to fight his own demons, too. He says that after receiving no help from the Army when he was medically discharged in 2009, he referred himself to a doctor to try to get help. He now does a lot of work with Veterans United Against Suicide. It is extremely important to him to help fellow soldiers. Andrew T.'s answer has been to find solace and comfort through his family and where he lives. 'I am living proof that it doesn't need to be all about counselling. I found my peace in the New Forest, and I would love to help others find it too.'

**

After three years and over a hundred questions posed, my final question to these soldiers was, 'Despite all that has happened and what you now know, would you do it all again?' The answers I received were pretty much what I expected: varied, brutally honest, and with some opting not to answer the question at all. What it shows is that Army life can be rewarding and fulfilling in equal measure, but it requires a level of sacrifice and hardship that takes a toll on both mind and body, especially during a time of conflict, change, and upheaval.

Soldier G. said, 'Absolutely ... I wouldn't swap it for anything ... When I was young I wanted to be a soldier and I have lived my dream. I have met so many of my school mates that have not done that.' Both Angus T. and Soldier B. were unequivocal: 'Absolutely, 100 per cent.'

Owen C. said, despite struggling after retirement, he would do it all again in a heartbeat. 'I have made friends from all over the country with different backgrounds and lifestyles but they are mates ... We could bump into each other tomorrow and we would get right back to the last time we met as if it was just this morning.'

Shaun G. said he loved his time in the Army, but when asked if he would do it all again he said, 'Probably not. The Army we knew no longer exists, and all my memories are of the good old days ... those sorts of tours and experiences will never happen again. Not saying the Army is crap now, it's just a different Army.'

Conrad P. said, 'Looking back now I wish I had gone to college and had experienced that life and been involved in university sport. But, joining the Army at 16 shaped my life.'

Paul H. now wishes he had done something other than join the Army. 'I met some great people, made some fantastic friends, and had some brilliant times. But being honest, I wish I had used my brain more and followed my family into British Steel. You give away 24 years of your life and there is not even a thank you.'

Doug K. sometimes has second thoughts.

> At times I think not, but where would I be if I hadn't joined? Still living in Hull, looking forward to cheap holidays to break the monotony of a mundane job. Drinking in the same pub night after night with the same grey people. Instead I travelled, so many places I wouldn't have dreamed of ... How many council estate lads from Hull got to do that? So was it worth it? Yes. Would I do it again? Yes ... in a heartbeat.

Stuart B. said he was 'Army barmy' since he was a young boy.

I spent nearly all my 25 years' service with 3 Para with only two postings to the Mortar Div. I wouldn't change a thing … All I ever wanted was to be a soldier and I do not regret it in the slightest. I had an amazing career alongside legends. I have been very lucky to have served during a period of turmoil ensuring I have remained busy for the majority of the time and practised the things I've trained for. On the down side I've lost many good friends along the way.

Since posing the final question I have been pondering the same, wondering whether I would do it all again. I was a decade ahead of the soldiers whom I interviewed, and although there was some service overlap, I was spared the worst, serving my last nine years either on ceremonial duties or in non-operational training units. Even so, I have found myself struggling with the question.

There is no doubt in my mind that I am the person I am today because of my regiment and the British Army, and for that I am so grateful. However, for many reasons I am still unsure that if I had my time again I would still join up. When I was 16, I felt there was no other option; coming from a military family, I was subconsciously drawn to be in a uniform of one colour or another. But today, with the luxury of hindsight, I might have chosen another path – I just don't know.

This uncertainty reinforces what I know to be true about this generation of soldiers. They have served through a period of history in the British Army that is without question truly unprecedented. Despite all they have had to put up with – the changes, the upheavals, the ever-increasing number of operational commitments, budget cuts, equipment shortages, and devastating losses – I am amazed that most would do it all again.

Glossary of Terms

3 Para	3rd Battalion, Parachute Regiment
3 RRF	3rd Battalion, Royal Regiment of Fusiliers
ABC	American Broadcasting Corporation
ANP	Afghan National Police
APC	Armoured Personnel Carrier
ASAP	As Soon As Possible
ATR	Army Training Regiment
BAOR	British Army of the Rhine
BCR	Battlefield Casualty Replacements
BG	Battle Group
Blue on Blue	Refers to an incident of friendly fire
CIA	Central Intelligence Agency
CO	Commanding Officer
CQMS	Company Quartermasters Sergeant
CRE	Commission for Racial Equality
CSM	Company Sergeant Major
CVR(T)	Combat Vehicle Reconnaissance (Tracked)
DC	District Centre
DUP	Democratic Unionist Party
ECHR	European Court of Human Rights
Endex	The end of a military exercise
FBU	Fire Brigade Union
GDP	Gross Domestic Product
GDR	German Democratic Republic
GFA	Good Friday Agreement
Glasnost	The policy of more open and transparent government
Green on Blue	Attacks on Coalition forces by Afghan forces
HCR	Household Cavalry Regiment
HESH	High Explosive Squash Head
HMS	Her Majesty's Ship
HQ	Headquarters
ICTY	International Tribunal for the Former Yugoslavia

IFOR	NATO Implementation Force in Bosnia
IHAT	Iraq Historic Allegations Team
IRA	Irish Republican Army
ISAF	International Security Assistance Force
JNA	Yugoslav Army
JNCO	Junior Non-Commissioned Officer
KFOR	NATO Peacekeeping Mission in Kosovo
KKIA	King Khalid International Airport
LEWT	Light Electronics Warfare Team
MBT	Main Battle Tank
MFC	Mortar Fire Controller
MLRS	Multiple Launch Rocket System
MOD	Ministry of Defence
MP	Member of Parliament
MSR	Main Supply Route
NATO	North Atlantic Treaty Organization
NBC	Nuclear, Biological, and Chemical
NORAID	Irish Northern Aid Committee
NSC	National Security Council
NUM	National Union of Miners
OC	Officer Commanding
Perestroika	The policy of restructuring the economic and political system
POW	Prisoner of War
PRT	Provincial Reconstruction Team
PSNI	Police Service of Northern Ireland
PTSD	Post-Traumatic Stress Disorder
QDG	Queen's Dragoon Guards
QRF	Quick Reaction Force
RAC	Royal Armoured Corps
RAF	Royal Air Force
REME	Royal Electrical and Mechanical Engineers
RMP	Royal Military Police
RPG	Rocket Propelled Grenade
RRF	Rapid Reaction Force
RSDG	Royal Scots Dragon Guards
RUC	Royal Ulster Constabulary
SAS	Special Air Service
SDLP	Social Democratic and Labour Party
SDI	Strategic Defense Initiative
SDR	Strategic Defence Review
SFOR	NATO Stabilization Force in Bosnia

SHQ	Squadron Headquarters
SNCO	Senior Non-Commissioned Officer
SQMC	Squadron Quartermasters Corporal
TA	Territorial Army
TUC	Trades Union Congress
UNPROFOR	United Nations Protection Force
UNSCR	United Nations Security Council Resolution
USAF	United States Air Force
USMC	United States Marine Corps
VRS	Army of the Republika Srpska
WFM	Whole Fleet Vehicle Management
WMD	Weapon of Mass Destruction
WO	Warrant Officer
YTS	Youth Training Scheme

Bibliography

Asthana, N. C. and Nirmal, Anjali. *Urban Terrorism: Myths and Realities.* Jaipur: Painter Publishers, 2009.

Bardon, Jonathan. *A History of Ulster.* Newtownards: The Blackstaff Press, 1992.

Baumann, Robert F. et al. *Armed Peacekeepers in Bosnia.* Fort Leavenworth: CSI Press, 2004.

Bergan, Peter and Reynolds, Alec. 'Blowback Revisited', *Foreign Affairs*, Nov/Dec 2005 issue.

Bishop, Stephanie L. 'US & Great Britain: Restrictions on Homosexuals in the Military as a Barricade to Effectiveness', *Penn State International Law Review*, Vol. 14, Article 13, 1996.

Butler, David and Butler, Gareth. *British Political Facts 1900–1994.* London: Macmillan, 1994.

Campbell, Alastair. *The Blair Years: The Alastair Campbell Diaries.* London: Knopf, 2007.

Crampton, R. J. *The Balkans since the Second World War.* London: Routledge, 2013.

de la Billière, General Sir Peter. *Storm Command – A personal account of the Gulf War.* London: Harper Collins, 1995.

Dodd, Tom. *The Armed Forces Bill, Paper 95/125.* London: House of Commons Library, 1995.

Dorman, Andrew M. *Blair's Successful War: British Intervention in Sierra Leone.* Farnham: Ashgate Publishing, 2009.

Engel, Jeffrey A. *When the World Seemed New – George H. W. Bush and the End of the Cold War.* New York: Houghton Mifflin Harcourt, 2017.

English, Richard. *Armed Struggle: The History of the IRA.* London: Oxford University Press, 2004.

Fairweather, Jack. *A War of Choice. Honour, Hubris and Sacrifice: The British in Iraq.* London: Vintage, 2012.

Ferguson, James. *A Million Bullets.* London: Corgi, 2009.

Flynn, Mick. *Bullet Magnet.* London: Phoenix, 2010.

Flynn, Mick. *Trigger Time.* London: Orion, 2011.

Freedman, Lawrence. *A Choice of Enemies – America Confronts the Middle East.* New York: Perseus, 2008.

Gaddis, John Lewis. *The Cold War: A New History.* London: Penguin, 2005.

Gazzini, Tarcisio. *The Changing Rules on the Use of Force in International Law.* Manchester: Juris Publishing, 2005.

Glaurdic, Josip. *The Hour of Europe: Western Powers and the Break Up of Yugoslavia.* New York: Yale University Press, 2011.

Gona, Uki. *The Real Odessa: Smuggling Nazis to Peron's Argentina.* London: Granta, 2002.

Gregory, Derek. *The Colonial Present: Afghanistan, Palestine, Iraq.* Malden: Blackwell Publishing Ltd, 2004.

Hall, Edmund. *We Can't Even March Straight.* London: Vintage, 1995.

Hardiman, Adrian. 'Long Revolution: The 1916 Rising in Context' (Conference paper). Cork: Ireland, 2006.

Harnden, Toby. *Bandit Country – The IRA and South Armagh.* London: Hodder and Stoughton, 1999.

Hawdon, James. *The Causes and Consequences of Group Violence: From Bullies to Terrorists.* Lanham: Lexington Books, 2014.

Healey, Dennis. *The Time of My Life.* London: Methuen, 2015.

Heaney MC, Steve and Lewis, Damien. *Operation Mayhem*. London: Orion, 2014.

Hoare, Marko Atilla. *Genocide and Resistance in Hitler's Bosnia: The Partisans and the Chetniks*. New York: Oxford University Press, 2006.

Hynek, Nik and Marton, Peter. *Statebuilding in Afghanistan*. London: Routledge, 2012.

Jackson, Mike. *Soldier*. London: Bantam Press, 2007.

Judah, Tim. *Kosovo: War and Revenge*. New York: Yale University Press, 2002.

Lee, Christopher. *This Sceptered Isle – Twentieth Century*. London: Penguin, 1999.

Maley, William. *The Afghanistan Wars*. London: Palgrave Macmillan, 2009.

Marx, Karl. *The Eighteenth Brumaire of Louis Bonaparte*. Peking: Foreign Language Press, 1978.

McCann, Eamonn. *War and an Irish Town*. Chicago: Haymarket Books, 2018.

McFaul, Michael. *From Cold War to Hot Peace*. New York: Houghton Mifflin Harcourt, 2018.

Milne, Seumas. *The Enemy Within – The Secret War against the Miners*. London: Verso, 2004.

Mowbray, Alasdair. *Cases and Materials on the European Convention on Human Rights*. Oxford: Oxford University Press, 2007.

Moynahan, Brian. *The British Century – A Photographic History of the Last Hundred Years*. London: Endeavour, 1997.

Nielsen, Suzanne C. 'An Army Transformed: The US Army's Post-Vietnam War Recovery and the Dynamics of Change in Military Organizations', *The Letort Papers*, US Army War College, 2010.

Penfold, Peter. *Atrocities, Diamonds and Diplomacy: The Inside Story of the Conflict in Sierra Leone*. Barnsley: Pen & Sword, 2012.

Perritt, Henry H. *Kosovo Liberation Army: The Inside Story of an Insurgency*. Champaign: University of Illinois Press, 2008.

Reagan, Ronald. *An American Life*. New York: Simon and Schuster, 2011.

Ripley, Tim and Chappell, Mike. *Security Forces in Northern Ireland (1969–92)*. London: Osprey, 1993.

Schinella, Anthony. *Bombs without Boots – The Limits of Airpower*. Washington, DC: Brookings Institution Press, 2019.

Sebetsyen, Viktor. *Revolution 1989: The Fall of the Soviet Empire*. New York: Pantheon Books, 2009.

Skinner, Kieran et al., ed. *Reagan: A Life in Letters*. New York: Simon and Schuster, 2003.

Smith, Rupert. *The Utility of Force – The Art of War in the Modern World*. New York: Vintage Books, 2008.

Stewart, Bob. *Broken Lives*. London: Harper Collins, 1993.

Strachan, Hew. *The British Army, Manpower and Society into the Twenty-first Century*. London: Frank Cass, 2000.

Taylor, Pete. *Behind the Mask: The IRA and Sinn Fein*. New York: TV Books, 1999.

Walker, R. K. *The Hunger Strikes*. Londonderry: Lagan, 2006.

Walsh, Dermot. *Bloody Sunday and the Rule of Law in Northern Ireland*. London: Palgrave Macmillan, 2000.

Watson, Graham and Rinaldi, Richard A. *The British Army in Germany: An Organizational History 1947–2004*. London: Tiger Lily Publications LLC, 2005.

Wither, James A. 'Battling Bullying in the British Army 1987–2004', *The Journal of Power Institutions in Post-Soviet Societies*, Issue 1 (2004).

Wright, Lawrence. *The Looming Tower: Al Qaeda and the Road to 9/11*. New York: Knopf, 2006.

Zelikow, Philip and Rice, Condoleezza. *Germany Unified and Europe Transformed*. New York: Harvard University Press, 1995.

Endnotes

Preface

1. Seymour Melman, 'The Peace Dividend; What to do with the Cold War money?' *New York Times*, 17 Dec 1989.
2. SO2 Media Projects, Army Media and Communications, email to author, dated 19 Feb 2019.

Chapter One

1. GOV. UK, 'Oath of Allegiance – Form and Procedure', https://www.gov.uk/government/uploads/system/uploads/attachment_data/file/632336/oathofallegiance.pdf (accessed 24 Jan 2018).
2. BBC Wales, 'Margaret Thatcher: A "Marmite" prime minister, says Rhodri Morgan', 8 Apr 2013 https://www.bbc.com/news/av/uk-wales-22072074/margaret-thatcher-a-marmite-prime-minister-says-rhodri-morgan (accessed 1 Feb 2018).
3. 'Maggie, the 'Iron Lady''', *The Sunday Times*, 24 Jan 1976.
4. HL Deb 19 Feb 1985, cc 474–8.
5. David Butler and Gareth Butler, *British Political Facts 1900–1994* (London: Macmillan, 1994), 375.
6. BBC News, 'Nottinghamshire coal mining ends with Thoresby closure', 10 Jul 2015. http://www.bbc.com/news/uk-england-nottinghamshire-33380495 (accessed 17 Feb 2018).
7. Adam Vaughan, 'UK runs without coal power for days in a row'' *The Guardian*, 24 April 2018.
8. Simon Rogers, 'How Britain changed under Margaret Thatcher in 15 Charts', *The Guardian*, 8 April 2013.
9. Sarfraz Manzoor, 'The Diamond Decade: The 1980s', *The Telegraph*, 31 May 2012.
10. Discovery Channel, 'Able Archer 1983 – The Brink of Apocalypse', YouTube https://www.youtube.com/watch?v=2EI3_jCIkkA.
11. Jamie Doward, 'How a NATO war game took the world to brink of nuclear disaster', *The Guardian*, 2 Nov 2013.
12. Ronald Reagan, *An American Life* (New York: Simon and Schuster, 2011), 585.
13. Ibid.
14. Ibid, 588–589.
15. Tom O'Connor, 'Russia takes the lead in Syria while Afghanistan war is "worse than it's ever been", former U.S. Defence Chief says', *Newsweek Business*, 7 Feb 2018.
16. Peter Bergan and Alec Reynolds, 'Blowback Revisited', *Foreign Affairs*, Nov/Dec 2005 issue.
17. Jeffrey A. Engel, *When the World Seemed New – George H. W. Bush and the End of the Cold War* (Boston: Houghton Mifflin Harcourt, 2017), 3.
18. Michael Meyer, 'The picnic that brought down the Berlin Wall', *Los Angeles Times*, 13 Sep 2009.
19. Victor Sebetsyen, *Revolution 1989: The Fall of the Soviet Empire* (New York, Pantheon Books, 2009).

20. BBC, On This Day 1950–2005, 3 December 1989: Malta summit ends Cold War, http://news. bbc.co.uk/onthisday/hi/dates/stories/december/3/newsid_4119000/4119950.stm (accessed 4 May 2018).
21. Ibid.
22. Karl Marx, *The Eighteenth Brumaire of Louis Bonaparte* (Peking: Foreign Language Press, 1978), 9.

Chapter Two

1. James K. Wither, 'Battling Bullying in the British Army 1987–2004', *The Journal of Power Institutions in Post-Soviet Societies*, Issue 1(2004): 12.
2. Ibid, 18.
3. Howell Raines, 'British Army Stung by Tales of Brutality in Ranks', *The New York Times*, 6 Nov 1987.
4. Ibid.
5. The Queen's Regulation for the Army, revised 1996, IAC 13206, HMSO, Part 6, Para 5.201A.

Chapter Three

1. Engel, *When the World Seemed New*, 58.
2. Joshua R. Itzkowitz Shifrinson, 'Russia's got a point: The US broke a NATO promise', *Los Angeles Times*, 30 May 2016.
3. Tom de Castella, 'Five years that shaped the British Army', *BBC News Magazine*, 10 Mar 2015.
4. www.parliament.uk, 'Select Committee on Defence – Eighth Report', https://publications. parliament.uk/pa/cm199798/cmselect/cmdfence/138/13805.htm (accessed 10 April 2018).
5. HC Deb 25 Jul 1990, cc 468ff.
6. Major Robert A Nelson, 'The Battle of the Bridges: Kuwait's 35th Brigade on 2nd August, 1990', *Armor – Professional Development Bulletin of the Armor Branch PB-17-95-5*, Vol. CIV No. 5 (1995): 26.
7. BBC, On This Day 1950–2005, 2 August 1990: Iraq invades Kuwait, http://news.bbc.co.uk/ onthisday/hi/dates/stories/august/2/newsid_2526000/2526937.stm (accessed 5 Dec 2018).
8. Ibid.
9. Con Coughlin, 'This is the way Saddam sees it', *The Telegraph*, 26 Jan 2003.
10. Margaret Thatcher Foundation, 'George Bush (Sr) Library', Bush & MT meet at Aspen (2 Aug 1990), www.margaretthacher.org/archive/us-bush.asp (accessed 4 Dec 2018).
11. Ibid.
12. Engel, *When the World Seemed New*, 394.
13. Ibid, 414.
14. Jamie McIntyre, 'While weakened, Iraq's military still a threat', CNN (4 Nov 1997), http://www. cnn.com/WORLD/9711/04/iraq.us.militaries/ (accessed 10 Dec 2018).
15. Dominic Tierney, '"The Mother of All Battles": 20 years later', *The Atlantic*, 28 Feb 2011.
16. Lawrence Freedman, *A Choice of Enemies – America Confronts the Middle East* (New York: Perseus, 2008), 228.
17. *Time*, 'Are we ready for this', 3 Sep 1990 http://content.time.com/time/magazine/0,9263, 7601900903,00.html (accessed 10 Dec 2018).
18. Engel, *When the World Seemed New*, 402.
19. General Sir Peter de la Billière, *Storm Command – A Personal Account of the Gulf War* (London: Harper Collins, 1995), 93.
20. Philip Zelikow and Condoleezza Rice, *Germany Unified and Europe Transformed* (Harvard University Press: New York, 1995), 175.

21. Engel, *When the World Seemed New*, 318.
22. 'Sir Geoffrey Howe savages Prime Minister over European stance in resignation speech', *The Times*, 14 Nov 1990.
23. de la Billière, *Storm Command*, 152.
24. Investigation Team's Findings, https://gulflink.health.mil/aljubayl/n10_s04.htm (accessed 8 Jan 2019).
25. de la Billière, *Storm Command*, 209.
26. Ibid, 196.
27. Ibid, 264.
28. Ibid, 300.
29. Ibid, 293.
30. Steve Coll, 'U.S. scrambled to shape view of Highway of Death', *Washington Post*, 11 Mar 1991.
31. Paul Gilkes, 'Where did the gold bars found in that military tank ever end up?' *Coin World*, 28 Aug 2018, https://www.coinworld.com/news/precious-metals/2018/08/what-happened-to-gold-bars-found-in-tank.all.html (accessed 11 Mar 2019).
32. Ibid, 308.
33. Human Rights Watch, 'Persian Gulf', *U.S. Cluster Bomb Duds a Threat*, https://www.hrw.org/news/2003/03/18/persian-gulf-us-cluster-bomb-duds-threat (accessed 16 Jan 2019).
34. David Hambling, 'After Cluster Bombs: Raining Nails', *Wired*, https://www.wired.com/2008/05/after-cluster-b/ (accessed 16 Jan 2019).

Chapter Four

1. Adam Clymer, 'War in the Gulf: Public Opinion; Poll finds deep backing while optimism fades', *The New York Times*, 22 Jan 1991.
2. William B. Ries, 'Britain welcomes home Gulf War veterans', UPI Archives, 21 June 1991, https://www.upi.com/Archives/1991/06/21/Britain-welcomes-home-Gulf-War-veterans/5092677476800/ (accessed 23 Jan 2019).
3. BBC News, 'Remember the Kurdish uprising of 1991, 7 Apr 2016', https://www.bbc.com/news/in-pictures-35967389 (accessed 24 Jan 2019).
4. Hussain Al-Qatari and Jon Gambrell, 'Iraq, Saddam and the 1991 Gulf War looms large over George H. W. Bush's legacy', *Chicago Tribune*, 1 Dec 2018.
5. Joel Kupersmith and Michael O'Hanlon, 'Gulf War illness 25 years after Desert Storm', *Health Affairs*, www.healthaffairs.org/do/10.1377/hblog20160804.056038/full/ (accessed 28 Jan 2019).
6. Claire Bates and Justin Parkinson, 'Why hasn't the mystery of Gulf War Syndrome been solved?' *BBC News Magazine*, 19 Jan 2016.
7. Joel Kupersmith and Michael O'Hanlon, 'Gulf War illness 25 years after Desert Storm,' *Health Affairs*, www.healthaffairs.org/do/10.1377/hblog20160804.056038/full/ (accessed 28 Jan 2019).
8. David Evans, 'British Jury blames U.S. pilots for 'friendly fire' deaths', *Chicago Tribune*, 19 May 1992.
9. de la Billière, *Storm Command*, 197.
10. TheyWorkForYou, 'Army (Restructuring) – in the House of Commons at 3.31pm on 23rd Jul 1991', https://www.theyworkforyou.com/debates/?id=1991-07-23a.1031.0 (accessed 30 Jan 2019).
11. Tom de Castella, 'Five years that shaped the British Military', *BBC News Magazine*, 10 Mar 2015.
12. Major John Christianson, 'The search for suitable strategy: Threat-Based and Capabilities-Based Strategies in a Complex World' (A monograph, School of Advanced Military Studies, 2016), 2–3.
13. Tom de Castella, 'Five years that shaped the British Military', *BBC News Magazine*, 10 Mar 2015.
14. Ibid.
15. Ibid.

Chapter Five

1. Paul Kelso, 'Floods, inundation, and other unspeakable words', *The Guardian* online, https://www.theguardian.com/society/2002/apr/25/asylum.uknews1 (accessed 11 July 2020).
2. Tom Dodd, The Armed Forces Bill, Research Paper 95/125, 8 Dec 1995, House of Commons Library, 35.
3. Ibid, 36.
4. Ibid, 34.
5. Dennis Healey, *The Time of My Life* (London: Methuen, 2015).
6. David Newman, 'I was tortured by Army bullies', *Sunday Mirror*, 25 Aug 2002.
7. Mark Smalley, 'Colour Barred?', *BBC News*, 11 Sep 2006, http://news.bbc.co.uk/2/hi/uk_news/magazine/5333874.stm (accessed 25 Mar 2018).
8. Dennis Healey, *The Time of My Life*.
9. Christopher Bellamy, 'Army pledges to stamp out racism in ranks', *The Independent*, 28 Mar 1996.
10. TheyWorkForYou, 'New schedule – in the House of Commons at 9.19pm on 9th May 1996', https://www.theyworkforyou.com/debates/?id=1996-05-09a.512.2&s=Racism+household+cavalry#g514.0 (accessed 11 Feb 2019).
11. Christopher Bellamy, 'Army pledges to stamp out racism in ranks', *The Independent*, 28 Mar 1996.
12. Sean Rayment, 'Army's top general makes history by addressing conference on homosexuality', *The Telegraph*, 11 Oct 2008.
13. GOV.UK, 'Local Government Act 1988', https://www.legislation.gov.uk/ukpga/1988/9/section/28 (accessed 13 Mar 2018).
14. Tom Dodd, The Armed Forces Bill, Research Paper 95/125, 8 Dec 1995, House of Commons Library, 39.
15. BBC News UK, 'Head to head: Gays in the Military', 27 Sep 1999, http://news.bbc.co.uk/2/hi/uk_news/458752.stm (accessed 14 Feb 2019).
16. GOV.UK, 'Army Act, 1955', http://www.legislation.gov.uk/ukpga/1955/18/pdfs/ukpga_19550018_en.pdf (accessed 13 Mar 2018).
17. Stephanie L. Bishop, 'US & Great Britain: Restrictions on Homosexuals in the Military as a Barricade to Effectiveness', *Penn State International Law Review*, Vol. 14, Article 13 (1996): 625.
18. Edmund Hall, *We Can't Even March Straight* (London: Vintage, 1995), 3.
19. Ibid, 4.
20. BBC News, 'Delight and despair at gay ban ruling', 27 Sep 1999, http://news.bbc.co.uk/2/hi/uk_news/458842.stm (accessed 14 Feb 2019).
21. BBC News, 'Brigadier quits over gays in the military', 27 Jan 2000, http://news.bbc.co.uk/2/hi/uk_news/620178.stm (accessed 13 Mar 2018).
22. Stephanie L. Bishop, 'US & Great Britain: Restrictions on Homosexuals in the Military as a Barricade to Effectiveness', *Penn State International Law Review*, Vol. 14, Article 13 (1996): 627.
23. House of Commons Publications, 'Letter from the Minister of State for the Armed Forces on Racism within the Armed Forces', 27 Mar 1998, https://publications.parliament.uk/pa/cm199899/cmselect/cmdfence/273/273r07.htm (accessed 18 Feb 2019).
24. Mark Smalley, 'Colour Barred?', *BBC News*, 11 Sep 2006. http://news.bbc.co.uk/2/hi/uk_news/magazine/5333874.stm (accessed 25 Mar 2018).
25. Semus Milne, 'General goes to war on racists in the Guards', *The Guardian*, 20 Jul 1999.
26. Ibid.
27. Ibid.
28. Chris Arnot and David Brindle, 'Race against time', *The Guardian,* 9 Aug 2000.
29. Ibid.

30. Mark Smalley, 'Colour Barred?', *BBC News*, 11 Sep 2006. http://news.bbc.co.uk/2/hi/uk_news/magazine/5333874.stm (accessed 25 Mar 2018).

Chapter Six

1. James Hawdon, *The Causes and Consequences of Group Violence: From Bullies to Terrorists*, ed. John Ryan and Marc Lucht (Lanham: Lexington Books, 2014), 5.
2. DW – Made for Minds, 'Serbia, WW1, and the question of Guilt', https://www.dw.com/en/serbia-wwi-and-the-question-of-guilt/a-17550497 (accessed 28 Feb 2019).
3. Uki Gona, *The Real Odessa: Smuggling Nazis to Peron's Argentina* (London: Granta, 2002), 202.
4. Marko Atilla Hoare, *Genocide and Resistance in Hitler's Bosnia: The Partisans and the Chetniks* (New York: Oxford University Press, 2006), 146–147.
5. Josip Glaurdic, *The Hour of Europe: Western Powers and the Break Up of Yugoslavia* (New York: Yale University Press, 2011), 290.
6. Tara John, 'The story of this shocking image from a prison camp in Bosnia continues 25 years later', *Time Magazine*, 22 Nov 2017.
7. Colonel Bob Stewart, *Broken Lives* (London: Harper Collins, 1993), 79.
8. Albina Sorguc and Anja Vladisavljevic, 'Bosnia Marks Anniversary of Ahmici Village Killings', 16 Apr 2019, *Balkan Transitional Justice*, https://balkaninsight.com/2019/04/16/bosnia-marks-anniversary-of-ahmici-village-mass-killings/ (accessed 4 Feb 2019).
9. Paul Welsh, 'Return to the land he never really left', *Independent*, 14 Aug 1999.
10. Colonel Bob Stewart, DSO, MP, 'Recent speech in Parliament to remember the Holocaust', https://www.bobstewart.org.uk/news/recent-speech-parliament-remember-holocaust (accessed 5 Feb 2019).
11. BBC News, 'Martin Bell', YouTube video, 0:45, 11 May 2015, https://www.youtube.com/watch?v=WVR75YaDcW4
12. Stewart, *Broken Lives*, 299.
13. Ibid, 310.
14. United Nations Peace-keeping, 'Former Yugoslavia – UNPROFOR', https://peacekeeping.un.org/mission/past/unprof_b.htm (accessed 27 Feb 2019).
15. Ibid.
16. Ibid.
17. Ibid.
18. Think Defence, *British Army Medium Weight Capability: Turning Points in the Balkans*, https://www.thinkdefence.co.uk/british-army-medium-weight-capability/turning-points-in-the-balkans/ (accessed 27 Feb 2019).
19. Stewart, *Broken Lives*, 270.
20. Gillian Sandford, 'Surviving Serbia', *The Observer*, 23 Jun 2001.
21. Radio Free Europe – Radio Liberty, 'At Genocide Trial, Prosecutor says Mladic wanted Muslims to "Vanish Completely"', *Serbia*, 5 Dec 2016, https://www.rferl.org/a/serbia-bosnia-mladic-trial-muslim-vanish-completely/28157335.html (accessed 2 May 2019).
22. NATO review, 'The Peacekeeping Challenge', General Sir Rupert Smith: DSACEUR, https://www.nato.int/docu/review/2001/COPYRIGHT/EN/index.htm (accessed 4 May 2019).
23. General Rupert Smith, *The Utility of Force – The Art of War in the Modern World* (New York: Vintage Books, 2008), 357.
24. Tracy Wilkinson, 'Rapid-Reaction Force is slow to move into action', *Los Angeles Times*, 17 Jul 1995.

25. Human Rights Watch, 'The Fall of Srebrenica and the failure of UN Peacekeeping – Bosnia and Herzegovina', 15 Oct 1995, https://www.hrw.org/report/1995/10/15/fall-srebrenica-and-failure-un-peacekeeping/bosnia-and-herzegovina (accessed 13 May 2019).
26. Marlise Simmons, 'Dutch peacekeepers are found responsible for deaths', *The New York Times*, 6 Sep 2019.
27. BBC News, 'Dutch state liable for over 300 Srebrenica deaths', 16 Jul 2014, https://www.bbc.com/news/world-europe-28313285 (accessed 6 May 2019).
28. Florence Hartmann and Ed Vulliamy, 'How Britain and the US decided to abandon Srebrenica to its fate', *The Guardian*, 4 Jul 2015.
29. Robert F. Baumann et al., *Armed Peacekeepers in Bosnia* (Fort Leavenworth: CSI Press, 2004), 35.
30. Florence Hartmann and Ed Vulliamy, 'How Britain and the US decided to abandon Srebrenica to its fate', *The Guardian*, 4 Jul 2015.
31. Tarcisio Gazzini, *The Changing Rules on the Use of Force in International Law* (Manchester: Juris Publishing, 2005), 69.
32. Smith, *The Utility of Force*, 368.
33. Ibid, 366.
34. Ibid, 371.
35. Rick Atkinson and Christine Spolar, 'Army opens river bridge', *The Washington Post*, 1 Jan 1996.
36. SFOR, 'SFOR Mission', https://www.nato.int/sfor/organisation/mission.htm (accessed 19 May 2019).
37. Brown University, 'Susan Allee, How did NATO's intervention in Bosnia set a precedent?', *The Choices Program* video, 12 Feb 2008, https://www.choices.edu/video/how-did-natos-intervention-in-bosnia-set-a-precedent/ (accessed 1 May 2019).
38. Steven Erlanger, 'NATO at crossroads in Bosnia: Serb power struggle is seen as defining moment', *The New York Times*, 31 Aug 1997.
39. BBC News, 'Hague probes Karadzic "deal" claim', 26 Oct 2007, http://news.bbc.co.uk/2/hi/europe/7062288.stm (accessed 21 May 2019).
40. Christopher Bellamy, 'Three British soldiers die in Bosnia Blast', *The Independent*, 29 Jan 1996.
41. Ibid.
42. Richard Norton-Taylor, 'TV drama comes under fire from army', *The Guardian*, 19 Nov 1999.
43. Ibid.
44. Ibid.

Chapter Seven

1. Joseph Lee, *The Modernisation of Irish Society* (Dublin: Gill and Macmillan, 1973), 2.
2. Adrian Hardiman, conference paper, 'Long Revolution: The 1916 Rising in Context' (Cork: Ireland, 2006), 225–226.
3. Toby Harnden, *Bandit Country – The IRA and South Armagh* (London: Hodder and Stoughton, 1999), 146–147.
4. Eamonn McCann, *War and an Irish Town* (Chicago: Haymarket Books, 2018), 114.
5. Johnathan Bardon, *A History of Ulster* (Newtownards: The Blackstaff Press, 1992), 666–667.
6. James Downey, 'Army on Armageddon Alert', *Irish Independent*, 2 Jan 2001.
7. Richard English, *Armed Struggle: The History of the IRA* (Oxford: Oxford University Press, 2004), 136.
8. General Sir Mike Jackson, *Soldier* (London: Bantam Press, 2007), 90.
9. R. K. Walker, *The Hunger Strikes* (Londonderry: Lagan, 2006), 27.
10. Jackson, *Soldier*, 83–84.

11. BBC News, 'Bloody Sunday: PM David Cameron's full statement', 15 June 2010, https://www.bbc.com/news/10322295 (accessed 12 Aug 2019).

12. Ibid.

13. Haroon Siddique and Megan French, 'Bloody Sunday inquiry: key findings', *The Guardian*, 15 Jun 2010.

14. Ibid.

15. Jackson, *Soldier*, 93.

16. General Sir Michael Rose, 'It wasn't Blair who brought peace to Ulster but brave British soldiers about to be branded as criminals', *The Daily Mail*, 15 June 2010.

17. Ibid.

18. Dermot Walsh, *Bloody Sunday and the Rule of Law in Northern Ireland* (London: Palgrave Macmillan, 2000), 133–134.

19. Al Jazeera, 'Head to Head', Transcript: Martin McGuinness https://www.aljazeera.com/programmes/headtohead/2014/03/transcript-martin-mcguinness-201432611584520903.html (accessed 20 Nov 2019).

20. Jo Thomas, 'British soldiers kill a teenager in West Belfast', *The New York Times*, 16 Jan 1985.

21. David McKittrick, 'Soldier gets life for joyrider murder', *The Independent*, 5 Jun 1993.

22. Ibid.

23. John Mullin, 'Grudging verdict after judge says defence a farrago of deceit and lies', *The Guardian*, 11 Mar 1999.

24. Jo Thomas, 'British soldiers kill a teenager in West Belfast', *The New York Times*, 16 Jan 1985.

25. Harnden, *Bandit Country*, 400.

26. Ibid, 416.

27. Ibid, 418.

28. Ibid, 422.

29. Matthew L. Ward, 'Long before verdict, Lockerbie changed airport security', *New York Times*, 31 Jan 2001.

30. Ibid.

31. David McKittrick, 'Sinn Fein ready to accept Mitchell Principles', *Independent*, 21 May 1996.

32. World Atlas, 'Most expensive terror attacks in the world', https://www.worldatlas.com/articles/the-price-of-terrorism-the-most-expensive-terrorist-attacks-in-the-world.html (accessed 29 Jul 2019).

33. Ulster University, 'Conflict and Politics in Northern Ireland', *A Chronology of the Conflict – 1996*, https://cain.ulster.ac.uk/othelem/chron/ch96.htm#Jun (accessed 29 Jul 2019).

34. Conor Humphries, 'Gerry Adams: Face of the IRA who helped cement Northern Ireland peace', *Reuters*, 18 Nov 2017.

35. Harnden, *Bandit Country*, 424.

36. David Blevins, 'Why were IRA suspects sent comfort letters', *Sky News*, 24 Mar 2015, https://news.sky.com/story/why-were-ira-suspects-sent-comfort-letters-10366493 (accessed 29 Jul 2019).

37. Ibid.

38. Ibid.

39. www.parliament.co.uk, 'Commons Select Committee', Publications – Northern Ireland Affairs Committee, Letter from John Reid to Tony Blair, https://www.parliament.uk/documents/commons-committees/northern-ireland-affairs/Letter-from-John-Reid-to-Tony-Blair-4-May-2001.pdf (accessed 30 Apr 2019).

40. Ibid.

41. Ibid.

42. BBC News, 'Sinn Fein rejects on-the-run bill', 20 Dec 2005, http://news.bbc.co.uk/2/hi/uk_news/northern_ireland/4546648.stm (accessed 29 Jul 2019).

43. David Blevins, 'Why were IRA suspects sent comfort letters', *Sky News*, 24 Mar 2015, https://news.sky.com/story/why-were-ira-suspects-sent-comfort-letters-10366493 (accessed 29 Jul 2019).

44. Criminal Justice Inspectorates, 'HM Inspectorate of Constabulary and Fire & Rescue Services', PSNI Historical Enquiries Team, https://www.justiceinspectorates.gov.uk/hmicfrs/our-work/article/inspections-of-the-police-service-of-northern-ireland-het/ (accessed 29 Jul 2019).

45. Owen Bowcott and Ben Quinn, 'Up to 200 ex-soldiers and police facing Troubles investigations', *The Guardian*, 25 April 2019.

Chapter Eight

1. www.parliament.uk, 'Select Committee on Defence', The Historical Context, https://publications.parliament.uk/pa/cm199798/cmselect/cmdfence/138/13805.htm (accessed 19 Apr 2018).

2. Ibid.

3. www.parliament.uk, 'Parliamentary Business', 3 Feb 1993, https://publications.parliament.uk/pa/cm199293/cmhansrd/1993-02-03/Debate-1.html (accessed 14 Aug 2019).

4. Ibid.

5. www.parliament.uk, 'Select Committee on Defence', The Historical Context, https://publications.parliament.uk/pa/cm199798/cmselect/cmdfence/138/13805.htm (accessed 19 Apr 2018).

6. www.parliament.uk, 'Select committee on Defence Eighth Report', Main Proposals, https://publications.parliament.uk/pa/cm199798/cmselect/cmdfence/138/13806.htm (accessed 23 Jan 2010).

7. Ibid.

8. Hew Strachan, *The British Army, Manpower and Society into the Twenty-first Century* (London: Frank Cass, 2000), 180.

9. Ibid.

10. James Dunn, 'Soldiers who shared photographs of their disgusting meals – including mouldy eggs and maggot-infested tomatoes – are warned by senior staff they may face legal action', *Daily Mail*, 24 March 2016.

11. ukpublicspending.co.uk, 'Recent UK Defense Spending', https://www.ukpublicspending.co.uk/uk_defence_spending_30.html (accessed 24 Jan 2020).

12. www.parliament.uk, 'The UK's commitment to 2%', https://publications.parliament.uk/pa/cm201516/cmselect/cmdfence/494/49404.htm (accessed 24 Jan 2020).

13. National Archives, 'Strategic Defense Review', https://webarchive.nationalarchives.gov.uk/20121018172816/http://www.mod.uk/NR/rdonlyres/65F3D7AC-4340-4119-93A2-20825848E50E/0/sdr1998_complete.pdf (accessed 24 Jan 2020).

14. RESDAL, 'United Kingdom – Strategic Defense Review – Factsheets – Army', https://www.resdal.org/Archivo/gb-fact-army.htm#34 (accessed 24 Jan 2020).

15. Claire Bates, 'When foot-and-mouth disease stopped the UK in its tracks', *BBC News Magazine*, 17 Feb 2016, https://www.bbc.com/news/magazine-35581830 (accessed 26 Jan 2020).

16. www.parliament.uk, 'Select Committee on Defense – Third report', https://publications.parliament.uk/pa/cm200304/cmselect/cmdfence/57/5707.htm (accessed 27 Jan 2020).

17. MOD, 'JSP 835: Alcohol and Substance Misuse and Testing', Version 2.0, 1 Nov 2013, https://assets.publishing.service.gov.uk/government/uploads/system/uploads/attachment_data/file/425401/20131101-JSP_835-V2_0-U.pdf (accessed 28 Jan 2020).

18. Ibid.

19. RUSI, 'British Army Loses "Battalion" a year to Drug-Use Discharges', 13 Dec 2007, https://rusi.org/rusi-news/british-army-loses-batallion-year-drug-use-discharges (accessed 28 Jan 2020).

20. Will Worley, 'Army insists it has not relaxed drug rules after it is revealed fresh recruits who use narcotics will not be dismissed', *Independent*, 23 October 2017.
21. MOD, 'JSP 835: Alcohol and Substance Misuse and Testing', Version 2.0, 1 Nov 2013, https://assets.publishing.service.gov.uk/government/uploads/system/uploads/attachment_data/file/425401/20131101-JSP_835-V2_0-U.pdf (accessed 28 Jan 2020).
22. Ben Riley-Smith, 'Battalion's worth of soldiers sacked for drug taking every year', *The Telegraph*, 11 Jul 2015.
23. Network, 'Army Ends Zero-Tolerance Drugs Policy,' 1 Oct 2019, https://www.forces.net/news/army/army-ends-zero-tolerance-drugs-policy (accessed 28 Jan 2020).

Chapter Nine

1. Louisa Brooke-Holland, 'Women in Combat', *Briefing Paper No. 7521*, House of Commons Library, 4 Mar 2016, https://researchbriefings.parliament.uk/ResearchBriefing/Summary/CBP-7521#fullreport (accessed 29 Jan 2020).
2. Simon Rogers, 'How Britain changed under Margaret Thatcher in 15 Charts', *The Guardian*, 8 April 2013.
3. Louisa Brooke-Holland, 'Women in Combat', *Briefing Paper No. 7521*, House of Commons Library, 4 Mar 2016, https://researchbriefings.parliament.uk/ResearchBriefing/Summary/CBP-7521#fullreport (accessed 29 Jan 2020).
4. National Army Museum, 'Fit to fight: Women in the Army today', https://www.nam.ac.uk/explore/fit-fight-woman-army-today (accessed 29 Jan 2020).
5. Louisa Brooke-Holland, 'Women in Combat', *Briefing Paper No. 7521*, House of Commons Library, 4 Mar 2016, https://researchbriefings.parliament.uk/ResearchBriefing/Summary/CBP-7521#fullreport (accessed 29 Jan 2020).
6. Ibid.
7. Harriet Agerholm, 'Former British Army commander says having women in the army will cost lives on the battlefield', *Independent*, 10 Jul 2016.
8. Christopher Bellamy, 'The £100 million babies', *Independent (Indy/Life)*, 13 Jul 1994.
9. Ibid.
10. HC Deb, 25 May 1994, Vol. 244 cc 410–418.
11. Ibid.
12. army.mod.uk, 'All British Armed Forces roles now open to women', 25 Oct 2018, https://www.army.mod.uk/news-and-events/news/2018/10/women-in-ground-close-combat-roles/ (accessed 5 Feb 2020).

Chapter Ten

1. Paul Latawski and Martin A. Smith, 'NATO, Kosovo and humanitarian intervention', Manchester openhive, https://www.manchesteropenhive.com/view/9781526137784/9781526137784.00007.xml#ch01en18a (accessed 6 Feb 2020).
2. Global Policy Forum, 'The Blair Doctrine', 22 Apr 1999, https://www.globalpolicy.org/component/content/article/154/26026.html (accessed 6 Feb 2020).
3. R. J. Crampton, *The Balkans Since the Second World War* (London: Routledge, 2013), 275.
4. Endrit Metolli, '1999: Tony Blair Kosovo Speech', YouTube video, 3:34, 13 Dec 2016, https://www.youtube.com/watch?v=KbzKq_d9-pI (accessed 7 Feb 2020).

5. James Goldgeier and Gorana Grgic, 'The Kosovo War in retrospect', *Texas National Security Review*, 24 Mar 2019, https://warontherocks.com/2019/03/the-kosovo-war-in-retrospect/ (accessed 7 Feb 2020).
6. Henry H. Perritt, *Kosovo Liberation Army: The Inside Story of an Insurgency* (Champaign: University of Illinois Press, 2008), 82.
7. Ibid, 90.
8. Thomas A. Emmert, 'Why Serbia will fight for "Holy" Kosovo; and the peril for western armies approaching the Balkan tripwire', *Washington Post*, 13 June 1993.
9. Tim Judah, *Kosovo: War and Revenge* (New York: Yale University Press, 2002), 140.
10. Julius Strauss, 'Massacre that started long haul to justice', *The Telegraph*, 30 Jun 2001.
11. James Goldgeier and Gorana Grgic, 'The Kosovo War in retrospect', *Texas National Security Review*, 24 Mar 2019, https://warontherocks.com/2019/03/the-kosovo-war-in-retrospect/ (accessed 7 Feb 2020).
12. R. J. Crampton, *The Balkans Since the Second World War* (London: Routledge, 2013), 275.
13. Martin Walker, Richards Norton-Taylor, and Martin Kettle, 'Blair pushes for ground assault', *The Guardian*, 20 Apr 1999.
14. Jackson, *Soldier*, 299.
15. Ibid, 306
16. Steven Erlanger, 'NATO was closer to ground war in Kosovo than is widely realized', *The New York Times*, 7 Nov 1999.
17. Jackson, *Soldier*, 336.
18. BBC News, 'Confrontation over Pristina Airport', 9 Mar 2000, http://news.bbc.co.uk/2/hi/europe/671495.stm (accessed 10 Feb 2020).
19. Jackson, *Soldier*, 341.
20. NATO, 'KFOR – Contributing Nations', https://jfcnaples.nato.int/kfor/about-us/welcome-to-kfor/contributing-nations (accessed 11 Feb 2020).
21. Jackson, *Soldier*, 310.
22. Simon Hattenstone and Eric Allison, 'Post Traumatic Stress Disorder – You don't ever get over it', *The Guardian*, 18 Oct 2014.
23. Phil McNulty, 'Kosovo v England: Excitement for final 2020 qualifying game', *BBC Sport*, 17 Nov 2019, https://www.bbc.com/sport/football/50448139 (accessed 11 Feb 2020).
24. Michael McFaul, *From Cold War to Hot Peace* (New York: Houghton Mifflin Harcourt, 2018), 51.
25. President of Russia, 'Vladimir Putin answered questions from Russian Journalists', 16 Oct 2016, http://en.kremlin.ru/events/president/news/53103 (accessed 9 Feb 2020).
26. Janine di Giovanni, 'Sierra Leone, 2000: A Case History in Successful Interventionism', *The New York Review of Books*, https://www.nybooks.com/daily/2019/06/07/sierra-leone-2000-a-case-history-in-successful-interventionism/ (accessed 12 Feb 2020).
27. Ibid.
28. Ibid.
29. Steve Heaney MC and Damien Lewis, *Operation Mayhem* (London: Orion, 2014), 28.
30. Janine di Giovanni, 'Sierra Leone, 2000: A Case History in Successful Interventionism', *The New York Review of Books*, https://www.nybooks.com/daily/2019/06/07/sierra-leone-2000-a-case-history-in-successful-interventionism/ (accessed 12 Feb 2020).
31. Ibid.
32. Heaney and Lewis, *Operation Mayhem*, 50.
33. Ibid.
34. BBC Radio 4, 'The Brigadier who saved Sierra Leone', 15 May 2010, http://news.bbc.co.uk/1/hi/programmes/from_our_own_correspondent/8682505.stm (accessed 12 Feb 2020).
35. Janine di Giovanni, 'Sierra Leone, 2000: A Case History in Successful Interventionism', *The New York Review of Books*, https://www.nybooks.com/daily/2019/06/07/sierra-leone-2000-a-case-history-in-successful-interventionism/ (accessed 12 Feb 2020).

36. Andrew M. Dorman, *Blair's Successful War: British Intervention in Sierra Leone* (Farnham: Ashgate Publishing, 2009), 94–95.

37. Peter Penfold, *Atrocities, Diamonds and Diplomacy: The Inside Story of the Conflict in Sierra Leone* (Barnsley: Pen and Sword, 2012), 182.

38. Heaney and Lewis, *Operation Mayhem*, xvi.

Chapter Eleven

1. 'Reaction from around the world', *New York Times*, 12 Sep 2001.

2. Ibid.

3. David Graves, 'Palace breaks with tradition in musical tribute', *The Telegraph*, 14 Sep 2001.

4. 'Reaction from around the world', *New York Times*, 12 Sep 2001.

5. Suzanne Daley, 'After the attacks: The alliance; for the first time, NATO invokes Joint Defense Pact with U.S.', *The New York Times*, 13 Sep 2001.

6. Tom Rogan, 'I can hear you: 17 years ago today, George W. Bush's Greatest Moment', *Washington Examiner*, 14 Sep 2019.

7. Gallup, 'Presidential approval ratings – George W. Bush', https://news.gallup.com/poll/116500/presidential-approval-ratings-george-bush.aspx (accessed 30 Sep 2019).

8. congress.gov, 'Public Law 107-40-SEPT. 18, 2001', Joint Resolution, https://www.congress.gov/107/plaws/publ40/PLAW-107publ40.pdf (accessed 30 Sep 2019).

9. Rita Siemion, 'The 9/11 War Authorization and Iran: An important lesson for Congress', *Human Rights First*, 1 Jul 2019, https://www.humanrightsfirst.org/blog/911-war-authorization-and-iran-important-lesson-congress (accessed 5 Oct 2019).

10. 'Bush gives Taliban ultimatum', *The Telegraph*, 21 Sep 2001, https://www.telegraph.co.uk/news/1341196/Bush-gives-Taliban-ultimatum.html (accessed 8 Oct 2019).

11. Hans Spross and Waslat Hasrat-Nazimi, 'Withdrawing from Afghanistan –1989 and 2014', *Deutsche Welle*, 14 Feb 2014, https://www.dw.com/en/withdrawing-from-afghanistan-1989-and-2014/a-17431139 (accessed 9 Oct 2019).

12. Abbas Nasir, 'The legacy of Pakistan's loved and loathed Hamid Gul', Al Jazeera, 17 Aug 2015, https://www.aljazeera.com/indepth/opinion/2015/08/legacy-pakistan-loved-loathed-hamid-gul-150817114006616.html (accessed 8 Oct 2019).

13. Quil Lawrence, 'Chaos after Soviet withdrawal gave rise to Taliban', All Things Considered (NPR), 7 Dec 2010, https://www.npr.org/2010/12/07/131884473/Afghanistan-After-The-Soviet-Withdrawal (accessed 9 Oct 2019).

14. Ibid.

15. William Maley, *The Afghanistan Wars* (London: Palgrave Macmillan, 2009), 288.

16. Dwight John Zimmerman, '21st Century Horse Soldiers – Special Operations Forces and Operation Enduring Freedom', 16 Sep 2011, *Defense Media Network*, https://www.defensemedianetwork.com/stories/operation-enduring-freedom-the-first-49-days-4/ (accessed 10 Oct 2019).

17. *Armed Forces Journal*, 'Special Forces and Horses,' 1 Nov 2006, http://armedforcesjournal.com/special-forces-and-horses/ (accessed 10 Oct 2019)

18. PBS, *Frontline*, 'Bush's War – Part One,' 35.15, https://www.pbs.org/video/frontline-bushs-war-part-1/ (accessed 25 Aug 2019).

19. Independent News online, 'Refugees say Taliban leader's son killed', 11 Oct 2001, https://archive.fo/20120804231808/http://www.iol.co.za/index.php?sf=522&set_id=1&click_id=3&art_id=qw1002832921692B232 (accessed 10 Oct 2001).

20. HC Deb 26 Oct 2001 Vol 373 cc 549–64.

21. Defense – Aerospace, 'Operation Fingal', http://www.defense-aerospace.com/articles-view/release/3/8013/uk-confirms-offer-to-lead-afghan-force-(dec.-20).html (accessed 15 Oct 2019).

22. Para Data, 'Afghanistan (Operation Fingal)', https://www.paradata.org.uk/event/afghanistan-operation-fingal (accessed 19 Nov 2019).

23. Alec Russell, '9/11 report condemns 'failure of imagination''', *The Telegraph*, 23 Jul 2004.

24. PBS, *Frontline*, 'Bush's War,' 24 Mar 2008 (1:03:44), https://www.pbs.org/video/frontline-bushs-war-part-1/ (accessed 25 Aug 2019).

25. Council on Foreign Affairs, 'The US war in Afghanistan', https://www.cfr.org/timeline/us-war-afghanistan (accessed 22 Aug 2019).

Chapter Twelve

1. Julian Borger, 'Blogger bares Rumsfeld's post 9/11 orders', *The Guardian*, 24 Feb 2006.

2. Ibid.

3. Ibid.

4. PBS, *Frontline*, 'Bush's War – Part One' (11:03), https://www.pbs.org/video/frontline-bushs-war-part-1/ (accessed 25 Aug 2019).

5. Ibid (12.40).

6. Simon Tisdall, 'There is no doubt about it: Tony Blair was on warpath from early 2002', *The Guardian*, 18 Oct 2015.

7. Forces Network, 'Former Royal Navy Head "Told of Iraq Invasion months before decision was announced"', https://www.forces.net/news/former-royal-navy-head-told-of-iraq-invasion-months-decision-was-announced (accessed 27 Mar 2019).

8. Ian Burrell, 'The media failed us during the Iraq war and now it faces the consequences', *Independent*, 5 Jul 2016.

9. Ibid.

10. U.S. Department of State, Bureau of Public Affairs, 'Saddam's Chemical Weapons Campaign: Halabja, March 16, 1988', https://2001-2009.state.gov/r/pa/ei/rls/18714.htm (accessed 8 Dec 2019).

11. BBC News, 'On This Day 16 Mar 1988', http://news.bbc.co.uk/onthisday/hi/dates/stories/march/16/newsid_4304000/4304853.stm (accessed 8 Dec 2019).

12. Stephen Pelletiere, 'A war crime or an act of war', *New York Times*, 31 Jan 2003.

13. Hillel Fradkin and Lewis Libby, 'The First Gulf War and its Aftermath', Hudson Institute, 14 Oct 2015, https://www.hudson.org/research/11787-the-first-gulf-war-and-its-aftermath (accessed 25 Jan 2019).

14. Iraq Liberation Act, Pub.L 105–338, 112 Stat. 3178 (1998).

15. Joint Resolution to authorize the use of United States Armed Forces against Iraq, Pub.L, 107–243, 116 Stat. 1498 (2002).

16. Oona A. Hathaway, 'The Soleimani Strike Defied the U.S. Constitution', *The Atlantic*, 4 Jan 2020.

17. Patrick Wintour, 'When Blair stood on the brink', *The Guardian*, 25 Apr 2003.

18. David Margolick, 'The Night of the Generals', *Vanity Fair*, 16 Sep 2013.

19. Dan Murphy, 'Iraq War: Predictions made, and results', *The Christian Science Monitor*, 22 Dec 2011.

20. Vernon Loeb, 'Rumsfeld faulted for troop dilution', *Washington Post*, 30 March 2003.

21. David Margolick, 'The Night of the Generals', *Vanity Fair*, 16 Sep 2013.

22. Ibid.

23. Vernon Loeb, 'Rumsfeld faulted for troop dilution', *Washington Post*, 30 March 2003.

24. Jackson, *Soldier*, 406.

25. Jack Fairweather, *A War of Choice. Honour, Hubris and Sacrifice: The British in Iraq* (London: Vintage, 2012), 14.

26. Philip Johnston, 'Tanks, guns and boots all failed Army in desert', *The Telegraph*, 1 Aug 2002.

27. Jackson, *Soldier*, 396.

28. Ibid.

29. Frontline, 'Operation Iraqi Freedom: A Chronology of the six-week invasion of Iraq', *Blue Ridge PBS*, https://www.pbs.org/wgbh/pages/frontline/shows/invasion/cron/ (accessed 8 Jan 2020).

30. CNN, '$1bn bill to fix oil field says UK', 27 March 2003, https://www.cnn.com/2003/BUSINESS/03/27/sprj.irq.oil/index.html (accessed 8 Jan 2020).

31. Frontline, 'Operation Iraqi Freedom: A Chronology of the six-week invasion of Iraq', *Blue Ridge PBS*, https://www.pbs.org/wgbh/pages/frontline/shows/invasion/cron/ (accessed 8 Jan 2020).

32. WO1 (Retd) M. Flynn, conversation with author, 4 April 2020.

33. GOV.UK, 'Operations in Iraq', *Fatality Notice: LCoH Matty Hull*, https://www.gov.uk/government/fatalities/lance-corporal-of-horse-matty-hull (accessed 10 Jan 2020).

34. WO1 (Retd) M. Flynn, conversation with author, 4 April 2020.

35. Mark Townsend, 'Why won't the US tell us how Matty died?', *The Observer*, 3 Feb 2007.

36. Ron Jensen, 'U.S. military wants to stop friendly fire', *Stars and Stripes*, 2 Mar 2003.

37. Mark Townsend, 'Why won't the US tell us how Matty died?', *The Observer*, 3 Feb 2007.

38. ENVagency, 'Invasion of Iraq: How the British and Americans got it wrong', YouTube video, 6:31, 2 Dec 2011, https://www.youtube.com/watch?v=BcxzigtuR9w (accessed 15 Jan 2020).

39. David Willis, 'Applause as Marines enter Basra', BBC, 22 Mar 2003, http://news.bbc.co.uk/2/hi/middle_east/2875777.stm (accessed 15 Jan 2020).

40. ENVagency, 'Invasion of Iraq: How the British and Americans got it wrong', YouTube video, 7:15, 2 Dec 2011, https://www.youtube.com/watch?v=BcxzigtuR9w (accessed 15 Jan 2020).

41. Frontline, 'Operation Iraqi Freedom: A Chronology of the six-week invasion of Iraq', *Blue Ridge PBS*, https://www.pbs.org/wgbh/pages/frontline/shows/invasion/cron/ (accessed 8 Jan 2020).

42. Kevin Canfield and Tara Weiss, 'Quick taking of Basra may also help war image', *The Hartford Courant*, 19 March 2003.

43. 'UK Forces destroy breakaway tank squadron', *The Guardian*, 27 Mar 2003, https://www.theguardian.com/world/2003/mar/27/iraq9 (accessed 16 Jan 2020).

44. 'Glaring failures caused US to kill RAF crew', *The Guardian*, 31 Oct 2006, https://www.theguardian.com/uk/2006/oct/31/military.iraq (accessed 16 Jan 2020).

45. Robert Mendick, 'Dragged from their vehicle, beaten and then executed', *The Telegraph*, 16 Oct 2016.

46. 'Scotland says goodbye to fallen Black Watch hero', *The Herald*, 22 April 2003, https://www.heraldscotland.com/news/11989047.scotland-says-goodbye-to-fallen-black-watch-hero-perth-at-standstill-for-lance-corporal/ (accessed 16 Jan 2020).

47. Wayback Machine Internet Archive, 'Board of Inquiry Report', https://web.archive.org/web/20110608011154/http://www.mod.uk/NR/rdonlyres/C2384518-7EBA-4CFF-B127-E87871E41B51/0/boi_challenger2_25mar03.pdf (accessed 16 Jan 2020).

48. 'Commander blamed over Iraq friendly fire tragedy', *Evening Standard*, 13 July 2007, https://www.standard.co.uk/news/commander-blamed-over-iraq-friendly-fire-tragedy-6597499.html (accessed 16 Jan 2020).

49. 'British: Airstrike likely killed "Chemical"', CNN, 6 Apr 2003, https://www.cnn.com/2003/WORLD/meast/04/07/sprj.irq.chemical.ali/ (accessed 16 Jan 2020).

50. ENVagency, 'Invasion of Iraq: How the British and Americans got it wrong', Youtube video, 57:20, 2 Dec 2011, https://www.youtube.com/watch?v=BcxzigtuR9w (accessed 15 Jan 2020).

51. Fairweather, *A War of Choice*, 28.

52. Frontline, 'Interview: Lt. Gen. James Conway', *Blue Ridge PBS*, https://www.pbs.org/wgbh/pages/frontline/shows/invasion/interviews/conway.html#basra (accessed 16 Jan 2020).

53. PBS, *Frontline*, 'Bush's War – Part One' (1:11:30), https://www.pbs.org/video/frontline-bushs-war-part-1/ (accessed 25 Aug 2019).

54. Fairweather, *A War of Choice*, 43.

55. PBS, *Frontline*, 'Bush's War – Part Two' (35:44), 25 Mar 2008, https://www.pbs.org/video/frontline-bushs-war-part-2/ (accessed 25 Aug 2019).

56. Fairweather, *A War of Choice*, 53.

57. Ibid, 61.

58. Sean Rayment, '*A War of Choice: The British in Iraq 2003–2009* by Jack Fairweather; review', *The Telegraph*, 5 Jan 2012.

59. Stephen Fiddler, 'How the British Army lost Basra', *Financial Times*, 20 Aug 2007.

60. 'Military Official: Iranian millions funding insurgency', *CNN*, 28 Sep 2006, https://www.cnn.com/2006/WORLD/meast/09/28/iraq.iran/index.html (accessed 19 Jan 2020).

61. Michael Rose, 'Enough of the excuses: Blair must be impeached over Iraq', *The Guardian*, 10 Jan 2006.

62. Jethro Mullen, 'Tony Blair says he's sorry for Iraq War "mistakes", but not for ousting Saddam', CNN, 26 Oct 2015, https://www.cnn.com/2015/10/25/europe/tony-blair-iraq-war/index.html (accessed 4 Dec 2019).

63. Ibid.

64. 'Daily Mail Comment: Blair's weasel words insult Iraq war dead', *Daily Mail*, 25 Oct 2015.

65. Roy Greenslade, 'UK newspapers reject Tony Blair's Iraq war apology', *The Guardian*, 26 Oct 2015.

66. Jackson, *Soldier*, 392.

67. National Audit Office, 'Report by the Comptroller and Auditor General', HC 1097 Session 2001–2002: 1 August 2002, https://www.nao.org.uk/wp-content/uploads/2002/08/01021097.pdf (accessed 16 Dec 2019).

68. Ibid.

69. Ibid.

70. Philip Johnston, 'Tanks, guns and boots all failed in desert', *The Telegraph*, 1 Aug 2002.

71. Ben Fenton, 'Families call for inquest into Redcap deaths', *The Telegraph*, 18 Nov 2004.

72. BBC News, 'Kit delays led to soldier's death', 18 Dec 2006, http://news.bbc.co.uk/2/hi/uk_news/england/bradford/6190337.stm (accessed 11 Dec 2019).

73. Ibid.

74. James Sturcke, 'Snatch Land Rovers: The "mobile coffins" of the British Army', *The Guardian*, 1 Nov 2008.

75. Ibid.

76. Mark Bulstrode, 'Snatch Land Rovers blamed for dozens of deaths', *Independent*, 9 Mar 2010.

77. Joe Shute, 'General Sir Lord Dannatt: "Going to Iraq was an error of near biblical proportions"', *The Telegraph*, 1 Oct 2016.

78. Fairweather, *A War of Choice*, 12.

79. Sinan Antoon, 'Fifteen years ago, America destroyed my country', *New York Times*, 19 Mar 2018.

Chapter Thirteen

1. Jackson, *Soldier*, 394.

2. Ibid, 389.

3. Mathew Tempest, 'Blair declares war on Taliban', *The Guardian*, 2 Oct 2001.
4. www.parliament.uk, 'Select Committee on Defence – Third Report', https://publications. parliament.uk/pa/cm200304/cmselect/cmdfence/57/5707.htm (accessed 27 Jan 2020).
5. Ibid.
6. Cadic's Universe, 'Afghanistan: The Battle for Helmand (BBC)', YouTube video, 7:00, 23 Sep 2017, https://www.youtube.com/watch?v=8mScn60Yd5Y (accessed 16 Feb 2020).
7. BBC News, 'UK to target terrorists', http://news.bbc.co.uk/2/hi/uk_news/4935532.stm (accessed 5 Mar 2020).
8. Max Hastings, 'An honest man who spoke for his men', *Daily Mail*, 14 Oct 2006.
9. James Ferguson, *A Million Bullets* (London: Corgi, 2009), 73.
10. Nik Hynek and Peter Marton, *Statebuilding in Afghanistan* (London: Routledge, 2012), 28.
11. Ferguson, *A Million Bullets*, 74.
12. Cadic's Universe, 'Afghanistan: The Battle for Helmand (BBC)', YouTube video, 10:48, 23 Sep 2017, https://www.youtube.com/watch?v=8mScn60Yd5Y (accessed 16 Feb 2020).
13. Hynek and Marton, *Statebuilding in Afghanistan*, 29.
14. Cadic's Universe, 'Afghanistan: The Battle for Helmand (BBC)', YouTube video, 11:06, 23 Sep 2017, https://www.youtube.com/watch?v=8mScn60Yd5Y (accessed 16 Feb 2020).
15. Hynek and Marton, *Statebuilding in Afghanistan*, 28.
16. Cadic's Universe, 'Afghanistan: The Battle for Helmand (BBC)', YouTube video, 12:05, 23 Sep 2017, https://www.youtube.com/watch?v=8mScn60Yd5Y (accessed 16 Feb 2020).
17. Ibid, 14:22.
18. Hynek and Marton, *Statebuilding in Afghanistan*, 29.
19. Cadic's Universe, 'Afghanistan: The Battle for Helmand (BBC)', YouTube video, 16:37, 23 Sep 2017, https://www.youtube.com/watch?v=8mScn60Yd5Y (accessed 16 Feb 2020).
20. Ferguson, *A Million Bullets*, 124.
21. Mick Flynn, *Trigger Time* (London: Orion, 2011), 60.
22. Ferguson, *A Million Bullets*, 158.
23. Ibid, 194.
24. Ferguson, *A Million Bullets*, 24.
25. Michael Evans, 'Extra 1,400 UK troops to be sent to Afghanistan', *The Times*, 26 Feb 2007.
26. Ministry of Defense, 'British fatalities – Operations in Afghanistan', https://www.gov.uk/ government/fields-of-operation/afghanistan (accessed 26 Feb 2020).
27. Ian Drury, 'Army "nearly seized up" fighting on two fronts: Dannatt tells Iraq inquiry forces were dangerously overstretched', *Daily Mail*, 29 July 2010.
28. Joe Shute, 'General Sir Lord Dannatt: "Going to Iraq was an error of near biblical proportions"', *The Telegraph*, 1 Oct 2026.
29. Christina Lamb, 'Over and out: former para on why he quit the Army after Afghanistan', *The Sunday Times*, 20 July 2008.
30. Datablog, 'British dead and wounded in Afghanistan, month by month', *The Guardian*, https:// www.theguardian.com/news/datablog/2009/sep/17/afghanistan-casualties-dead-wounded-british-data (accessed 27 Feb 2020).
31. Ministry of Defense, 'British fatalities – Operations in Afghanistan', https://www.gov.uk/ government/fields-of-operation/afghanistan (accessed 26 Feb 2020).
32. Alix Culbertson, 'British troops fired astonishing 46 million bullets at Taliban fighters', *The Daily Express*, 8 Apr 2015.

Chapter Fourteen

1. Marco Grannangeli, 'Army crisis as soldier numbers plunge with even Queen's guards and SAS overstretched', *The Daily Express*, 3 Mar 2019.
2. BBC News, 'Afghan Conflict: Top court backs war crimes probe', 5 Mar 2020, https://www.bbc.com/news/world-asia-51751717 (accessed 6 Mar 2020)
3. PMC, 'Mental health consequences of overstretch in the UK armed forces: first phase of a cohort study', https://www.ncbi.nlm.nih.gov/pmc/articles/PMC1988977/ (accessed 14 Aug 2019)
4. Ibid.
5. Patrick Hill, Sean Rayment, Amy Sharpe, 'At least 13,000 hero soldiers left homeless after leaving the military – and almost all have PTSD', *Daily Mirror*, 13 Jan 2018.
6. Max Pemberton, 'Too many ex-servicemen in prison', *The Telegraph*, 11 Jan 2010.
7. Joel Adams, 'Retiring soldiers should face psychological exams to help them avoid prison, says former army chief', *The Telegraph*, 17 Sep 2018.
8. Lord Dannatt, 'To let soldiers suffer in silence is a dereliction of duty', *Daily Mail*, 13 Jan 2018.
9. Lucy Fisher, 'Alarm over surge in suicides by veterans of Afghanistan war', *The Times*, 2 Mar 2020.
10. Office for National Statistics, 'Suicides in the UK: 2018 registrations,' https://www.ons.gov.uk/peoplepopulationandcommunity/birthsdeathsandmarriages/deaths/bulletins/suicidesintheunitedkingdom/2018registrations (accessed 6 Jul 2020).
11. Armed Forces and Veterans Breakfast Clubs, https://www.afvbc.net (accessed 23 April 20

Index